INTERPRETING BIBLICAL TEXTS

THE
PROPHETIC
LITERATURE

GENERAL EDITORS

Gene M. Tucker, *Old Testament*

Charles B. Cousar, *New Testament*

INTERPRETING
I·B·T
BIBLICAL TEXTS

THE
PROPHETIC
LITERATURE

Marvin A. Sweeney

ABINGDON PRESS
Nashville

THE PROPHETIC LITERATURE

Library of Congress Cataloging-in-Publication Data

Sweeney, Marvin A. (Marvin Alan), 1953–
   The prophetic literature / Marvin A. Sweeney.
      p. cm.
   Includes bibliographical references and index.
   ISBN 0-687-00844-1 (binding: adhesive, perfect : alk. paper)
   1. Bible. O.T. Prophets—Criticism, interpretation, etc. I. Title.

   BS1505.52.S94 2005
   224'.061—dc22

                                                      2005012613

05 06 07 08 09 10 11 12 13 14—10 9 8 7 6 5 4 3 2 1

MANUFACTURED IN THE UNITED STATES OF AMERICA

For

_____

David L. Petersen

Contents

ACKNOWLEDGMENTS

One of the best aspects of the completion of a book project is to thank those who have helped to see a book through to its completion. Several people have played some very important roles in the writing of this volume.

First, I would like to thank Gene M. Tucker, the Old Testament Editor of the Interpreting Biblical Texts series, for his invitation to contribute this volume. It has been my pleasure to work with him before as volume editor for my FOTL commentary on Isaiah 1–39 (*Isaiah 1–39, with an Introduction to Prophetic Literature* [FOTL 16; Grand Rapids and Cambridge: Eerdmans, 1996]). He is a perceptive editor whose suggestions inevitably save me from many embarrassments and result in a much stronger, clearer, and far more interesting volume.

Second, I would like to thank my former student assistant, Faye Ellen Ellwood, now an alumna of the Claremont School of Theology. Faye Ellen was a student in my most recent CST course on Prophecy and Prophetic Literature, and wrote her M.A.T.S. thesis on the book of Jonah. Her reading of the rough draft of the manuscript was invaluable, particularly since it provided insights from one who would represent the primary readers of this volume, viz., students.

Third, I would like to thank my students over the past twenty-two years at the University of Miami, the Hebrew Union College-Jewish Institute of Religion, the Academy for Jewish Religion, the Claremont School of Theology, and the Claremont Graduate University, for their insights and their eagerness to learn from the prophetic literature of the Hebrew Bible. This volume is a product of dialogue with them during the course of the many classes I have taught on this topic.

Fourth, I would like to thank my many colleagues in the field of prophetic literature. I have learned much from reading their works and discussing various aspects of the prophetic literature in scholarly meetings, private conversation, e-mail communications, and so on., over the course of many years. I had the occasion to reflect on this most recently at the Society of Biblical Literature meeting in San Antonio (November, 2004) where I read a paper on Amos in a room filled with many of those from whom I have learned so much.

Fifth, I would like to thank my wife, Muna, and our daughter, Leah, for the love and support that make everything possible, and for always reminding me what is most important in life.

Finally, I would like to thank David L. Petersen, formerly of the University of Illinois and the Iliff School of Theology, and now of the Candler School of Theology at Emory University. David was my undergraduate advisor at the University of Illinois, and played a very important role in introducing me to the study of the prophetic literature and in preparing me for graduate study in the field. In the years since my undergraduate days, he has continued to serve as a valued mentor, colleague, and friend. I continue to learn from him at every opportunity. It is therefore my distinct pleasure to dedicate this volume to David, in recognition of his considerable expertise in the study of prophetic literature and his role in stimulating me to engage this utterly fascinating and challenging body of literature.

Marvin A. Sweeney
January 2005/Shevat 5765
Claremont, California

N.B., in keeping with some streams of Jewish tradition, this volume employs terms such as YHWH, G-d, L-rd, and so forth, in reference to the Deity. Such use is intended to convey the sanctity of the divine Name.

FOREWORD

Biblical texts create worlds of meaning, and invite readers to enter them. When readers enter such textual worlds, which are often strange and complex, they are confronted with theological claims. With this in mind, the purpose of this series is to help serious readers in their experience of reading and interpreting, to provide guides for their journeys into textual worlds. The controlling perspective is expressed in the operative word of the title—*interpreting*. The primary focus of the series is not so much on the world *behind* the texts or out of which the texts have arisen (though these worlds are not irrelevant) as on the world *created by* the texts in their engagement with readers.

Each volume addresses two questions. First, what are the critical issues of interpretation that have emerged in the recent history of scholarship and to which serious readers of the texts need to be sensitive? Some of the concerns of scholars are interesting and significant but, frankly, peripheral to the interpretative task. Others are more central. How they are addressed influences decisions readers make in the process of interpretation. Thus the authors call attention to these basic issues and indicate their significance for interpretation.

Second, in struggling with particular passages or sections of material, how can readers be kept aware of the larger world created by the text as a whole? How can they both see the forest and examine the individual trees? How can students encountering the story of David and Bathsheba in 2 Samuel 11 read it in light of its context in the larger story, the Deuteronomistic History that includes the books of Deuteronomy through 2 Kings? How can readers of Galatians fit what they learn into the theological coherence and polarities of the larger perspective drawn from all the letters of Paul? Thus each volume provides an overview of the literature as a whole.

The aim of the series is clearly pedagogical. The authors offer their own understanding of the issues and texts, but are more concerned about guiding the reader than engaging in debates with other scholars. The series is meant to serve as a resource, alongside other resources such as commentaries and specialized studies, to aid students in the exciting and often risky venture of interpreting biblical texts.

Gene M. Tucker
General Editor, *Old Testament*
Charles B. Cousar
General Editor, *New Testament*

LIST OF ABBREVIATIONS

AB	Anchor Bible
ABD	*Anchor Bible Dictionary,* ed. D. N. Freedman, et al. 6 volumes. New York: Doubleday, 1992.
AnBib	Analecta biblica
ANEP	*The Ancient Near East in Pictures Relating to the Old Testament,* ed. J. Pritchard. Princeton: Princeton University Press, 1969.
ANET	*Ancient Near Eastern Texts Relating to the Old Testament,* ed. J. Pritchard. Princeton: Princeton University Press, 1969.
BBET	Beiträge zur biblischen Exegese und Theologie
BEATAJ	Beiträge zur Erforschung des Alten Testament und des antiken Judentums
BETL	Bibliotheca ephemeridum theologicarum lovaniensium
BibInt	*Biblical Interpretation*
BibSem	The Biblical Seminar
BZAW	Beihefte zur Zeitschrift für die alttestamentliche Wissenschaft

ConBOT   Coniectanea biblica: Old Testament Series
ContCom   Continental Commentaries
CurBS   *Currents in Research: Biblical Studies*
CRINT   Compendia rerum iudaicarum ad Novum Testamentum
DJD   Discoveries in the Judaean Desert
EncJud   *Encyclopaedia Judaica*, ed. C. Roth, et al. Jerusalem: Keter, n.d.
ETL   *Ephemerides theologicae lovanienses*
FOTL   Forms of the Old Testament Literature
HCOT   Historical Commentary on the Old Testament
HKAT   Handkommentar zum Alten Testament
HSM   Harvard Semitic Monographs
HSS   Harvard Semitic Studies
HUCA   *Hebrew Union College Annual*
ICC   International Critical Commentary
IDBSup   Interpreter's Dictionary of the Bible: Supplementary Volume, ed. K. R. Crim. Nashville: Abingdon, 1976.
IEJ   *Israel Exploration Journal*
Int   *Interpretation: A Journal of Bible and Theology*
JBL   *Journal of Biblical Literature*
JR   *Journal of Religion*
JSOT   *Journal for the Study of the Old Testament*
JSOTSup   Journal for the Study of the Old Testament: Supplement Series
JSPSup   Journal for the Study of the Pseudepigrapha: Supplement Series
LXX   Septuagint
MT   Masoretic Text
NCB   New Century Bible
OBO   Orbis biblicus et orientalis
OBT   Overtures to Biblical Theology
OPIAC   *Occasional Papers of the Institute for Antiquity and Christianity*
OTL   Old Testament Library
SBLDS   Society of Biblical Literature Dissertation Series
SBLMS   Society of Biblical Literature Monograph Series
SBLSymS   Society of Biblical Literature Symposium Series
VT   *Vetus Testamentum*
VTSup   Supplements to Vetus Testamentum
ZAW   *Zeitschrift für die alttestamentliche Wissenschaft*

CHAPTER 1

THE PROPHETS IN
JEWISH AND
CHRISTIAN SCRIPTURE

The prophetic books of the Hebrew Bible present some of the most profound theological literature in both the Tanak, the Jewish version of the Bible, and the Old Testament, the first portion of the Christian version of the Bible. Indeed, the prophetic books of the Bible grapple with the foundational theological questions of evil and righteousness as they attempt to come to grips with the problems posed by the Babylonian destruction of Jerusalem and the Temple and the prospects for the restoration of both in the aftermath of the Babylonian exile. Of course, the long history of the prophetic books indicates that such questions were not limited to the Babylonian exile and the postexilic restoration. Earlier invasions by Aram and Assyria, among others, the destruction of the northern kingdom of Israel in 722/1 B.C.E., and the prospects for restoration during the reign of King Josiah of Judah (640–609 B.C.E.) had already opened such questions for the people of Judah and Israel in their efforts to understand their relationship with their G-d, YHWH, and their role in the world which YHWH created. Is YHWH indeed a righteous deity? What are Judah's and Israel's responsibilities in relation to YHWH? What role do the nations play in YHWH's plans for Judah/Israel and creation at large? These questions and others are addressed throughout the prophetic books, and they are just as significant today, particularly in the aftermath of the Shoah or Holocaust, for both Jews and Christians.[1]

It is essential for readers to grasp the literary character of the prophetic books in order to discern their respective understandings of the significance of Judah's and Israel's relationship with YHWH and the events that they portray. The reading of the prophetic literature has been fragmented by more than a century of modern critical work that sought to reconstruct the words and persons of the historical prophets and the events of their times.[2] The one-sided focus on historical reconstruction, with its identification of later editorial additions to the authentic words of the prophets, tended to obscure the literary coherence of the prophetic books and the overarching theological programs that they are designed to convey. The work of historical or diachronic reconstruction is necessary to the overall interpretation of the prophetic literature, but it must follow and work in conjunction with the synthetic or synchronic literary analysis of whole prophetic books in order to provide a credible reading of their presentation of the prophets. This is not to say that prophetic books must be read uncritically as the work of the prophets themselves—the prophetic books are the products of later editors or redactors who shaped earlier materials into their current forms. Rather, an understanding of the synchronic forms of the prophetic books (i.e., without regard to historical setting or the history of composition) helps readers to understand the overall framework in which the prophet is presented, and an understanding of the diachronic formation of the prophetic books (i.e., with consideration of historical setting and the history of composition) helps readers to understand how the prophet has been shaped.

The first step in a reading of the synchronic literary form of the prophetic literature is an assessment of the roles that the prophetic books play within the overall structure and theological program of the Bible. Such an assessment requires readers to recognize the differences between the Jewish Tanak and the Christian Old Testament.[3] Many assume that the Tanak and the

(Protestant) Old Testament are one and the same because they contain the same biblical books, but such a view is mistaken. The Old Testament itself shows great variety. The Roman Catholic version of the Old Testament contains a number of books that appear only as the Apocrypha in Protestant versions of the Bible. Other Christian Bibles, e.g., the Greek Septuagint of the Eastern Orthodox churches, the Syriac Peshitta of the Syrian churches, and the Ethiopian versions of the Bible contain books that might not appear in Western Christian Bibles. Furthermore, there are major differences in the structure or order of books in the Christian and Jewish versions of the Bible that have a profound impact on the theological reading of each. Although there is variation in the orders of the various Christian Bibles, we will focus on the Western Protestant tradition to illustrate the differing roles of the prophetic books in the Jewish and Christian versions of the Bible.

All forms of the Christian Bible are divided into two fundamental portions, viz., the Old Testament and the New Testament, which reflects the fundamental theological viewpoint of Christianity. The term "testament" means "covenant," and the terminology reflects Christianity's understanding of the progressive revelation of G-d to the world throughout human history. The Old Testament represents a first stage of G-d's revelation to the world through the Mosaic covenant with Israel. The New Testament represents a second stage of G-d's revelation to the world at large through the life, death, and resurrection of Jesus Christ, who is understood to be the son of G-d in Christianity. Christianity anticipates a third stage of divine revelation through the second coming of Christ, which will see the final culmination of G-d's plans for the salvation of humanity.

The Old Testament revelation of the Mosaic covenant to Israel in the Christian Bible therefore represents only a stage in the revelation of G-d that anticipates the revelation of Jesus Christ in the New Testament. The various forms of Christianity differ in their respective understandings of whether or not and how the Mosaic covenant with Israel continues in Judaism following the New Testament period. Nevertheless, the preparatory character of the Old Testament is clear in the basic four-part structure of the Christian Old Testament. Although many argue that Old Testament's structure depends on the logical organization of the

Greek Septuagint, which was itself likely the product of the Hellenistic Jewish community of Alexandria, it plays a constitutive role in defining Christianity's theological reading of the Old Testament.[4] The first portion is the Pentateuch, viz., Genesis, Exodus, Leviticus, Numbers, and Deuteronomy, which presents the earliest history of creation and the formation of Israel, including the revelation of the Mosaic covenant. The second portion is the Historical Books, viz., Joshua, Judges, Ruth, 1–2 Samuel, 1–2 Kings, 1–2 Chronicles, Ezra–Nehemiah, and Esther, which presents the history of Israel from the entry into the promised land through the Persian period immediately prior to the Greco-Roman period of the New Testament when Judah/Israel found itself under the rule of foreign powers. The third section of the Old Testament shifts from concern with the past to concern with the timeless present, insofar as its books, Job, Psalms, Proverbs, Ecclesiastes, and Song of Solomon, take up concern with fundamental questions of epistemology, human spirituality, and human behavior in the world. Finally, the Prophets, the fourth section of the Old Testament, including Isaiah, Jeremiah, Lamentations, Ezekiel, Daniel, and the twelve books of the Minor Prophets, assess the fall of Israel and Judah to foreign powers and the prospects for their restoration following the Babylonian exile. Because the prophetic books contend that the sins of Judah and Israel led to their punishment and that YHWH intends to restore Judah and Israel following the period of their punishment, the Prophets occupy a key position in the Christian Bible. Appearing at the conclusion of the Old Testament and immediately prior to the New Testament, they point to the revelation of Jesus Christ as the means by which G-d's intended restoration of Israel at the center of the nations will be realized.

Indeed, the New Testament displays a structure like that of the Old Testament, insofar as it, too, is organized to anticipate the second coming of Christ. The Gospels present the earliest history of Jesus' revelation to the world; the Acts of the Apostles present Christianity's earliest history following the lifetime of Christ; the Epistles take up the timeless questions of Christian faith, practice, and organization, and the book of Revelation or the Apocalypse of John points to the anticipated second coming of Christ.

18

The organization of the Jewish Tanak is quite different from the Christian Old Testament,[5] and this difference reflects a very distinctive theological viewpoint. There is no New Testament in Judaism because the revelation of divine Torah to Israel through Moses at Sinai continues to be the operative covenant of Judaism to this day. Furthermore, the Tanak is organized into three major sections, the Torah or "Instruction,"[6] the Nevi'im or "Prophets," and the Ketuvim or "Writings." The first letter of the Hebrew name for each section forms the acronym TaNaK by which the Jewish version of the Bible is known. The Torah, "Instruction," Genesis, Exodus, Leviticus, Numbers, and Deuteronomy, again presents the earliest history of Israel from creation through the Mosaic revelation, and thereby represents the ideal construction of Israel as a holy people centered on the Tabernacle, a precursor for the Jerusalem Temple. The position of the Nevi'im, "Prophets," at the center of the Tanak, however, entails a very different function for the prophetic books in the Jewish form of the Bible. First, the Prophets are constructed quite differently into two subsections. The *Nevi'im Rishonim,* "Former Prophets," include Joshua, Judges, Samuel, and Kings, and relate the history of Israel from entry into the promised land through the Babylonian exile. Although these books present historical narrative, they emphasize a theological evaluation of the reasons for the destruction of Israel and Judah together with some inklings of potential restoration. The *Nevi'im Aḥronim,* "Latter Prophets," include Isaiah, Jeremiah, Ezekiel, and the Book of the Twelve Prophets, which again provide an assessment of the reasons for the punishment of Israel and Judah and the prospects for their restoration. Overall, they are concerned with the disruption of the holy ideal for Israel articulated in the Torah and the possibility of the reconstruction of that holy ideal. Because the Prophets appear at the center of the Tanak, they do not point beyond the Bible itself, but to the next segment of the Bible, the *Ketuvim,* "Writings," which express the reconstitution of that ideal. The *Ketuvim* include Psalms, Job, Proverbs, the Five Megillot or Scrolls (Ruth, Song of Songs, Qohelet/Ecclesiastes, Lamentations, Esther), Daniel, Ezra–Nehemiah, and Chronicles. Altogether, these books are concerned with holy life for Israel around the Temple and within the world of creation; Psalms express spirituality, Job and Proverbs examine the epistemological foundations of divine creation, the *Megillot* are each associated with a festival, Daniel projects the restoration of holiness in the world, Chronicles expresses Israel's history around the Temple from creation through Cyrus's decree of restoration, and Ezra–Nehemiah express Judah's/Israel's restoration around the holy Temple in Jerusalem as the ideal for Jewish life.

Altogether, the *Tanak*'s presentation of the holy ideal for Israel in the world, its disruption, and its restoration, represents a combination of linear and cyclical understandings of the course of human history and Israel's relationship with G-d. The Prophets play a key role in that presentation, insofar as they both sum up the reasons for that disruption and provide the rationale for restoration. Such an understanding has enabled Judaism both to weather periods of challenge and persecution and to develop progressively through the course of human history into modern times. The Prophets occupy a very different role at the conclusion of the Christian Old Testament. Within the linear presentation of the Old Testament, the Prophets again sum up the reasons for Israel's punishment and prepare the reader for the revelation of Jesus Christ in the New Testament. Such a perspective provides Christianity with a clear sense of historical progression and development into the modern age as Christianity anticipates the culmination of human history through the second coming of Christ.

The formation of the Jewish *Tanak* and the Christian Old Testament clearly depends not on the original authors of the biblical books, but on the decisions and perspectives of later thinkers and leaders who organized the Bible into its present forms in order to articulate their respective understandings of the significance of the Bible. Although such organization—or even the concept of a Bible—was likely entirely foreign to the authors of the prophetic books or even to the prophets themselves, it clearly plays a very important role in the continuing life and relevance of the prophetic books to later generations of readers in both Judaism and Christianity.

In the next chapter we turn to the question of the reading of the individual prophetic books in their present synchronic literary forms and to the diachronic reconstruction of the prophetic books and the prophetic figures that they present.

SELECTED BIBLIOGRAPHY

Barton, John. "The Significance of a Fixed Canon of the Hebrew Bible." Pages 67-83 in *Hebrew Bible/Old Testament: The History of Its Interpretation. Volume I: From the Beginnings to the Middle Ages (Until 1300). Part 1: Antiquity.* Edited by M. Sæbø. Göttingen: Vandenhoeck & Ruprecht, 1996.

Beckwith, Roger T. *The Old Testament Canon of the New Testament Church and Its Background in Early Judaism.* Grand Rapids: Eerdmans, 1986.

———. "Formation of the Hebrew Bible." Pages 39-86 in *Mikra: Text, Translation, Reading, and Interpretation of the Hebrew Bible in Ancient Judaism and Early Christianity.* Edited by M. Mulder. CRINT 2/1. Assen: Van Gorcum. Philadelphia: Fortress, 1988.

Blenkinsopp, Joseph. *Prophecy and Canon: A Contribution to the Study of Jewish Origins.* Notre Dame: University of Notre Dame Press, 1977.

Campenhausen, H. von. *The Formation of the Christian Bible.* London: Adam and Charles Black, 1972.

Leiman, Sid. *The Canonization of Hebrew Scripture: The Talmudic and Midrashic Evidence.* Hamden: Connecticut Academy of Arts and Sciences/Archon, 1976.

Morgan, Donn F. *Between Text and Community: The Writings in Canonical Interpretation.* Minneapolis: Fortress, 1990.

Sanders, James A. *Canon and Community: A Guide to Canonical Criticism.* Philadelphia: Fortress, 1984.

Sundberg, A. C. *The Old Testament of the Early Church.* Harvard Theological Studies 20. Cambridge: Harvard University Press, 1964.

Sweeney, Marvin A. "Tanak versus Old Testament: Concerning the Foundation for a Jewish Theology of the Bible." Pages 353-72 in *Problems in Biblical Theology: Essays in Honor of Rolf Knierim.* Edited by H. T. C. Sun and K. L. Eades with J. M. Robinson and G. I. Moller. Grand Rapids: Eerdmans, 1997.

CHAPTER 2

READING PROPHETIC BOOKS

Reading the prophetic books of the Hebrew Bible calls for an understanding of the nature of prophecy and the social roles of prophets in ancient Israel and Judah as well as the larger world of the ancient Near East.[1] It also calls for an understanding of the specific forms of literary presentation and linguistic expression that one encounters when reading prophetic literature.[2]

A. PROPHETS IN THE ANCIENT WORLD

Although many think of prophets as persons who predict the future, prophets are concerned primarily with the events and circumstances of their own times and with influencing people within their own societies. Many prophets speak about potential future events, but they do so as part of their interest in persuading their contemporaries to adopt a specific course of action or attitude that they think best represents the will of G-d and the best interests of the people. Although prophecy was a recognized profession in the ancient Near Eastern world—and prophets, diviners, and other types of shamans appear frequently in other cultures and times as

23

well—such a role tends to be expressed in contemporary Western culture by other types of figures, such as religious or political leaders, educators, journalists, artists, writers, musicians, attorneys, and others who are concerned with charting the directions of our society and the actions and viewpoints of people who live within it. Both men and women functioned as prophets in the ancient world, and their success was determined by the extent to which people understood them to speak the truth on behalf of their respective gods.

Prophets are well known throughout the ancient Near Eastern world in Egypt, Canaan, Aram (ancient Syria), Mesopotamia, and Israel and Judah.[3] Although some might like to think of prophets as persons from all walks of life who suddenly find themselves possessed of divine spirit and compelled to speak on G-d's behalf, most prophets in the ancient world appear to be well-trained professionals who have mastered a set of skills, such as oracular divination, poetic and musical expression, ritual action, and so on, and who might function within the contexts of well-recognized institutions, such as temples, royal palaces, or even roving bands.[4]

The literature of ancient Egypt, for example, presents many examples of prophetic activity and roles. The "Admonitions of Ipu-Wer"[5] present the warnings of a well-educated prophetic figure from 2300 to 2050 B.C.E. who warned his pharaoh of a breakdown in Egypt's well-ordered society and called upon the pharaoh to restore order in the land:

> He is the herdsman of all men. Evil is not in his heart . . . . Then he would smite down evil; he would stretch his arm against it.[6]

The "Prophecy of Neferti"[7] (or Nefer-rohu) relates how the Fourth Dynasty Pharaoh, Snefru (r. 2613ff. B.C.E.), called upon the lector-priest, Nefer-rohu, to entertain the court with his choice speeches. Nefer-rohu surprised the court with his descriptions of threats to Egypt:

> Foes have arisen in the east, and Asiatics have come down into Egypt. . . . No protector will listen. . . . This land is helter-skelter, and no one knows the result which will come about.[8]

The lector-priest ultimately predicts the reign of the Twelfth Dynasty Pharaoh, Amenis (Amen-em-het I, r. 1990ff. B.C.E.), who actually did bring order to the land, although many scholars suspect that this text was written specifically to support his rise to power. Finally, the Sphinx Stela presents a text in which the god, Harmakhis, who lived in the Sphinx, appeared to Thut-Mose IV (r. 1421–1413 B.C.E.) in a dream as he slept in the shadow of the great monument.[9] Because Thut-mose had cleared the Sphinx of sand, Harmakhis granted him kingship:

> See me, look at me, my son, Thut-moses! I am thy father, Harmakhis-Khepri Re-Atum. I shall give thee my kingdom upon earth at the head of the living. . . .Thine is the land in its length and its breadth . . . . Approach, thou! Behold, I am with thee; I am thy guide.[10]

Whereas prophets in Egypt are especially known for poetic composition and dream interpretation, prophets in Mesopotamia are especially well known for the reading of omens and oracular divination. The ancient Babylonians saw the cosmos as part of an interlocking totality, in which the gods expressed themselves by showing signs to human beings. If two events occurred together, for example, if a fox walks into a village and then the village is destroyed by earthquake, the Babylonians believed that the fox was meant as an omen of danger. Extensive lists of omens were recorded during the Old Babylonian period (1894–1595 B.C.E.) for use by *baru* priests, who were specialists in the interpretation of omens. Such *baru* priests were professionally trained in the omen literature of the time as well as in the reading of the movements of stars and planets that were identified with individual gods; divination techniques, such as the reading of oil patterns on water or the patterns of incense smoke; the reading of animal entrails and livers, and so forth, in an effort to determine the will of the gods.[11]

The Mari tablets, which contain the royal correspondence of King Zimri-lim (r. 1730–1700 B.C.E.) of the Mesopotamian city of Mari, provide an especially rich library of prophetic activity, insofar as the king frequently consulted with prophets of varying types. One type, known as the *apilu*, "answerer," apparently provided oracular answers to questions that were put to a deity. The *apilu* was generally associated with the temple of a specific deity, and was not hesitant to criticize the king or other officials as the occasion requires:

"Am I not Addu, the lord of Halab, who has raised you . . . and who made you regain the throne of your father's house? I never ask anything of you. When a man or a woman who has suffered an injustice addresses himself to you, respond to his appeal and give him a verdict. This is what I ask of you, this which I have written to you, you will do. You will pay attention to my word . . ." This is what the *apilum* of Addu, lord of Halab, said to me. (A.2925)[12]

The *muḫḫu*, "ecstatic," was known to engage in the behavior of trance possession, including irrational acts such as the drawing of his own blood, to deliver rational oracles on behalf of the deity that he represented:

Speak to my lord: the message of Lanasum governor of Tuttu, your servant, "My lord has written me as follows, 'Now I will offer a sacrifice to Dagan. I will sacrifice one head of cattle and six sheep.' At present the sacrifice of my lord has arrived in the city safe and sound, and it has been offered to Dagan. The whole country is greatly cheered. And the *muḫḫu*-ecstatic got up before Dagan and spoke as follows, 'I am not given pure water to drink. Write to your lord so that he may give me pure water to drink.' Now by this message I am sending to my lord a piece of his hair and his hem." (A.455)[13]

Finally, the *assinu*, a term of uncertain meaning, appears to be a special type of male prophet who takes on feminine characteristics when speaking on behalf of the female deity, e.g., Annunitum or Ishtar of Arbela, with whom he was associated:

Speak to my lord: the message of the lady Shibtu, your servant, "The palace is all right. Ilihaznaya, the *assinu* of the goddess Annunitum came and—several lines lost—that man is plotting many things against this land, but he will not succeed. My lord will see what the god will do to that man. You will overcome him and you will stand on him. His time is near; he will not live long." (X.6)[14]

Prophecy is well represented in Canaan and Aram (Syria) as well, although the types of prophetic expression appear to resemble those of Mesopotamia. Ecstatic *muḫḫu* prophets are mentioned in the Ugaritic tables from the Mediterranean coast, "my brothers bathe in their own blood like *muḫḫu*," and the portrayal of Elijah's encounter with the prophets of Baal in 1 Kgs 18 notes their ecstatic dancing and the drawing of blood. An eleventh century B.C.E. Egyptian text, "The Journey of Wen-Amon to Phoenicia"[15] describes the efforts of an official from the Temple of Amon at Karnak to procure timber from the Phoenicians to construct a ceremonial barge for the deity. He was continually frustrated in his efforts until a young boy was seized by trance possession, and declared, "Bring up the god! Bring the messenger who is carrying him! Amon is the one who sent him out! He is the one who made him come!" Although the Prince of Byblos became somewhat more cooperative, he continued to demand Wen-Amon's papers authorizing the trip. Nevertheless, the episode provides us with an example of ecstatic prophetic behavior.

The *baru* priest also appears to be well represented, especially in areas that were heavily influenced by Aram. The Balaam narrative in Num 22–24 portrays the typical actions of a *baru* priest who offered seven bulls and seven rams on seven altars as part of a ritual in which he prepared to deliver oracles that would curse Israel prior to its entry into the promised land. Although the narrative is clearly formulated as a parody of Balaam—his ass sees the angel of YHWH before the great Aramean seer is able to do so, and he is unable to speak anything but the blessings for Israel that YHWH places in his mouth[16]—it nevertheless presents the social reality of a very well-known type of oracle diviner in the ancient world. Indeed, the Deir 'Alla inscription, which presents an oracle of Balaam ben Beor that was originally mounted on the side of a building at the site just east of the Jordan River, indicates that Balaam was a known figure in ancient Israel and Aram.[17] Since the inscription is dated to the early eighth century B.C.E., it would likely have been produced during the period that the Arameans subdued Israel following Jehu's revolt against the house of Omri (see 2 Kgs 9–10, esp. 10:32-33; cf. 2 Kgs 12:17-18). The inscription itself resembles the Egyptian oracles cited above insofar as they portray the chaos of the land that calls for a leader to establish order:

> The gods came to him one night in a vision . . . and they spoke to Balaam the son of Beor, saying, "Would that someone do something without hesitation to reveal what message there is."[18]

27

Like the Egyptian examples, the Balaam inscription is a well-crafted poetic composition that apparently justifies the intervention of a powerful ruler who would restore order to the land. Unfortunately, we do not know if it calls for the rule of an Aramean or other foreign monarch who displaced Israel in the Transjordan, or an Israelite monarch who restored Israelite rule following a period of Aramean hegemony.

When we consider the prophets represented in the Hebrew Bible, we find a variety of terms that are employed to describe the prophets and prophetic activity. Our English term, "prophet," is derived from the Greek term, "*prophetēs*," which refers to "one who speaks forth," i.e., on behalf of a god, but the Hebrew terms employed for prophets tend to emphasize their perception of YHWH and the significance of events or their identification with YHWH or G-d. Thus, Samuel, for example, is called *ro'eh*, "seer" (1 Sam 9:9), which would emphasize his capacity to see or perceive YHWH speaking to him in the sanctuary at Shiloh (1 Sam 3) or YHWH's designation of Saul as king. Gad (2 Sam 24:11), Amos (Amos 7:12), Iddo (2 Chr 9:29), Jehu (2 Chr 19:2) are called, *hozeh*, "visionary," and the prophetic experiences of Isaiah (Isa 1:1), Nahum (Nah 1:1), Obadiah (Obad 1), Habakkuk (Hab 2:2), and Ezekiel (Ezek 7:13) are labeled *hazon*, "vision," or *hazut*, "vision" (Isa 21:2), and Nathan's experiences is called, *hizayon*, "vision" (2 Sam 7:17). The Levitical Temple singers, Heman (1 Chr 25:5), Asaph (2 Chr 29:30), and Jeduthan (2 Chr 35:15) are also called *hozeh*. Although these terms are generally translated as "vision" or the like, they are used in relation to the words of YHWH heard by the prophet as well, and are best understood as "perception." Moses (Deut 33:1), Samuel (1 Sam 9:6-10), Shemaiah (1 Kgs 12:22), Elijah (1 Kgs 17:18-24), Elisha (2 Kgs 4:7-42), and others (1 Sam 2:27; 1 Kgs 13:1-31; 2 Kgs 23:6-7) are called, *iš 'elohim*, "man of G-d," to indicate their identification with the Deity. By far the most commonly employed term is *nabi'*, "prophet," which is employed for Abraham (Gen 20:7), Moses (Deut 34:10), Aaron (Exod 7:1), Samuel (1 Sam 3:20), Elijah (1 Kgs 18:36), the prophetic bands from the time of Elijah and Elisha (1 Kgs 20:35; 2 Kgs 4:1), Jeremiah (Jer 1:5), Ezekiel (Ezek 2:5), Nathan (2 Sam 7:2), Isaiah (2 Kgs 19:2), Habakkuk (Hab 1:1), Haggai (Hag 1:1), Zechariah (Zech 1:1), Hananiah (Jer 28:1), and many others as well. Unfortunately, interpreters are not entirely certain as to what the term means, although the verb *nb'* can be used to describe ecstatic prophetic experience with song and music (Num 11:25; 1 Sam 10:11; 1 Kgs 18:29) or the simple announcement of a divine word (1 Kgs 22:8; Jer 29:27; Ezek 37:10). The feminine form of the term, *nebi'ah,* "prophetess," is applied to Miriam (Exod 15:20), Deborah (Judg 4:4), Huldah (2 Kgs 22:14), Noadiah (Neh 6:14), and the wife of Isaiah (Isa 8:3).

The narratives of the Hebrew Bible also point to a variety of roles for prophets, although they are consistent in presenting prophets as persons who purportedly speak on behalf of YHWH or another god. In reading these narratives, however, we must bear in mind that their presentation of the prophetic figures may well reflect the realities of the times in which these works were composed, i.e., the early Second Temple period for the final forms of the Pentateuch and the Deuteronomistic History and the mid–Second Temple period for the Chronicler's work. Although these works contain much earlier tradition, scholars are often at odds in dating earlier layers of composition.

Moses is identified in the Pentateuch as the prophet par excellence (Deut 34:10-12; cf. 18:15-22; Hos 12:14 [NRSV 12:13]) and as a Levite (Exod 2:1-4; Num 26:59). Throughout the Pentateuchal narratives Moses functions as both prophet and priest in communicating YHWH's Torah to Pharaoh and the people of Israel (e.g., Exod 5; Lev 1). He joins Aaron, Nadab, Abihu, and the seventy elders of Israel for a meal before YHWH, which symbolizes the eating of sacrificial offerings in the Temple (Exod 24:1-11), although Moses continued alone, much as the priests would approach YHWH in the Holy of Holies of the Temple to receive YHWH's revelation (Exod 24:12–30:38). He later isolates himself in the tent of meeting outside of the Israelite camp to function as an oracular prophet for YHWH (Exod 33). His other roles also appear to be bound up with his identity as a Levitical priest. He functions as the chief judicial officer for Israel, much as the Levitical priests serve as the chief judges of the nation (see Exod 18; Deut 18:8-13), and he plays an important role in battle, much as a Levitical priest would accompany soldiers in war (Exod 17; Deut 20). He leads Israel in singing a hymn of praise for YHWH at the Red Sea, much as the Levitical singers, who are also identified as prophets, would lead in singing at the Temple (Exod 15; 1 Chr 25).

Moses' sister Miriam, who is identified as a prophetess and Levite, plays a similar role in leading the singing of the Israelite women (see Exod 15:20-21).

The judge Deborah is called a prophet, and like Moses, she makes judicial decisions on behalf of the people. She speaks on behalf of YHWH to call out Barak and the men of Israel for war, and she leads the soldiers of Israel in battle against the forces of Sisera, and later leads the people in singing a liturgical hymn following their victory (Judg 4–5).

Samuel shows a combination of roles like that of Moses and Deborah. Although he is born as a member of the tribe of Ephraim and not of the priestly tribe of Levi, he is raised in the sanctuary at Shiloh under the supervision of the high priest, Eli, and he functions as a priest throughout his lifetime (see, e.g., 1 Sam 1–3; 7:3-14). Such a role apparently reflects an ancient Israelite tradition that designated the firstborn sons for service to YHWH (N.B., Samuel is the firstborn of his mother, Hannah), although this practice was superseded when the tribe of Levi was later designated to serve as Israel's priests (see Num 3:40-51; 8:5-26; cf. Exod 22:28-29; 34:19-20; Gen 22). His prophetic experience, such as his call by YHWH in the Shiloh sanctuary (1 Sam 3) and his designation of Saul as king at YHWH's behest (1 Sam 8; 9:1–10:16), have been noted above. Samuel acts as judge for the people (1 Sam 7:15-17). He presides as priest when the people go to war (1 Sam 7:3-14; 13–15). Ultimately, he is the representative of YHWH, who designates Saul and David as Israel's first two kings (1 Sam 8–12; 16), and who rejects Saul's kingship (1 Sam 13–15).

The prophet Nathan appears to fill a less variegated role as a spokesperson for YHWH and an active member of David's royal court. Although Gad had been David's prophet prior to David's accession to kingship (1 Sam 22:5), Nathan appears only in Jerusalem. There is no indication of priestly identity, although some note that David's sons were priests (2 Sam 8:18) and that David had a son named Nathan (2 Sam 5:14, but there is no indication that this is the prophet Nathan). He informs David of YHWH's desire not to have a Temple and YHWH's decision to grant David a royal dynasty (2 Sam 7). He speaks on behalf of YHWH to upbraid David for his adultery with Bath Sheba and his murder of her husband, Uriah the Hittite (2 Sam 12:1-14). Finally, he plays an important role together with Bath Sheba in convincing the aged David to designate his son, Solomon, as the next king of Israel (1 Kgs 1).

The prophet Ahijah the Shilonite may well be a member of the priestly line of Eli, given his identification with Shiloh and the temple once located there (see 1 Sam 1–3), but this must remain uncertain. He does function as a spokesperson for YHWH in his oracular announcement of kingship for Jeroboam ben Nebat and his criticism of Solomon (1 Kgs 11:26-40). He appears to function as a professional oracle diviner in 1 Kgs 14:1-18 when the wife of Jeroboam comes to him with payment to request his assistance in healing her sick son (cf. Isaiah in Isa 38, who plays a similar role in healing Hezekiah). His oracular denunciation of Jeroboam and his announcement of the destruction of his dynasty indicate divine judgment against a king regarded as evil throughout the Deuteronomistic History.

Other prophets presented in the narratives that portray Israel's history play similar roles as oracular prophets. Shemaiah advises Rehoboam against war with Jeroboam following northern Israel's revolt (1 Kgs 12:21-24). The anonymous man of G-d from Judah condemns Jeroboam at Beth El, and the old prophet of Beth El likewise delivers an oracle that condemns his Judean counterpart (1 Kgs 13). We should note, however, that the Beth El prophet is accused of lying in the narrative, and that his tomb becomes a well-known landmark in the vicinity of the Beth El, which may suggest some association with the sanctuary.

Although Elijah is identified only as a prophet, his actions carry some overtones of priestly identity. He prepares a sacrifice at Mount Carmel during the course of his conflicts with the prophets of Baal and Asherah (1 Kgs 18), and his encounter with YHWH at Mount Horeb suggests the pattern of the priest before YHWH in the Holy of Holies (1 Kgs 19; cf. Moses in Exod 33:12-23). He is known for healing the son of the widow at Zarephath and for providing her with food (1 Kgs 17:8-24). He isolates himself on a mountain as an oracle diviner (2 Kgs 1), and he spares no efforts in his oracular criticism of King Ahab and Queen Jezebel of Israel (1 Kgs 21) and their son Ahaziah (2 Kgs 1). Elijah appears to be a loner, but the narratives about him and his successor Elisha indicate bands of professional prophets who serve as disciples to the master (1 Kgs 18; 2 Kgs 2).

Elijah's contemporary, Micaiah ben Imlah, opposes such a prophetic guild that supports Ahab in his oracular condemnation of the king (1 Kgs 22). Micaiah's condemnation is especially noteworthy because he claims to have stood in the heavenly royal court of YHWH, and functions as a messenger would on behalf of an earthly king.

Elisha clearly functions as an oracular diviner, although he also serves as the head of a priestly band or guild (2 Kgs 2–8). He performs his oracles to music (2 Kgs 3:14-20). He is especially known for his miraculous actions, including the feeding of a widow and her son and the healing of the son much like Elijah (2 Kgs 4). His power includes the capacity to bring sickness, such as leprosy, together with the power to heal (2 Kgs 5; 8), and he provides wartime oracles (2 Kgs 6–7; 13:14-21). He is instrumental in anointing Jehu as the next monarch and he plays a role in instigating Jehu's revolt, although he does not play an active role in the hostilities (2 Kgs 9–10).

The narrative portrayal of Isaiah as oracle diviner in 2 Kgs 18–20 largely matches the portrayal of the prophet in Isaiah 36–39. Hezekiah makes his inquiry from the Temple. Although the narrative does not make it clear that Isaiah was located in the Temple, Hezekiah receives an oracular response to his inquiry from the prophet Isaiah.

Finally, the prophetess Huldah functions as an oracle diviner in answering King Josiah's inquiry concerning the significance of the Torah scroll discovered in the Temple (2 Kgs 22:3-20). She apparently lived outside of the Temple precincts in the Mishneh quarter, located west of the city of David and the Temple Mount, with her husband Shallum, who was a royal official. Although she clearly understands that Josiah is righteous, she nevertheless announces that he will die prior to the destruction of Jerusalem in keeping with the anonymous oracular announcement in 2 Kgs 21:10-15 that Jerusalem would be destroyed because of the sins of his grandfather Manasseh.

The prophetic literature itself for the most part does not appear in narrative form, although narratives do appear within prophetic books. The prophetic books are instead organized largely as presentations of oracular material that may (or may not) be framed or supplemented with narrative of various sorts that provides some understanding of the context in which the oracles are delivered.

B. GENRES OF PROPHETIC LITERATURE AND SPEECH

Prophetic books begin with a superscription or other narrative introduction which identifies the prophet who is the subject of the book.[19] They may include narrative material by or about the prophet to provide a historical, social, theological, ideological, or literary context by which the reader might understand the prophet's sayings and actions. Not all of the prophetic material necessarily derives from the prophet to whom the book is attributed (e.g., Isa 40–66), but it is presented as if it is the product of the prophet in question.

The superscription generally includes a brief identification of the prophet, date, or subject (e.g., Isa 1:1; Hos 1:1; Joel 1:1; Amos 1:1; Mic 1:1; Nah 1:1; Zeph 1:1; Hag 1:1; Zech 1:1). Three books begin with a more elaborate narrative introduction that includes elements of the superscription (Jer 1:1-3; Ezek 1:1-3; Jonah 1:1). The superscription may also identify the book generically as the "words" (Jer 1:1; Amos 1:1), "vision" (Isa 1:1; Obad 1:1; Nah 1:1), "pronouncement" (Hab 1:1; Mal 1:1), or "book" (Nah 1:1) of the prophet. Most frequently it identifies the book as the "word of YHWH" which came to the prophet (e.g., Ezek 1:1-3; Hos 1:1; Joel 1:1; Jonah 1:1; Mic 1:1; Zeph 1:1; Hag 1:1; Zech 1:1; Mal 1:1). The prophetic books may also include superscriptions for textual blocks within the book (e.g., Isa 2:1 [Isa 2–4]; 13:1 [Isa 13–23]; Jer 46:1 [Jer 46–51]) or for individual compositions (e.g., Isa 14:28; 15:1; 30:6; 38:9; Jer 7:1; 11:1; Hab 3:1; Hag 2:1, 10; Zech 1:7; 7:1; 9:1; 12:1). Several prophets, including Jeremiah, Zechariah, and especially Ezekiel, employ first-person autobiographical language that functions as a superscription, e.g., "The word of YHWH came to me (saying)" (Jer 2:1; Ezek 6:1; 7:1; Zech 6:9).

Some consider prophetic books to be completed collections of the message of the prophet, but there is little evidence for such a contention. There are no criteria by which to determine if a prophetic book is a complete collection of the sayings of a prophet or not. Scholars simply do not know whether or not material stemming from the prophet in question failed to be included, either intentionally or accidentally, in the book that bears the prophet's name. The existence of two distinct forms of the book of Jeremiah in the Greek and Masoretic traditions, each with a different structure, arrangement and, to some extent, contents, certainly testifies to the fact that the full inclusion of the prophet's materials, or material attributed to the prophet, is not a criterion for the definition of a prophetic book. Second, not all of the material in a prophetic book necessarily stems from or relates to the prophet. The oracles of Second and Third Isaiah in Isa 40–55; 56–66 and those of Second and Third Zechariah in Zech 9–12; 13–14 attest to the fact that the writings of later anonymous authors can be included within a prophetic book as a means to represent an extension or fulfillment of the prophet's message. Third, prophetic books can only be labeled as collections in the most general sense. Each book has a distinctive structure that indicates a specific intention in composing the book in the first place. They are not haphazard or incoherent collections of prophetic oracles, but well-planned compositions with specific aims.

Many interpreters argue that prophetic books are arranged according to a tri-partite schema that includes (1) judgment against Israel/Judah; (2) judgment against the nations; and (3) promise for Israel/Judah and the nations, but close attention to the structure and themes of individual texts demonstrates that this view cannot be upheld. Although, prophetic books tend to focus on the punishment and restoration of Israel/Judah, the specific structural principle varies book by book. It may be chronological (e.g., Ezekiel, Haggai, Zechariah); generic (e.g., Isaiah; Obadiah, which are presented as prophetic visions; Nahum, which is presented as a prophetic disputation; Habakkuk, which is presented as a prophetic pronouncement followed by a prayer). It may also appear as a simple narrative (Jonah).

The setting for the composition and reading of prophetic books appears to be the Jerusalem Temple. A number of prophetic books contain liturgical texts (e.g., Isa 12; 33; Hab 3; the hymns of Second Isaiah and Amos; the lament-response form of Joel; and the partial acrostic of Nahum). The liturgical forms of these texts indicate that they were read as part of the Temple liturgy. Their similarities with the Psalms, and the references to the prophetical roles of the Temple Levitical singers, demonstrate the potential use of prophetic texts in the Temple liturgy.[20]

Prophetic literature contains a wide variety of narratives written by or about prophets. Such narratives point to the literary setting of prophecy, in which later tradents attempted to preserve traditions about the prophets or to reflect on the significance of the prophet's words or activities. Some are autobiographical in form, which suggests that the actual writing of prophetic literature began with the prophets themselves. Prophets must therefore be considered as writers as well as speakers, since prophecy is both a literary and an oral phenomenon. Prophets cannot be considered solely as irrational ecstatic shaman figures, but as clear rational thinkers who reflect upon and interpret their ecstatic experiences. Such reflection and writing by both the prophets themselves and by their tradents suggest continuity between the original prophets and their later redactors.

One of the most characteristic genres of prophetic literature is the prophetic vision report.[21] It is generally autobiographical, and recounts what a prophet claims to see or hear. It typically contains (1) an announcement of the vision that states what the prophet "saw"; (2) a transition to the vision indicated by the Hebrew expression *wehinneh*, "and behold"; and (3) the vision itself. Prophetic vision reports were likely set in the context of divination where they functioned as a means to answer individuals who approached a prophet to determine divine intentions (see 2 Kgs 8:7-15; Ezek 14; 20; Jer 38:21-23). In their present literary contexts, they authenticate and convey the prophetic message.

The prophetic word report is a narrative genre that also authenticates and conveys a prophetic message.[22] It generally begins with the prophetic word formula, which combines the phrase *debar yhwh* ("the word of YHWH") with the verb *hayah* ("to be, happen"), the preposition *'el* ("unto"), and the name of the prophet or the pronoun "me" (e.g., *haddabar 'ašer hayah 'el yirmeyahu me'et yhwh*, "the word which was unto Jeremiah from YHWH" [Jer 35:1]; *wayehi debar yhwh 'elay le'mor*, "and the word of YHWH was unto me saying" [Ezek 14:2]). Other narrative elements specify the setting of the prophetic word, and a quotation of the word of YHWH to the prophet then follows (e.g., Jer 21:1-10; 32:1-44; Ezek 14:1-11; 20:1-44).

The symbolic action report is a first- or third-person narrative that describes an act by the prophet intended to symbolize YHWH's intentions or actions toward the people.[23] The symbolic action frequently confirms a prophetic word or vision (e.g., Hos 1;

3; Isa 7:3; 8:1-4; 20:1-6; Jer 13:1-11; 16:1-4, 5-7, 8-9; 32:1-15; Ezek 4:1–5:17; 12:1-20; 37:15-28; cf. 1 Kgs 11:29-39; 22:11).

The prophetic vocation account presents an autobiographical narrative of the prophet's experience of having been called by YHWH, ordained, or commissioned to convey YHWH's message.[24] There are two basic types. One presents a vision in the heavenly court of YHWH in which the Deity commissions the prophet to speak (e.g., Isa 6; Ezek 1–3; cf. 2 Kgs 22:19-23). The other emphasizes a very personal experience of YHWH in which the coming word of G-d replaces the visionary experience (e.g., Jer 1:4-10; cf. Exod 3–4; Judg 6:11-14). The vocation accounts share a number of consistent elements, including a divine confrontation, an introductory word, a commission, an objection, a reassurance, and a sign. The form is derived from settings in which ambassadors or messengers present their credentials (e.g., Gen 24:35-48). Its purpose is to authenticate the prophet as YHWH's representative.

The prophetic story is a narrative in which the prophet plays a central role.[25] There are a variety of subgenres, based primarily on content and aim.

The prophetic legend focuses on the prophet as an exemplar of virtue, goodness, piety, power, and divine favor in order to edify its audience or to inculcate religious devotion. The "simple legenda" (2 Kgs 2:19-22, 23-24; 4:1-7, 38-41, 42-44; 6:1-7; 13:20-21) recount the performance of a miracle that demonstrates the prophet's or the holy man's power over nature employed for the benefit and veneration of the people. The "elaborations of the legenda" (2 Kgs 1:2-17a; 4:8-37) display a fully developed plot which explains the circumstances of the miracle. The "vita" (see the Elisha cycle in 1 Kgs 19:19–2 Kgs 13:19; esp. 2 Kgs 2:1-18 on the ascension of Elijah) attempts to describe the origins and end of the prophet or holy man. The genre presupposes a large existing body of legenda, and results in the presentation of a "biography of legenda."

The "political legenda" (2 Kgs 6:8-23; 6:24–7:20) place the prophet in the arena of politics in order to overcome an opponent who attempts to belittle the holy man's abilities. The details of political events found in these legenda are commonly found in historiography. Like historiography, "prophetic historiography" (2 Kgs 9:1-10:28; 2 Kgs 18:13–19:37 [cf. Isa 36–37]; 2 Kgs 20:12-19 [cf. Isa 39]) treats a series of continuous political events, avoids supernatural explanations, attempts to be historically accurate, and suggests causal relationships. It differs, however, in that a prophetic word is often sufficient cause for an event, and the adherence to or rejection of that word is frequently the cause of the success or failure of major characters. The "prophetic biography" does not attempt to glorify the prophet as "Holy Man." Instead, it contains details of political events in the lifetime of the prophet, and it aspires to authenticity and historical accuracy.

The "ethical legenda" (e.g., Num 20:1-13; 2 Kgs 4:1-7, 18-37; 5; 20:1-11 [cf. Isa 38]) emphasize the power of prayer and the word of YHWH in order to concentrate on the *significance* rather than the *fact* of the miracle. The "exemplum" (e.g., 1 Kgs 22:1-28) employs the example of a historically recognized prophet or the opponents of a prophet to teach a moral, whereas the closely related "parable" (e.g., Jonah; 1 Kgs 13) instructs by means of an imaginary incident. The "epic" (e.g., 1 Kgs 16:29–19:18) surpasses the miracle-working primitivism of the legenda to focus on an idea that dominates the prophet's life struggle, for example, the choice of YHWH over Baal in the Elijah cycle. Finally, the "martyrology" (Jer 38:28b; 39:3, 11-14; 40:1-6) presents a believer who, at the risk of his life, testifies to the existence of God before nonbelievers.

Although the forms of prophetic literature testify to the extensive writing activities of the prophets, the prophets appear to have functioned first and foremost as speakers. Prophetic literature contains a wide variety of characteristic prophetic speech genres. Many of these forms appear to be derived from social settings outside of prophecy itself, which demonstrates that the prophets were well rooted in the life of the people and aware of the world around them.

One of the most basic speech forms employed by the prophets is the oracle.[26] An oracle is a divine communication presented through an intermediary such as a priest, prophet, or seer. It may be delivered in response to an inquiry (cf. Num 22:7-12, 19-20; Josh 7:6-15; Judg 1:1-2; 1 Sam 23:2, 10-11; 2 Sam 5:23-24), or it may be unsolicited. The oracle has no specific form, but it is generally indicated by presence of the oracular formula, *ne'um yhwh*, "utterance of YHWH," at its beginning, middle, or end. Examples appear throughout prophetic literature, frequently in conjunction with other prophetic speech forms (Isa 14:4-23; Isa 17:1-6; 30:1-5;

41:10-16; Jer 1:4-10; 30:1-3; Ezek 11:7-13; 24:9-14; Hos 11:1-11; Amos 2:6-16; Nah 2:14; Zeph 1:2-3; and so forth; cf. Num 24:3-9, 15-24). The setting of the oracle appears to be a formal oracular inquiry through dreams, Urim, or the prophets (1 Sam 28:6), perhaps in a cultic context (cf. Num 22–24).

The prophetic pronouncement *(maśśa')* is a standard prophetic form of discourse in which the prophet attempts to explain how YHWH's actions will be manifested in the realm of human affairs.[27] The genre has no specific formal structure, other than an identification of the text as a *maśśa'*, "pronouncement, burden, oracle"), in a superscription (e.g., Isa 13:1; 14:28; 30:6; Nah 1:1; Hab 1:1; Zech 9:1; 12:1; Mal 1:1). The term itself is derived from the verb *nś'*, "to lift up," and it may well have been employed in a setting of oracular inquiry (Jer 23:16-40; cf. Num 24:3, 21, 23).

The messenger speech appears frequently in prophetic literature, although it is hardly a unique prophetic form.[28] It is essentially a report of an oral message delivered by a messenger, in which the words dictated by the sender are repeated literally to the recipient (cf. Gen 32:1-5). The form is identified by the appearance of the messenger formula, *koh 'amar* (PN), "thus says (PN)." In prophetic literature it appears as *koh 'amar yhwh*, "thus says YHWH," or as *'amar yhwh*, "says YHWH," since YHWH is the one who sends the prophet as a messenger; otherwise, it has no distinguishing characteristics.

The most basic form of prophetic speech is the prophetic announcement or prophecy.[29] It can only be considered as a genre in the broadest sense in that it has no specific form other than an unsolicited announcement by a prophet of future events or future actions by YHWH. It complements the solicited prophetic oracle discussed above. The prophetic announcement can appear in a number of variations that announce both judgment and salvation.

One of the most widely recognized subgenres of the prophetic announcement is the prophetic judgment speech in which the prophet speaks on behalf of YHWH to announce disaster to individuals, groups, or nations.[30] It includes a statement of the reasons for judgment, a logical connective, such as *laken*, "therefore," and the announcement of judgment, often in combination with the messenger formula (e.g., Mic 3:9-12; Isa 8:6-8; Jer 11:9-12). In cases where a punishment is decreed without reason, the announcement of judgment functions separately as an independent genre (e.g., 2 Kgs 20:1 [Isa 38:1]; Jer 22:10, 11-12; 22:24-27). The genre appears to be heavily influenced by juridical language.

A variation of the prophetic judgment speech is the prophetic proof saying in which a prophet announces punishment against an individual, group, or nation, and argues that the punishment will convince the recipient to recognize YHWH.[31] Examples appear in 1 Kgs 20:13, 28; Isa 41:17-20; 49:22-26; Ezek 12:19-20; 25:6-7; and 25:8b-11. The primary form contains two elements: (1) the announcement of punishment and (2) the recognition formula, "and you shall know that I am YHWH" (e.g., Ezek 12:19-20).

The counterpart to the prophetic judgment speech is the prophecy of salvation in which a prophet speaks on behalf of YHWH to announce salvation to individuals, groups, or the nation (e.g., Isa 7:7-9; Jer 28:2-4; 31:2-6; 34:4; Amos 9:11-12, 13-15; Mic 5:10-20).[32] The basic pattern of the prophecy of salvation includes a proclamation of deliverance followed by blessing, which may refer to prosperity in preexilic times and restoration of a state of well-being after the collapse in 587 B.C.E. It has a long history of use, but the most important developments in the form take place in the exilic and postexilic periods, especially in relation to the oracle of salvation found in Deutero-Isaiah (Isa 41:8-13, 14-16; 43:1-7; 44:1-5). The oracle of salvation originates in a cultic situation of lament calling for YHWH's intervention. This is illustrated in Deutero-Isaiah where the "promise of salvation" includes a "call of reassurance" which employs the characteristic reassurance formula, "fear not," the "basis of reassurance in the perfect tense or a nominal form," and the "future-oriented basis" which is identical with the "proclamation of salvation." This sets the pattern for the independent examples of the prophecy of salvation that appear in Deutero-Isaiah and in other prophetic writings. The origins of the prophetic announcement of salvation may also be traced to oracular inquiry.

A special form of the prophecy of salvation is the announcement of a royal savior, in which the prophet announces and describes the rule of a just and righteous king (e.g., Isa 11:1-10; 32:1-8; Jer 23:5-6; 33:15-16; and Mic 5:1-4).[33] There is no set structure, but characteristic elements include the announcement of the new king's reign, his names, a description of the righteousness and peace that will characterize his rule, and descriptions of social, cosmic, or political chaos that preceded and necessitated the new king's rule. The form appears extensively in Egypt and Mesopotamia, where it justifies the rule of a new king or usurper.

A special form of the prophetic announcement is the prophecy concerning a foreign nation.[34] The form is identified primarily by content in that it focuses on the punishment or destruction of a foreign nation by an enemy. Prophecies concerning foreign nations frequently appear in series (Isa 13–23; Jer 46–51; Ezek 25–32; Amos 1–2; Zeph 2:4-15), although they may appear individually as well (e.g., Isa 34; Obadiah; Nahum). The primary intent appears to be to identify the destruction of a foreign nation as an act by YHWH. The form ultimately addresses Israel even though it is ostensibly addressed to another nation. The setting of the form is in the holy war traditions where it functioned as a means to curse Israel's enemies (Deut 20:1-4; 1 Kgs 22).

The prophetic announcement of a sign is a characteristically prophetic form in which the prophet announces that an event will take place in the future that will confirm the prophetic word.[35] It includes three characteristic elements: (1) a declaration of an event as a sign from YHWH, e.g., "This shall be the sign to you from YHWH"; (2) a subordinate clause stating the significance of the sign; and (3) a description of the event that will constitute the sign (e.g., 1 Kgs 13:3; Isa 37:30-32 [2 Kgs 19:29-31]; Isa 38:7-8 [2 Kgs 20:9-10]; and Jer 44:29-30). The settings for such announcements vary according to the circumstances in which they were delivered, but they seem to be rooted in the practice of oracular inquiry of prophets (cf. Isa 7:10).

Other characteristic prophetic genres employ language derived from a variety of settings, including the legal, cultic, educational, and royal spheres of life. The trial genres relate to juridical procedure and a courtroom setting, which may be located in "secular law" as decided in the gates of a city (Ruth 4) and the royal court (1 Kgs 3:16-28; cf. 2 Sam 12:1-15) or in "sacred law" as decided in a cultic setting (Josh 7; Jer 26). The primary form is known as the "trial speech," the "rib-pattern" (i.e., "controversy"), or the "covenant lawsuit."[36] Examples appear in Isa 1; 41:1-5, 21-29; 42:18-25; 43:8-15; 43:22-28; 44:6-8; 50:1-3; Jer 2; Hos 4; and Mic 6. The form includes three basic elements: (1) the summons to trial; (2) the trial proper, which includes speeches by the plaintiff and defendant; and (3) the sentencing. The form may express YHWH's accusations against the gods of the nations or against Israel.

Various settings have been proposed, including standard court procedure, the cult, and international treaty formulations.

The prophetic disputation speech is frequently related to the trial genres in that they are designed to argue against a particular viewpoint and thereby support the interrogations that take place in a courtroom setting.[37] Although most of the examples appear in prophetic literature (Isa 8:16–9:6; 40:27-31; 49:14-25; Jer 31:29-30; 33:23-26; Ezek 11:2-12; 11:14-17; 12:21-28; 18:1-20; 20:32-44; 33:10-20, 23-29; 37:11b-13; Mic 2:6-11; Hag 1:2-11; Mal 1:2-5; 1:6–2:9, 10-16; 2:17–3:5, 6-12, and 13-21; cf. Nah), the original setting of the form does not appear to be law or even prophecy, but wisdom in which contrasting viewpoints are analyzed and evaluated (cf. Job). Three basic elements appear in the deep structure of the text: (1) the thesis to be disputed; (2) the counterthesis for which the speaker argues; and (3) the dispute or argumentation itself.

The woe oracle commonly appears in prophetic literature as a means to criticize specific actions and attitudes of people, and to announce punishment against them.[38] They may occur individually (Amos 5:18-20; 6:1-7; Isa 1:4; 3:11; 10:5) or in series (Isa 5:8-24; Hab 2:6-20). The form is identified by (1) the introductory exclamation *hoy*, "woe!" followed by a participle or a noun that describes the action or people in question; and (2) additional material employing various forms to elaborate upon the situation.

The prophetic instruction or prophetic Torah is a didactic form employed by prophets to offer guidance to an individual or group.[39] It is frequently linked to the priestly Torah, in which priests give authoritative instruction in response to a question concerning cultic purity or other sacred matters (e.g., Hag 2:11-13; Isa 1:10-17; Jer 7:21; Amos 5:21-24; Mic 6:6-8). It seems likely that both the priestly Torah and prophetic instruction ultimately derive from the more generalized instruction genre characteristic of the wisdom tradition (e.g., Prov 1–9; 22:17–24:22), which may reflect nothing more than the means by which literate persons were educated in ancient Israelite and Judean society. The specific form of prophetic instruction may vary, but characteristic wisdom forms, such as commands, prohibitions, rhetorical questions, calls to attention, exhortations, admonitions, parables, and so on, frequently appear.

The prophetic exhortation is an address form employed to persuade an audience to follow a particular course of action.[40] It complements the admonition, which attempts to persuade against a particular course of action. Together, the two forms constitute paranesis, which is an address to an individual or group that attempts to persuade with reference to a goal. The form varies in that it employs a variety of generic components, including calls to attention, commands, prohibitions, instructions, motive clauses, and so forth. The setting appears to be any situation of public or private address (see Deut 6–11; Josh 1:2-9; 1 Kgs 2:2-9; 1 Chr 28:8, 20-21; 2 Chr 15:7), although the form appears to be rooted in wisdom instruction (cf. Prov 1:8-19) or cultic instruction (Pss 1; 50; 95). In the discussion of prophetic literature, the form is generally associated with the motif of repentance. It makes little sense to maintain that the prophets simply announced judgment without attempting to influence their addressees. Otherwise, they had little reason to speak.

Finally, a number of prophetic texts may be classified as prophetic liturgies (Isa 12; 33; Jer 14; Joel 1–2; Habakkuk; Nahum).[41] There is no set form to a prophetic liturgy; rather, they employ standard liturgical genres such as hymns (Isa 12), prayers (Hab 3), complaints (Jer 14; Joel 1–2), entrance liturgies (Isa 33), oracles, thanksgiving songs (Isa 12), blessings, theophanies (Hab 3), Zion songs (Isa 2:2-4; Mic 4:1-4), and doxologies (Amos 4:13; 5:8-9; 9:5-6). Prophetic liturgies apparently reflect the cultic setting in which prophetic literature was performed and perhaps produced. Furthermore, the frequent use of standard liturgical forms by the prophets in their own speech, such as the complaint (e.g., Jer 15:10-18; 18:18-23; 20:7-9; Hab 1:2-17) and other liturgically based forms discussed above, further testifies to an association between the prophets and the cult.

In the following chapters we turn to the reading of the prophetic books in which the literary and speech genres appear as part of a larger effort to address the issues of divine action and human experience faced by the people of ancient Israel and Judah.

SELECTED BIBLIOGRAPHY

Ben Zvi, Ehud. "The Prophetic Book: A Key Form of Prophetic Literature." Pages 276-97 in *The Changing Face of Form*

Criticism for the Twenty-first Century. Edited by M. A. Sweeney and E. Ben Zvi. Grand Rapids and Cambridge: Eerdmans, 2003.

Ben Zvi, Ehud, and Michael H. Floyd, editors. *Writings and Speech in Israelite and Ancient Near Eastern Prophecy.* SBLSymS 10. Atlanta: Society of Biblical Literature, 2000.

Blenkinsopp, Joseph. *A History of Prophecy in Israel.* Louisville: Westminster John Knox, 1996.

Coggins, Richard, Anthony Phillips, and Michael Knibb, editors. *Israel's Prophetic Tradition: Essays in Honour of Peter Ackroyd.* Cambridge: Cambridge University Press, 1982.

Collins, Terence. *The Mantle of Elijah: The Redaction Criticism of the Prophetical Books.* The Biblical Seminar 20. Sheffield: Sheffield Academic Press, 1993.

Cryer, Frederick H. *Divination in Ancient Israel and Its Near Eastern Environment: A Socio-Historical Investigation.* JSOTSup 142. Sheffield: Sheffield Academic Press, 1994.

Floyd, Michael H. "Basic Trends in the Form-Critical Study of Prophetic Texts." Pages 298-311 in *The Changing Face of Form Criticism for the Twenty-First Century.* Edited by M. A. Sweeney and E. Ben Zvi. Grand Rapids and Cambridge: Eerdmans, 2003.

Heschel, Abraham Joshua. *The Prophets.* New York: Harper and Row, 1962.

Mays, James Luther, and Paul Achtemeier, editors. *Interpreting the Prophets.* Philadelphia: Fortress, 1987.

Nissinen, Martti, editor. *Prophecy in Its Ancient Near Eastern Context: Mesopotamian, Biblical, and Arabian Perspectives.* SBLSymS 13. Atlanta: Society of Biblical Literature, 2000.

Overholt, Thomas. *Channels of Prophecy: The Social Dynamics of Prophetic Activity.* Minneapolis: Fortress, 1989.

Petersen, David L. *The Roles of Israel's Prophets.* JSOTSup 17. Sheffield: JSOT Press, 1981.

———. *The Prophetic Literature: An Introduction.* Louisville: Westminster John Knox, 2002.

———. "The Basic Forms of Prophetic Literature." Pages 269-75 in *The Changing Face of Form Criticism for the Twenty-First Century.* Edited by M. A. Sweeney and E. Ben Zvi. Grand Rapids and Cambridge: Eerdmans, 2003.

Rad, Gerhard von. *Old Testament Theology. Volume 2: The Theology of Israel's Prophetic Traditions.* Trans. D. M. G. Stalker. New York: Harper & Row, 1965.

Rofé, Alexander. *The Prophetical Stories: The Narratives about the Prophets in the Hebrew Bible.* Jerusalem: Magnes, 1988.

Stacey, W. D. *Prophetic Drama in the Old Testament.* London: Epworth, 1990.

Steck, Odil Hannes. *The Prophetic Books and Their Theological Witness.* St. Louis: Chalice, 2000.

Sweeney, Marvin A. *Isaiah 1–39, with an Introduction to Prophetic Literature.* FOTL 16. Grand Rapids and Cambridge: Eerdmans, 1996.

———. "The Latter Prophets: Isaiah, Jeremiah, Ezekiel." Pages 69-94 in *The Hebrew Bible Today: An Introduction to Critical Issues.* Edited by S. L. McKenzie and M. P. Graham. Louisville: Westminster John Knox, 1998.

Tucker, Gene M. "Prophecy and Prophetic Literature." Pages 325-68 in *The Hebrew Bible and Its Modern Interpreters.* Edited by D. A. Knight and G. M. Tucker. Chico, Calif.: Scholars Press, 1985.

Westermann, C. *Basic Forms of Prophetic Speech, with a New Foreword by Gene M. Tucker.* Louisville: Westminster John Knox; Cambridge: Lutterworth, 1991.

———. *Prophetic Oracles of Salvation in the Old Testament.* Trans. K. Crim. Louisville: Westminster John Knox, 1991.

Wilson, Robert. *Prophecy and Society in Ancient Israel.* Philadelphia: Fortress, 1980.

CHAPTER 3

THE BOOK OF ISAIAH

The book of Isaiah is perhaps the best known of all the prophetic books of the Hebrew Bible. Isaiah generally appears as the first of the major prophetic books in both the Jewish Tanak and the Christian Old Testament. There are exceptions, however, since one Talmudic tradition places it as the third book of the Latter Prophets following Jeremiah and Ezekiel (*b. Baba Batra* 14b) and the Septuagint tradition places it as the second book of the Prophets following the Dodekapropheton (Book of the Twelve Prophets). Both Judaism and Christianity look to Isaiah as the primary prophet who announced the famous vision of world peace, in which all nations would journey to Mount Zion to learn YHWH's Torah and to hear YHWH's word, to turn their swords into plowshares and their spears into pruning hooks, and to learn war no more (Isa 2:2-4; cf. Mic 4:1-5). Although Isaiah anticipates a period of punishment, Judaism views Isaiah as a book of comfort (*b. Baba Batra* 14b) because it looks forward to the time when Jews will bring divine Torah to the world at large and exiled Jews from throughout the world will return home to Jerusalem. Christianity looks to Isaiah as the primary prophet who announced the coming of the Messiah, both as the Prince of Peace (Isa 9:1-6) and the Suffering Servant (Isa 52:13–53:12). Apart from Psalms, Isaiah is cited more frequently in the New Testament than any other book of the Christian Old Testament.

The book of Isaiah includes sixty-six chapters that present a combination of prophetic oracles and narrative materials concerning the prophet's vision of divine plans for Judah and Jerusalem. The received form of the book contains material that was written over the course of some four hundred years or more.[1] As indicated below, the composition of Isaiah apparently began in the time of the Assyrian invasions of Israel and Judah during the latter half of the eighth century B.C.E. It continued through the end of the Babylonian exile and the projected restoration of Jerusalem and Judah in the early Persian period during the latter half of the sixth century B.C.E., and it came to a conclusion in the late fifth century B.C.E. during the times of Nehemiah and Ezra.

Nevertheless, the superscription in Isa 1:1 attributes the entire book to the vision of the eighth century prophet, Isaiah ben Amoz, who lived during the reigns of the Judean kings Uzziah (783–742 B.C.E.), Jotham (742–735 B.C.E.), Ahaz (735–715 B.C.E.), and Hezekiah (715–687/6 B.C.E.). Major historical events of his lifetime would include the Syro-Ephraimitic War (735–734 B.C.E.) in which Aram and Israel formed an anti-Assyrian coalition that attacked Judah in an effort to force it into their alliance; the first Assyrian invasions of Aram and Israel (734–732 B.C.E.) by the Assyrian monarch Tiglath Pileser III, which resulted in the destruction of Damascus, Assyria's annexation of Israel's territory in the Transjordan, the Galilee, and the coastal plain, and Judah's subjugation to Assyria; Israel's revolt against Assyria (724–722/1 B.C.E.), including the destruction of Samaria and the deportation of large numbers of its surviving population by the Assyrian monarchs Shalmaneser V and Sargon II; and finally Sennacherib's invasion of Judah (701 B.C.E.) following Hezekiah's revolt. The book also addresses or presupposes events beyond the lifetime of the prophet. Such events include the assassination of Sennacherib in 681 B.C.E., apparently by his own sons; the downfall of the Assyrian Empire in the latter half of the seventh century B.C.E.; the Babylonian exile of Jerusalem and Judah in the sixth century

B.C.E.; the fall of Babylon to King Cyrus of Persia in 538 B.C.E.; and the restoration of Jerusalem from the late-sixth through the fifth centuries B.C.E.

The book of Isaiah presents the prophet as a royal counselor who advises the kings and people of Jerusalem and Judah during the crises of the latter half of the eighth century B.C.E. The book does not tell us whether or not Isaiah ben Amoz was a member of the royal family, but his oracles and actions are consistently based in the royal theology of the house of David. The royal Davidic or Zion covenant tradition maintains that YHWH had chosen Jerusalem/Zion and the house of David as the eternal representative institutions of YHWH's role as sovereign of all creation and that YHWH alone would defend Zion and David from all threats.[2] The presence of the Temple, built by the Davidic monarch Solomon in Jerusalem/Zion, would of course symbolize this theological tradition of YHWH's eternal covenant with David and Jerusalem. The royal orientation of the book of Isaiah is evident in Isa 6 in its presentation of YHWH who appears to Isaiah (and to the reader) as a divine monarch enthroned in the Jerusalem Temple, with a royal court of Seraphim (fiery angelic figures) singing YHWH's praises, "Holy, holy, holy is the L-rd of hosts; the whole earth is full of his glory" (Isa 6:3). The prophet's vision of YHWH presupposes that Isaiah stands by the columns at the entrance to the temple (see 1 Kgs 7:15-22) where he can view the holy of holies, i.e., where the ark of the covenant is located, at the other end of the Temple structure.[3] Other biblical traditions identify this location as the place where the king stands (2 Kgs 11:14; 23:3; 2 Chr 23:13; cf. 2 Chr 34:31).

The narrative presentation of Isaiah likewise illustrates the Davidic/Zion orientation of the book. The prophet appears to King Ahaz in Isa 7:1–9:6 to assure him of YHWH's protection at a time when the king is inspecting the defenses and water system of the city of Jerusalem at the conduit of the upper pool on the highway to the fullers' field in anticipation of an attack by the Syro-Ephraimitic coalition. Isaiah appears naked in the streets of Jerusalem in Isaiah 20 as a symbolic action during Sargon's campaign against the Philistine city of Ashdod in 720 B.C.E. to symbolize the fate of the Egyptian and Ethiopian armies that had come to relieve Ashdod. Such an act illustrates the futility of

Judah's attempts to rely on the assistance of foreign nations, such as Egypt and Ethiopia, rather than upon YHWH, particularly since Isaiah claims that YHWH had sent the Assyrian monarch to punish Ashdod in the first place. Following the arrogant demand for Jerusalem's unconditional surrender by Sennacherib's officers, again at the conduit of the upper pool on the highway to the fullers' field, Isaiah responds to King Hezekiah's plea for YHWH's assistance with an oracle that promised YHWH's complete defeat of the Assyrian army and the death of its blasphemous ruler (Isa 36–37). When Hezekiah became ill (Isa 38), the king's pious psalm prompts Isaiah's efforts to cure the sick monarch on YHWH's behalf. When Hezekiah allied with the Babylonians against Assyria (Isa 39), Isaiah condemns him for failing to place his trust in YHWH. Even though Isaiah does not appear at all in Isa 40–66, the latter part of the book continues to espouse the theology of the Zion/Davidic tradition by identifying King Cyrus of Persia as YHWH's chosen monarch and Temple builder (Isa 44:28; 45:1), Israel as the recipient of the eternal covenant tradition of David (Isa 55:3), Zion as the seat of YHWH's sovereignty throughout all creation (Isa 66:1), and Jerusalem as the city to which the exiled Jews will return (Isa 66:18-24).

The synchronic literary structure of the received form of the book of Isaiah is organized so that it will emphasize the royal Davidic/Zion covenant tradition in an effort to present the prophet's oracles in relation to the major events of Jerusalem's and Judah's experience in history from the time of the Assyrian invasions through the time of the Persian period restoration.[4] Although many interpreters argue that the structure of the book includes three basic parts, including Isa 1–39, which presents the eighth-century prophet Isaiah ben Amos, Isa 40–55, which presents the work of the anonymous exilic prophet Second Isaiah, and Isa 56–66, which presents the work of anonymous writers generally designated as Third Isaiah, such a model is based on a diachronic reconstruction of the book's compositional history, not on its synchronic literary features.[5]

Instead, the synchronic literary structure of the book includes two basic parts, Isa 1–33, which projects a scenario of judgment and restoration on the Day of YHWH for Jerusalem Israel/Judah, and the nations, including Assyria and Babylon, that will reveal

YHWH's sovereignty to the entire world of creation, and Isa 34–66, which no longer projects judgment, but instead presupposes that the judgment of the Day of YHWH against Babylon, Assyria, and the other nations has now taken place and that the time of Jerusalem's restoration is at hand. Whereas Isa 1–33 begins in Isa 1 with an address to the heavens and earth to witness YHWH's punishment of Israel, Judah, and Jerusalem, Isa 34–66 begins in Isa 34–35 with an address to the nations and all the earth to witness YHWH's punishment of the nations and restoration of the exiles to Jerusalem. Whereas the narrative concerning the Syro-Ephraimitic War in Isa 7:1–9:6 portrays King Ahaz's lack of trust in YHWH at a time when his nation faces invasion, the narrative in Isa 36–39 portrays King Hezekiah's appeal to YHWH at the time of the Assyrian invasion.[6] Whereas Isa 1–33 looks forward to the reign of a righteous Davidic monarch who will preside over a period of peace and restoration, Isa 34–66 argues that the reign of Cyrus of Persia and YHWH point to the realization of YHWH's plans for righteous rule in later times.[7]

Fundamentally, this two-part structure for the book is designed to address the problem of evil, that is, it presents its oracles and narratives in order to argue that the tragedies of the Assyrian invasions and the Babylonian exile were not the result of YHWH's failure to protect Jerusalem and the house of David from threats. Rather, these events were the result of YHWH's deliberate plans to reveal YHWH's divine sovereignty to the entire world. The book of Isaiah maintains that the nations act at YHWH's direction. Thus, YHWH brought the Assyrians to demonstrate to the people of Israel, Judah, and Jerusalem that YHWH was not simply the deity of a single nation, but the deity of all the nations of the world. When the Assyrians arrogantly claimed that they and not YHWH held power over Jerusalem, they were likewise condemned by YHWH, together with all the nations of the world that might exalt themselves. Following the Babylonian exile, the book of Isaiah maintains that it was YHWH who decreed that the time had come for Jews to return to their homeland in Jerusalem, Judah, and Israel, and that the nations of the world would acknowledge YHWH's worldwide sovereignty in bringing the exiled Jews home. The book looks forward to the time when this scenario would be realized.

In this respect, readers of the book must recognize that its purpose is not simply to preserve the oracles of Isaiah ben Amoz. Instead, the book's purpose is to present the oracles of the prophet in order to persuade the reader that Isaiah's oracles will be realized in the period of restoration following the return from Babylonian exile.[8] The book therefore addresses its reading audience in order to elicit a response, i.e., it calls upon its readers to adhere to YHWH in the aftermath of the Babylonian exile and to take part in the restoration of Jerusalem in fulfillment of the prophet's oracles.

Of course the structure and contents of the book of Isaiah are far more complex at both the synchronic and the diachronic levels. Isaiah 1–33 begins with a prologue in Isa 1 that lays out the basic themes of punishment and restoration for Jerusalem for the entire book. Isaiah 2–33 then lays out Isaiah's instruction concerning YHWH's projected plans for the Day of YHWH that will transform the entire earth. Within these chapters, Isa 2–4 focuses on the judgment and restoration of Jerusalem for its role as the center for YHWH's sovereignty in the world; Isa 5–12 focuses on YHWH's judgment against Israel and the restoration of righteous Davidic rule; Isa 13–27 focuses on YHWH's judgment against the nations and the subsequent gathering of Israel and the nations to Jerusalem in the aftermath of that punishment; and Isa 28–33 focuses specifically on YHWH's plans for Jerusalem and the emergence of the royal figure who will represent YHWH's sovereignty. Isaiah 34–66 begins in Isa 34–35 with the prophet's announcement concerning YHWH's punishment of the nations and the imminent restoration of Jerusalem; Isa 36–39 demonstrates these principles with a narrative that relates Assyria's defeat and Jerusalem's deliverance in the time of Hezekiah; Isa 40–54 draws upon earlier traditions concerning the covenants with Noah, Abraham, David, Jacob's exile and return, Sarah's barrenness and subsequent childbirth, the exodus through the wilderness, the portrayal of Zion as YHWH's bride, and so on, to argue that YHWH is now restoring Jerusalem; and Isa 56–66 presents a series of oracles that call upon the audience of the book to adhere to YHWH's covenant as Jerusalem is restored. The following structure outline provides an overview of the synchronic literary organization and message of the book according to the various literary blocks of material that comprise the book of Isaiah:

THE BOOK OF ISAIAH

THE VISION OF ISAIAH BEN AMOZ
PROPHETIC EXHORTATION TO JERUSALEM/JUDAH
TO ADHERE TO YHWH

(Isaiah 1–66)

This synchronic literary analysis of the book of Isaiah appears to have its diachronic dimensions as well. In pointing to a period of restoration for the city of Jerusalem and its population, the book of Isaiah presupposes the period of Persian rule in the late-sixth and fifth centuries B.C.E. Indeed, it posits that a member of the royal house of David no longer sits on the throne in Jerusalem, but that first King Cyrus of Persia will be designated as YHWH's messiah and Temple builder (Isa 44:28; 45:1) and later that YHWH will be recognized as the divine sovereign in Jerusalem (Isa 66:1). Even the oracles concerning the nations in Isa 13–23 seem to presuppose the period of Persian rule, since no oracle against Persia appears in these chapters and all of the nations listed, viz., Babylon, Assyria, Philistia, Moab, Aram, Israel, Ethiopia, Egypt, Babylon again, Dumah, Arabia, Jerusalem, and Tyre, were incorporated into the Persian Empire. Indeed, the oracle against Babylon in Isa 21 mentions Elam and Media, elements of the Persian Empire, as nations that would bring down Babylon. The Persians were known for their efforts to enable Jews to return to Jerusalem and to reestablish their life in the land around the

Temple according to Jewish law. Both Nehemiah the governor and Ezra the priest were appointed by the Persian authorities to return to Jerusalem and oversee efforts to restore Jewish life in the city. Insofar as Isaiah points to the restoration of Jerusalem under Persian rule and the restoration of divine Torah in the city and throughout the world, it would appear that the received form of the book presupposes the fifth century restoration efforts of Nehemiah and Ezra. Much of the material in Isa 56–66, and perhaps in other sections of the book, would have been composed during the Persian period restoration of the late-sixth through the fifth centuries B.C.E.

We may observe other stages in the composition of the book as well. The work of the so-called Second Isaiah, the anonymous prophet of the Babylonian exile, presupposes the events of the latter stages of the Babylonian exile during the years 545–538 B.C.E. when King Cyrus of Persia was advancing against Babylon and perhaps had already taken control of the city. The material in Isa 40–55, and perhaps in other sections of the book, such as Isa 2–4; 13–14; 24–27; 34–35; 36–39; and 60–62, appears to have been composed during this period. This suggests that a sixth century edition of the book, including much of Isa 2–55; 60–62, appeared at the end of the Babylonian exile in an effort to announce that the rise of Cyrus, the collapse of Babylon, and the potential return of Jews to Jerusalem were the fulfillment of the oracles of Isaiah ben Amoz. There are also indications of a late-seventh century edition of the book that supported the program of national restoration and religious reform sponsored by King Josiah ben Amon of Judah (r. 640–609 B.C.E.).[9] Such an edition would look to the collapse of the Assyrian Empire and the anticipated restoration of Davidic rule over all Israel during this period as the fulfillment of the oracles of Isaiah ben Amoz. Isaiah 7; 11–12; 32, and other texts appear to presuppose this period, and would contribute to an edition of the book that comprised Isa 5–12; 14–23; 28–32; 33; and 36–37. Of course a great deal of material also appears to derive from the prophet Isaiah ben Amoz himself, which suggests that an eighth century form of the book, which includes materials from Isaiah 1; 2–3; 5; 6; 8–10; 14–23; and 28–31, appeared during the prophet's lifetime or perhaps shortly thereafter. Such an edition would argue that the threat of the Assyrian Empire came directly from YHWH, but that Judah would

survive the onslaught under the rule of a righteous Davidic
monarch who would preside over an era of peace.

The balance of the discussion will therefore focus on each of
the major components of the book in an effort to explain both its
synchronic literary function within the received form of the book
and its diachronic dimensions in relation to the history of the
book's composition.[10]

ISAIAH 1

The prologue for the book in Isaiah 1 functions both as an introduction to the first part of the book in Isaiah 1–33 and to the book
as a whole.[11] It begins with the superscription in Isa 1:1, which
identifies the contents of the book. This includes its literary type
or genre as a prophetic vision, the prophet Isaiah ben Amoz to
whom the vision is ascribed, the subject of the vision concerning
Judah and Jerusalem, and the purported historical setting of the
prophet's visions during the reigns of the Judean kings Uzziah
(783–742 B.C.E.), Jotham (742–735 B.C.E.), Ahaz (735–715 B.C.E.),
and Hezekiah (715–687/6 B.C.E.). The superscription is clearly the
work of someone other than Isaiah. Although the book contains
material that was composed by both Isaiah ben Amoz and later
writers, including both narratives about the prophet and oracles
that presuppose much later times, the superscription identifies
the whole as the vision of Isaiah. The parenetic address in Isa 1:2-
31 lays out the basic themes that appear throughout the rest of the
book, i.e., Jerusalem's punishment and restoration, in the form of
a trial speech that includes elements of accusation (vv. 2-20) and
an announcement of Jerusalem's restoration once the punishment is complete (vv. 21-31). The passage appeals to the audience
to do justice by observing YHWH's Torah and to abandon past
practices of wrongdoing and idolatry. Although much of this
material appears to stem from Isaiah himself, the speech is organized to address the concerns with covenant observance and the
destruction of the wicked that appear in Isa 55–66 as well.

ISAIAH 2–4

The block of material in Isa 2–4 constitutes the first major
subunit of the large section in Isa 2–33 in which the prophet announces YHWH's plans to reveal worldwide sovereignty. Isaiah 2–4

is concerned specifically with the preparation of Jerusalem for this role.[12] As the site of YHWH's holy Temple, Jerusalem/Zion naturally stands at the center of all creation where YHWH will reveal divine Torah to the world at large.

Isaiah 2–4 begins with its own superscription in Isa 2:1, which again identifies the following material according to its genre or literary type as a prophetic word attributed to Isaiah ben Amoz and its concern with Judah and Jerusalem. The superscription is clearly written by someone other than Isaiah. Although some have argued that it once served as the superscription for an earlier edition of the book, it now serves only for chapters 2–4 which are concerned specifically with Judah and Jerusalem, whereas chapters 5–12 and 13–27 take up Israel and the nations respectively.

The initial oracle depicts the pilgrimage of the nations to Zion so that they might learn YHWH's Torah, which will in turn lead to the abandonment of war.[13] The pilgrimage by the nations reflects that made by the people of Judah at times of festival observance when they would go to the Jerusalem Temple to celebrate the holidays, bring their offerings to the Temple, and learn YHWH's teachings. This oracle serves as the basic premise for the three prophetic addresses that follow in Isa 2:5–4:6 which explain the process of Jerusalem's cleansing on the Day of YHWH by which this idyllic scenario will be achieved. Each address is easily identified by its introductory statement formulated with cohortative or imperative verbs that call the attention of the addressee to the following statements by the prophet.

The first address appears in Isa 2:5-9, which takes up the need for Jerusalem's cleansing so that it might serve in this role. The passage begins with an address to Jacob or Israel in verse 5, inviting Jacob to join the procession of the nations to walk in the light of YHWH. Verses 6-9, however, explain that Jacob is unfit for such a role, insofar the house of Jacob has forsaken the ways of YHWH by aligning itself with foreign powers who are bent on war and idolatry.

The second address in Isa 2:10-21 takes up the process of cleansing by announcing the Day of YHWH. It begins with a command to enter into the rocks to hide from YHWH's wrath. The concept of the Day of YHWH is rooted in the liturgy of the Jerusalem Temple where it expresses YHWH's efforts to defeat enemies and to manifest divine glory. Although it is frequently employed against foreign enemies who threaten Jerusalem, it may also be employed against the people of Israel or Jerusalem when YHWH's holiness is compromised. Here it is directed against those in the land who purportedly exalt themselves by relying on their power rather than upon YHWH. It does not specify whether they would attempt to threaten Jerusalem or defend it. This is a classic expression of the Zion tradition that maintains that YHWH alone will protect Jerusalem.

The third address in Isa 2:22–4:6 provides an extended discussion of the process by which Jerusalem and Judah will be cleansed in preparation for its role as the center for YHWH's worldwide sovereignty. Following the prophet's plea in Isa 2:22 to desist from self-reliance, a prophetic judgment speech in Isa 3:1–4:1 respectively threatens both the men and the women of Jerusalem with punishments for wrongdoing. The passage concludes in Isa 4:2-6 with a portrayal of the purified Jerusalem in which the surviving remnant of the people will be once again gathered around the Temple.

Although Isa 2–4 points ultimately to the restoration of Jerusalem that appears in Isa 55–66, much of its material appears to have been composed in earlier times. The idyllic portrayal of peace in Isa 2:2-4 corresponds closely to the concepts and scenario outlined in Isa 40–54, so that it appears to be the product of a sixth century writer. It contrasts sharply with Isaiah ben Amoz's own portrayals of warfare and violence throughout the book and particularly in Isa 2:6–4:1. The prophet's portrayal of exiled leaders and destitute women appears to reflect the aftermath of the Assyrian invasion of 701 when Sennacherib exiled large numbers of Jews, and it would certainly be relevant to the later Babylonian exile as well. The concluding portrayal of the restored remnant of the people around the Temple in Isa 4:2-6 also appears to derive from the sixth and fifth centuries when the Temple itself was destroyed and rebuilt.

ISAIAH 5–12

Isaiah 5–12 constitutes the second major subunit of the prophetic instruction concerning YHWH's plans to reveal worldwide sovereignty in Isa 2–33.[14] The subunit is specifically concerned with the significance of Assyrian judgment against Jacob/Israel and the threat posed by Assyria to Judah and Jerusalem as well, insofar as it portrays Assyria's invasions of the northern kingdom of Israel in conjunction with the Syro-Ephraimitic War of 734–732. Although Israel will suffer punishment in the scenario laid out in these chapters, it projects that Israel will ultimately return to righteous Davidic rule after the Assyrian king is brought down for his arrogance.

Isaiah 5–12 lacks its own superscription, but the shift in concern from Jerusalem and Judah to northern Israel and Judah is clear from the outset. The first oracle in Isa 5:1-7 explicitly refers to Israel and Judah, and it continues through the portrayal of the righteous Davidic monarch in Isa 11:1-16 who will reunite Israel and Judah. The block includes a mixture of prophetic oracles, autobiographical and third-person narrative, and liturgical poetry. It is organized to proclaim a prophetic announcement of judgment against Israel and Judah in Isa 5 and to explain the significance and results of that judgment in the establishment of righteous Davidic rule as a result of that judgment in Isaiah 6–12.

The initial subunit of this material in Isa 5:1-30 employs a combination of oracle types to announce YHWH's intentions to bring a foreign nation in judgment against Israel and Judah. The chapter begins in Isa 5:1-7 with an allegorical song that portrays the care given by a friend of the prophet to a vineyard in the hopes that it would produce good grapes. The prophet's friend does everything possible, clearing stones, planting vines, building watchtowers, digging a vat, and so on, to ensure a good grape harvest. But when the time came to harvest the fruit of the vineyard, it had only produced sour grapes. It is only when the prophet asks his audience what the friend should do about his failed vineyard that the meaning of the allegory becomes clear, i.e., the friend is YHWH, the vineyard is Israel, and the vines are Judah. A pun makes the final point. When YHWH looked for justice *(mišpaṭ)*, only bloodshed appeared *(mišpaḥ)*, and when YHWH looked for righteousness *(ṣedaqah)*, only outcry *(ṣeʻaqah)* resulted.

A series of woe oracles in Isa 5:8-24 then follows to illustrate the basis for the prophet's condemnation of Israel. Indeed, the emphasis on drunkenness and wine in these oracles indicates that they follow up on the initial theme of the vineyard in verses 1-7. He charges the leadership of Israel with abuse, insofar as they

take people's homes and land, drink and feast all day on the proceeds of extortion, and deny that YHWH would bother to do anything about it. Ultimately, the prophet contends that the people
have rejected YHWH's Torah. The passage concludes in Isa 5:25-
30 with the prophet's depiction of YHWH raising a hand to call for
a nation from far away to bring punishment against Israel.

The following block of material in Isa 6–12 is designed to provide an explanation of the reasons and expected outcome of the
judgment against Israel and Judah expressed in Isa 5. The narrative material in Isa 6:1–8:15 recounts the prophet's understanding
of the reasons for the punishment, whereas Isa 8:16–12:6 presents
the prophet's announcements concerning the impending fall of
the Assyrian king and the rise of a new righteous Davidic king.

The narratives in Isa 6:1–8:15 appear in their present position to
provide an explanation for YHWH's decision to bring punishment
on Israel and Judah. Many interpreters view these chapters as
Isaiah's *Denkschrift* or "memoir" because the autobiographical
style of the narratives suggests that Isaiah wrote a first-person
account of his experiences as a means to reflect upon the destruction of Israel and the subjugation of Judah by the Assyrians.[15]
Such a view of this material is only partially correct, however,
since a major portion of the narrative in Isa 7:1-25 is formulated
as a third-person narrative about the prophet. Although these narratives may have originally appeared as autobiography, a later
writer has reworked them to emphasize Isaiah's encounter with
Ahaz in chapter 7. As noted above, this narrative contrasts Ahaz's
refusal to place trust in Isaiah's promises of YHWH's protection at
a time of threat with Hezekiah's appeal to YHWH for protection in
a very similar situation of threat in Isa 36–39. The pointed contrast
between the two kings is an important link that binds together the
two major halves of the book of Isaiah.

Isaiah 6:1–8:15 contains two narrative subunits that explain the
reasons for YHWH's judgment. The first is the autobiographical
account in Isa 6:1-13 of Isaiah's vision of YHWH in the Temple.
Interpreters have debated whether this narrative represents
Isaiah's initial commission by YHWH to serve as a prophet or constitutes a later reflection on his failure to prevent the people from
suffering judgment.[16] Those who see it as a later reflection
assume that the book is presented in chronological order and note
that the narrative appears only after the oracles in Isa 1–5. There

is no clear indication that the book is presented in a strictly chronological order, and the initial reference to the year that King Uzziah died (ca. 742 B.C.E.) points to a time when a relatively secure and prosperous period in Israel's and Judah's history came to an end as the Assyrian Empire began to pose a threat to the region (see 2 Kgs 14–17).

The vision itself raises issues of tremendous theological importance. The vision of YHWH enthroned and surrounded by a court of winged, fiery angelic creatures *(śerap)* is derived from a Hebrew verb that means "to burn" and presents YHWH as a holy, divine monarch. Such a vision presupposes the imagery of the Holy of Holies in the Jerusalem Temple and the ark of the covenant that symbolizes YHWH's throne on earth (1 Sam 4:4; 6:2; Isa 37:16; 66:1; Pss 80:2; 99:1). Indeed, the three-room Temple built by Solomon employs the same basic structure as a royal palace in which the Holy of Holies is based on the pattern of a king's throne room.[17] The fiery Seraphs and the smoke that fills the "house," i.e., "Temple," recall the imagery of the Temple *menorot* (candelabra) and incense altars that are employed during festival worship. The call of the Seraphs, "Holy, holy, holy is the L-rd of Hosts; the whole earth is full of his glory," is an expression of YHWH's holy nature as divine monarch that appears in the liturgies of Judaism as the Kedushah and of Christianity as the Trisagion. Isaiah's lips are purified in a manner similar to the mouth purification rituals of ancient Near Eastern oracle diviners.[18] This enables Isaiah to respond to YHWH's call for someone to speak to the people on YHWH's behalf.

The prophet's commission, however, is very disturbing.[19] His task is to make sure that the people do not understand the judgment that will overtake them lest they repent and be saved from YHWH's judgment. As the narrative concludes, the imagery of the burning stump makes it clear that YHWH intends to destroy some 90 percent of the people until only a remnant remains. Such an image functions as a means to come to grips with the enormity of the disaster that overtook Israel and Judah during the Assyrian period and even the later Babylonian exile. In other words, by maintaining that the disaster was part of a divine plan, the prophet contends that YHWH is indeed sovereign over the world. Although many interpreters view this narrative as an expression of YHWH's holiness, one wonders what might have happened if

Isaiah had stood up and told YHWH that such an act is immoral and not fitting for a righteous deity. When Abraham (Gen 18), Moses (Exod 33; Num 14), Job, and Amos (Amos 7:1-6) posed such questions to YHWH, YHWH relented—at least in part—in each case. We may note that the book of Isaiah does end with a scenario of continued judgment; perhaps Isa 6 shows the reader the consequences of failing to challenge evil, even when it comes from the highest authority.

The narratives in Isa 7:1–8:15 present an account of Isaiah's actions in the Syro-Ephraimitic War (735–732 B.C.E.) when Aram and Israel formed an alliance to fight against Assyria and attacked Judah in an effort to force it into the alliance by removing the Davidic king (Jotham and then Ahaz) and replacing him with a ruler of their own choosing.[20] Overall, the narrative is designed to portray King Ahaz's refusal to trust in YHWH's promises of protection as a cause for Assyria's invasion of the region. The narrative portrays Isaiah's encounter with Ahaz while the king was inspecting Jerusalem's water system, a crucial element in the defenses of an ancient city expecting a siege, at the end of the conduit of the upper pool on the highway to the fullers' field (N.B., a fuller is one who does laundry). Isaiah's symbolically named son, Shear Yashuv, "a remnant will return," expresses Isaiah's belief that many Judeans would die in the attack, but YHWH would protect the city. When Ahaz balked at accepting Isaiah's assurances, the prophet demanded that the king test YHWH by asking another sign. When Ahaz refused this as well, Isaiah announced a sign in the birth of Immanuel, "G-d is with us," whose name indicates that YHWH would be with Judah to punish it for Ahaz's refusal to accept Isaiah's assurances. It is striking that Ahaz's refusal to test YHWH is actually a very pious act, but his failure to do so nevertheless results in an Assyrian invasion of the region that subjugates Judah as well as Israel. As in Isaiah 6, Ahaz's testing of divine authority might have averted the disaster. We readers must remember that Ahaz was a twenty-year-old king, who was faced with a choice of accepting invasion by the Syro-Ephraimitic coalition or subjugation by Assyria. Nevertheless, had he waited out the siege as Isaiah suggested, Assyria would have invaded anyway, but Ahaz would not have been so deeply indebted to Assyria for saving his life. The birth of a third baby to the prophet symbolically represents the Assyrian invasion, insofar as the boy is named Maher-Shalal-Hash-Baz, "the spoil speeds, the prey hastens."

The command by the prophet to bind up the testimony and seal the teaching among his disciples in Isa 8:16 marks the beginning of his announcements concerning the downfall of Assyria and the rise of a righteous Davidic king in Isa 8:16–12:6. The first portion of the prophet's announcements in Isa 8:16–9:6 envisions a long period of darkness and distress prior to the emergence of a righteous Davidic king who would preside over a period of peace, justice, and righteousness. Interpreters generally maintain that the prophet's oracle points to the birth of King Hezekiah, but the anonymity of the oracle has enabled it to be read generally as a reference to royal or messianic figures, such as Josiah, Cyrus, Zerubbabel, Jesus, Simon Bar Kochba, and so forth, in much later times as well. The prophet's statements reflect frustration on his part, but his comments are very important for understanding the formation of the book, particularly since his decision to wait for YHWH, "who is hiding his face from the house of Jacob," points to future action by YHWH that ultimately would be revealed in the Babylonian exile and the Persian period restoration of Jerusalem.

The second portion of the prophet's announcements in Isa 9:7–12:6 presents a far more detailed scenario of judgment and restoration. Isaiah 9:7–10:4 begins this segment with a series of oracles that express YHWH's judgment against the northern kingdom of Israel, which was destroyed by the Assyrians in 722/1 B.C.E. (see 2 Kgs 17). It continues in Isa 10:5–12:6 with a portrayal of the arrogance of the Assyrian king, who maintained that his own power enabled him to threaten Jerusalem much as the Egyptian Pharaoh had once threatened the Hebrew slaves (cf. Isa 2:10-21). Isaiah's oracles maintain that YHWH would bring down the Assyrian king just as one would chop down the branches of an olive tree at harvesttime. This in turn would allow for a new shoot to grow from the stump of Jesse to produce a new Davidic monarch who would reunite Israel and Judah, defeat the nations that oppress them, and return the exiles from Assyria just as YHWH had returned the slaves from Egypt in an earlier time. Indeed, the concluding hymn for this section in Isa 12:1-6 even cites statements from the song of the sea in Exod 15 (cf. Isa 12:2b, 5a with Exod 15:1b; see also Pss 105:1; 118:14).

Although many interpreters maintain that the Davidic oracle and the hymn in Isa 11:1–12:6 are postexilic compositions, the references to the new king as a little child (Isa 11:6-8), the reunification of Israel and Judah, and the return of exiles from Assyria suggest that this material was composed during the reign of King Josiah, who ascended the Judean throne at the age of eight and attempted to restore Israel and Judah in the aftermath of Assyria's collapse (see 2 Kgs 22–23). Although Isa 5–12 is heavily edited by later writers (e.g., Isa 7:1-25), much of the material in Isa 6; 8:1–10:34 appears to derive from Isaiah ben Amoz himself. Even so, this section is easily read in relation to the Babylonian and Persian periods as well.

ISAIAH 13–27

Isaiah 13–27 constitutes the third major component of Isaiah's instruction concerning YHWH's plans to reveal worldwide sovereignty in Isa 2–33. The subunit builds upon the earlier concerns with Jerusalem and Judah in Isa 2–4 and Israel and Judah in Isa 5–12 by focusing specifically on the role of the nations in YHWH's plans. Although this block of materials begins with a superscription in Isa 13:1, the superscription introduces only the oracle concerning Babylon in Isa 13:1–14:27. Nevertheless, Isa 13:1 marks the beginning of the subunit because it also qualifies the passage as "the oracle concerning Babylon that Isaiah son of Amoz saw," just as Isa 1:1 and 2:1 referred respectively to "the vision" and "the word" that "Isaiah son of Amoz saw." Furthermore, Isa 13:1 is the first in a series of superscriptions throughout chapters 13–23 that are formulated similarly as "the oracle (Hebrew, *massa'*) concerning . . ." to introduce each of the oracles concerning the nations that appear in this sub-unit, i.e., Isa 14:28 (Philistia); Isa 15:1 (Moab); Isa 17:1 (Damascus); Isa 19:1 (Egypt); Isa 21:1 (wilderness of the sea, i.e., Babylon); Isa 21:11 (Dumah); Isa 21:13 (desert plain, i.e., Arabia); Isa 22:1 (valley of vision, i.e., Jerusalem); and Isa 23:1 (Tyre). Although Isa 24–27 do not present individual oracles concerning the nations like Isa 13–23, chapters 24–27 are linked to chapters 13–23 by their common concern with the role of the nations in the world following the period of judgment when YHWH reveals divine sovereignty at Zion. The portrayal in Isa 24–27 of worldwide judgment and the gathering of the nations at Zion at the time of Israel's restoration provides a climactic conclusion for the oracles concerning the nations in Isa 13–23.

The literary structure for this text is relatively simple to discern. The oracles concerning the nations in chapters 13–23 constitute the first portion of this text. Each oracle begins with the characteristic superscription, "the oracle *(maśśa')* of . . ." identified above, and it continues with a prophetic oracle that discusses YHWH's judgment against the nation in question. Indeed, such oracles were typically delivered by prophets in Israel/Judah and the ancient Near East immediately prior to a battle to indicate a deity's intention to defeat an enemy nation (see, e.g., 1 Kgs 22; Num 22–24; cf. Deut 20:1-20). Chapters 13–23 therefore present a succession of nations, including Babylon (with comments concerning Assyria and Philistia as well) in Isa 13:1–14:32; Moab in Isa 15:1–16:13; Damascus (with comments concerning northern Israel, since both Aram and Israel formed the Syro-Ephraimitic coalition, and the recognition of YHWH by all the nations of the earth beyond even Ethiopia) in Isa 17:1–18:7; Egypt in Isa 19:1–20:6; Babylon (identified as the wilderness of the sea, a designation for the southern part of Babylonia ruled by Merodach-baladan in the late-eighth century) in Isa 21:1-10; Dumah, an oasis located in the Arabian Desert between Babylonia and Aram, in Isa 21:11-12; the desert plain, a designation for the Arabian Desert, in Isa 21:13-17; the valley of vision, a designation for Jerusalem, in Isa 22:1-25; and Tyre in Isa 23:1-18.

Many interpreters maintain that these chapters are intended to condemn all of the nations of the world, but even a cursory scan of the nations named herein indicates that it is a very selective list. Major nations, such as Persia, are missing, and even more familiar smaller countries, such as Edom and Ammon, are also absent. All of the nations found within these chapters did form part of the Persian Empire in the fifth century B.C.E., and the oracle concerning Babylon in Isa 21:1-10 names Elam and Media, two regions of the Persian Empire, as nations that led the assault against the Babylonians. Such an observation has two important consequences. First, it identifies YHWH's plans to judge the nations with the expansion of the Persian Empire in the late-sixth and fifth centuries B.C.E., which of course corresponds to the designation of Cyrus as YHWH's messiah and temple builder in Isa 44:28 and

45:1. Second, it suggests that the oracles concerning the nations were edited or composed in the Persian period as well. Although close study of the oracles indicates that most of them do in fact stem from Isaiah ben Amoz, several oracles, particularly the one concerning Babylon in Isa 13:1-22, appear to have been composed at the time of the rise of Persia in the late-sixth century. Other elements of the oracles concerning Moab (Isa 16:13-14), Egypt (Isa 19:18-25), and Tyre (Isa 23:15-18) appear to presuppose the interests of Josiah's program of reform and restoration. Although the oracles concerning the nations function well as an indication of YHWH's judgment against the nations in the received form of the book, major elements of Isa 13–23 appear to have functioned in relation to earlier editions of Isaiah as well.

Isaiah 24–27 forms the second portion of the textual block concerning the nations in Isa 13–27. This material is sometimes identified as "the Apocalypse of Isaiah" because it purportedly takes up the eschatological judgment and restoration of the world. Nevertheless, the passage does not portray the end of time. Prophetic literature is filled with mythological language concerning cosmic disruption that signals YHWH's judgment against Israel, Judah, or the nations within the framework of historical events, such as the Assyrian invasions of Israel (see Hos 4); Josiah's reform (Zeph 1); and the Babylonian invasions of Judah (Jer 4–6). Such language is also typical of the blessings and curses that appear at the conclusion of biblical law codes in Lev 26 and Deut 28–30. In the present case, Isa 24–27 looks forward to the nations' recognition of YHWH at Jerusalem, which in fact took place under Persian rule when the Persian Achaemenid dynasty enabled figures such as Nehemiah and Ezra to govern Judah under Jewish law. Such a policy was in fact characteristic of the Achaemenids, who preferred to allow self-governance to elements of the empire provided that they would accept Persian hegemony.

Isaiah 24–27 begins with a prophetic announcement concerning YHWH's punishment of the entire earth in Isa 24:1-23. The announcement employs the mythological language of cosmic destruction, particularly when it refers enigmatically to the breaking of the eternal covenant and the downfall of the city of chaos. The eternal covenant refers to the Noachic covenant that ensured stability of creation (Gen 9:1-17). The city of chaos has been the subject of considerable discussion,[21] although it must be recognized as a reference to the fall of Babylon, which is announced in the introductory oracle for the entire subunit in Isa 13–14. The second portion of this passage in Isa 25:1–27:13 constitutes a prophetic announcement of YHWH's blessing of the earth and the restoration of Zion/Israel at the center of the nations. This section employs a great deal of hymnic material that anticipates YHWH's victory over enemies, and it calls for a banquet for all the nations at Mount Zion once the victory is complete. Such a banquet refers to the worship of YHWH at Jerusalem Temple since sacrificial worship in antiquity enabled worshipers to enjoy a feast as part of the festivities. The concluding material, with its reference to YHWH's restored vineyard (Isa 27:2-6; cf. Isa 5:1-7; 11:1-16), points to the restoration of Israel among the nations.

Isaiah 24–27 is filled with inner-biblical references, in which the passage quotes or reworks earlier statements from other biblical material to portray the scenario of judgment and restoration.[22] Examples include Isa 24:2/Hos 4:9; Isa 24:17-18a/Jer 48:43-44a; Isa 24:20/Amos 5:2; Isa 24:23/Mic 4:7; and Isa 26:21/Mic 1:3. It is noteworthy that the quotations tend to universalize the earlier statement in keeping with the purposes of the present passage. The pattern of quotations and the general concern with the anticipated establishment of YHWH's sovereignty indicates that these chapters were composed in the late sixth century at the time of the fall of Babylon to Persia. References to the return of Israelite exiles from Assyria and Egypt suggest that Isa 27:2-13 may presuppose the Josianic period. In any case, the repeated references to "that day" in these chapters point to future fulfillment as expressed in Isaiah 34–66 and thus the role of these chapters in the final received form of the book.

Isaiah 28–33 constitute the fourth and concluding segment of Isaiah's instruction concerning YHWH's plans to reveal worldwide sovereignty in Isa 2–33. Chapters 28–33 build upon the previous blocks of material concerning Jerusalem and Judah (Isa 2–4), Israel and Judah (Isa 5–12), and the nations (Isa 24–27) by returning to a concern with Jerusalem that culminates in the announcement of a just and righteous royal savior. In keeping with prior references to a Davidic royal figure in Isa 9:1-6 and 11:1-16, the identity of the monarch is not disclosed, although later texts in the book identify him first with Cyrus (Isa 44:28; 45:1) and ultimately with YHWH (Isa 66:1). Indeed, the first-person statements concerning YHWH's exaltation and power in Isa 33:10, 13, 22 make it clear that this passage envisions YHWH as the righteous monarch, in keeping with the final received form of the book.

ISAIAH 28–33

Isaiah 28–33 lacks a superscription (see also Isa 5–12), but it is identified as a discrete textual block by its sequence of introductory "woe" oracles (Hebrew, *hoy*, "woe! alas! ah!," which appear at the head of each subunit in Isa 28:1; 29:1; 30:1; and 31:1. However, the concluding unit differs insofar as an introductory *hen*, "behold!" appears in place of the expected *hoy* to signal the announcement of the righteous king. The *hoy* in Isa 33:1 marks the prophet's announcement of the downfall of "the destroyer," i.e., Assyria or later Babylon, as the righteous king assumes his rule. Such a concern indicates that chapters 32 and 33 together form the concluding subunit of Isa 28–33. The result is a logical sequence of texts that outline YHWH's plans for the announcement of a royal savior in Jerusalem.

Isaiah 28 begins the sequence with a presentation of the prophet's instruction concerning YHWH's purpose in bringing Assyrian hegemony over Israel and Judah. The passage begins with a "woe" oracle in verses 1-4 addressed to the leaders of Israel that calls for them to be trampled underfoot because of their drunkenness and arrogance (cf. Isa 5:8-24). The prophet's instruction speech in verses 5-22 then provides the details of what will take place on "that day" by announcing that YHWH will assume leadership of the people (vv. 1-4) when the leaders of both Israel (vv. 7-13) and Judah (vv. 14-22) are removed. The passage concludes in verses 23-29 with the prophet's use of the allegory of the farmer to illustrate that just as a farmer must plow land and crush grain to produce food, so YHWH must bring punishment to produce the desired result.

Isaiah 29 then follows with the prophet's instruction concerning YHWH's purposes in bringing about an assault against Ariel or Mount Zion. *Ariel,* which many take to mean "mountain of G-d," is a poetic name that is used to identify the Temple Mount (see v. 8). Although some believe that it could be related to the Hebrew term, *har 'el,* "mountain of G-d," it appears to be an expression used for the altar for burnt offerings at the Jerusalem Temple (cf. the Akkadian word, *arallu,* "altar, hearth"). The "woe" oracle in verses 1-14 identifies YHWH as the cause of the assault against Ariel, which contrasts with the traditional view that YHWH's role is to defend Zion. A second "woe" speech in verses 15-24 points to YHWH's plans to overthrow Jerusalem's oppressors once the punishment is complete. The statements that the deaf and the blind will hear and understand the words of the prophet's scroll take up motifs from other parts of the book, such as the prophet's commission to ensure that the people remain blind and deaf in Isa 6, his decision to bind up the scroll during a time of darkness in Isa 8:16–9:6, and the announcements of the second part of the book, e.g., Isa 35:5; 42:18; 43:8, that the blind and deaf will understand YHWH's purposes.[23]

Isaiah 30 follows with an instruction speech by the prophet that is designed to explain YHWH's delay in delivering the people from Assyria. The "woe" speech in verses 1-26 begins with statements concerning YHWH's dissatisfaction with plans to send embassies to Egypt rather than to rely solely on YHWH's protection in keeping with the basic tenants of the Zion tradition (cf. Isa 7). The result will be a delay in deliverance, which has tremendous importance for understanding why the book projects deliverance following the Babylonian exile rather than after the downfall of Assyria. The chapter concludes in verses 27-33 with a theophanic announcement that YHWH will strike down Assyria. Because the fall of Assyria is associated with the fall of Babylon elsewhere in the book (see Isa 13:1–14:23 and 14:24-27; see also Isa 52:3-6), such an announcement implies that YHWH will also strike down Babylon.

Isaiah 31 builds upon the preceding chapter with the prophet's warnings against reliance on Egyptian aid against the Assyrians. The "woe" oracle in verses 1-5 warns that the Egyptians are human and therefore lack the power of YHWH. Isaiah compares YHWH to a lion, the symbol of Judah, who stands watch over prey. The metaphor conveys once again the prophet's view that YHWH will first punish the people before restoring them. Verses 6-9 then call upon the people to return to YHWH since they make it clear once again that YHWH's divine power will ultimately overthrow Assyria.

The climactic passage of this textual unit—and indeed of the first half of the book—appears in Isa 32–33, which presents the prophet's instruction concerning the rise of a royal savior in the context of the downfall of the destroyer or oppressor of the people. As noted above, Isa 32:1 begins with the particle, *hen*, "behold," rather than *hoy*, "woe," to signal the appearance of the righteous king. The first part of this text in chapter 32 is devoted entirely to announcing the appearance of the royal figure. It begins in verses 1-8 by pointing out how those whose eyes, ears, and minds will be opened as YHWH's restoration becomes apparent. Verses 9-19 call for lamentation until the time of peace and security for the people emerges together with the king, and verse 20 points to the happiness of the people at that time. The second part of this text appears in chapter 33, which like the previous chapters of this textual block begins with the particle *hoy*, "woe," in Isa 33:1. This chapter also announces the royal figure, but it does so in the context of announcing the fall of the destroyer, that is, Israel's oppressor. The oppressor is not identified, but the context of the book would call first for Assyria and then Babylon. This chapter includes five basic elements: an announcement of punishment addressed to the oppressor in verse 1; a petition to YHWH asking for relief in verses 2-4; an address to the people concerning YHWH's exaltation in Zion in verses 5-6; the prophet's announcement of punishment that leads ultimately to the royal figure in verses 7-13; and the vision of the royal figure in verses 17-24. As noted above, verses 10, 13, and 22 make it clear that YHWH is the anticipated king.

The presentation of YHWH as king is in keeping with the final received form of the book of Isaiah, which posits YHWH's kingship in Isa 6 and 66. Indeed, Isa 33 makes this assertion very clear with its statement in verse 22 that YHWH is our judge, ruler, and king, who will save us. Recent studies have emphasized that chapter 33 summarizes all of the basic themes of the book, often by taking up the language of other passages.[24] The anonymous presentation of the destroyer or oppressor likewise makes it easy to typologize the figure as the enemy of YHWH and apply it generally to figures named elsewhere in the book, such as Assyria or Babylon. Such characteristics suggest that Isa 33 was composed during the Persian period, and that it plays an important role in tying the major portions of the book together as the concluding segment of the first part of the book and an important transition into the following material in Isa 34–66.

The specific interest in identifying the rise of a righteous king in Isa 32 differs from Isa 33, however, in that it does not point to YHWH as that king. The concern with the king's righteousness and justice relates closely to the characteristics identified in Isa 11, and the placement of this chapter immediately following statements concerning the downfall of Assyria (and not Babylon) in Isa 30 and 31 point to the interests of King Josiah's program of religious reform and national restoration in the seventh century B.C.E. The purpose of such a text would be to point to Josiah as the king who would restore Israel and Judah once the Assyrian Empire had collapsed. The anonymity of the king would allow these chapters to be read in relation to the rise of Cyrus and the collapse of Babylon in the sixth century B.C.E. as well. Otherwise, Isa 28–31 appears to derive largely from Isaiah ben Amoz himself in the eighth century B.C.E. The prophet appears to be concerned with interpreting the problem of evil in his own day, i.e., to explain the disaster of Assyrian invasion as an act of punishment by YHWH and to point to YHWH's role as protector of Jerusalem once the punishment was completed. With the successive additions of Isa 32 and 33 in the context of the seventh, sixth, and fifth century editions of the book, Isaiah's words would be applied to much later times as well.

ISAIAH 34–66

Isaiah 34–66 constitutes the second half of the book of Isaiah. As noted above, these chapters are fundamentally concerned with the revelation of YHWH's plans for worldwide sovereignty at Zion. As part of this scenario, they presuppose that YHWH's punishment of Israel and the nations, particularly Babylon, is complete, and that the time for Jerusalem's restoration at the center of the nations is at hand. Within this section, Isa 40–54 presents prophetic instruction concerning the realization of YHWH's worldwide sovereignty at Zion, and Isa 55–66 calls upon the book's audience to adhere to YHWH's covenant.[25]

ISAIAH 34–35

Within this framework, Isa 34–35 functions as the introduction to the second half of the book. Although these chapters appear as part of the so-called First Isaiah materials in Isa 1–39, interpreters have argued that they represent the work of later writers, perhaps even Second Isaiah, from the exilic or postexilic periods. Apart from such diachronic considerations, Isa 34–35 displays some important parallels with Isa 1 that point to their introductory role in relation to Isa 34–66. Parallels include the calls to attention in Isa 34:1 and 1:2; the focus on YHWH's vengeance in Isa 34:8 and 1:24; the unquenchable burning of Edom in Isa 34:10 and of YHWH's enemies in 1:31; the mouth of YHWH that speaks in Isa 34:16 and 1:20; YHWH's sword of punishment in Isa 34:5, 6 and 1:20; the sacrificial blood and fat of cattle in Isa 34:6-7 and 1:11-15; the references to Sodom and Gomorrah in Isa 34:9-10 and 1:7-9, 10; and the references to wilting leaves in Isa 34:4 and 1:30. Whereas Isa 1 focuses on the punishment of Israel and the removal of its evildoers as the prelude for restoration, Isa 34–35 focuses on the punishment of the nations, particularly Edom, as the prelude for the restoration of Zion. Isaiah 34–35 employs the motif of the Day of YHWH to portray Edom's downfall, much as the Day of YHWH portrayed the downfall of the arrogant in Isa 2 and Babylon in Isa 13. It likewise anticipates YHWH's punishment against Edom in Isa 63:1-6.

Isaiah 34 emphasizes the punishment of the nations as a demonstration of YHWH's sovereignty. Edom serves as an example of YHWH's punishment against the nations because of its reputation for having aided the Babylonians in the destruction of the Jerusalem Temple (see Ps 137; Obadiah). During the fifth and fourth centuries B.C.E, the Edomites were displaced by Arabian nomadic groups known as the Nabateans. Isaiah 34:1-15 announces YHWH's judgment against Edom, and Isa 34:16-17 calls upon the readers of the book of Isaiah to confirm its condemnation of Edom and the nations as a command by YHWH. Isa 35 then focuses on the restoration of Israel's exiles to Zion. Much like Second Isaiah, this chapter employs motifs from the exodus and wilderness wandering traditions to make its points. Verses 1-2 announce the rejoicing and blossoming of nature as a symbol of YHWH's glory, and verses 3-10 call upon the exiles to take YHWH's highway through the wilderness to return to Zion. In addition, Isa 35 calls for the blind and the deaf to open their eyes and ears to recognize YHWH's act (cf. Isa 6; 32–33). Such motifs appear throughout Isa 40–48 as well. By combining YHWH's judgment against the nations and the involvement of the natural world, Isa 34–35 emphasizes the traditional viewpoint of the Zion/Davidic theological tradition that YHWH is sovereign of all creation.

Although both chapters function synchronically as the introduction to the second half of the final form of the book, only Isa 34, with its emphasis on Edom as the representative of the nations (cf. Isa 63:1-6) appears to have been composed in relation to the fifth century edition of the book. The affinities of Isa 35 with Second Isaiah suggest that it was composed as part of the sixth century edition of the book where it apparently served as a literary link that summed up the traditions of First Isaiah and provided an introduction for the work of Second Isaiah.

ISAIAH 36–39

Isaiah 36–39 constitutes the second element of the prophetic instruction concerning the realization of YHWH's sovereignty in Zion in Isa 34–54. Many interpreters consider these chapters as the conclusion to the First Isaiah tradition in Isa 1–39 because they present narrative accounts of Isaiah's interactions with King Hezekiah in relation to the Assyrian invasion of Judah in 701 B.C.E. Nevertheless, more recent interpretation points to the contrast in the portrayal of Hezekiah with that of King Ahaz (see Isa 7:1–9:6) in similar times of crisis.[26] Whereas Ahaz refused Isaiah's advice to rely solely on YHWH for the protection of Jerusalem at the time of the Syro-Ephraimitic invasion, Hezekiah turned to YHWH at the time of Sennacherib's invasion. Whereas Judah suffered subjugation to Assyria as a result of Ahaz's actions, the Assyrian army was defeated and driven from the land as a result of Hezekiah's piety.

As noted above, the parallels and contrasts in these narratives point to their roles in relation to the two halves of the book of Isaiah, i.e., whereas the Ahaz narratives illustrate the basis for YHWH's punishment of Jerusalem and Judah, the Hezekiah narratives illustrate the basis for YHWH's restoration of Jerusalem at the center of creation.

The portrayal of Hezekiah in relation to the focus on Zion's restoration in the second half of the book is not limited to the Assyrian siege of Jerusalem. A second narrative in Isa 38 portrays Isaiah's healing of Hezekiah following the king's prayer to YHWH. A third narrative in Isa 39 points to the Babylonian exile insofar as it portrays Isaiah's condemnation of Hezekiah for receiving a Babylonian delegation as he prepared for revolt against Assyria. Although Isaiah claims that some of Hezekiah's sons would be taken to Babylon, the Babylonian exile is the precursor for the return to Zion in the book of Isaiah.

The diachronic dimensions of these narratives must also be considered. They appear to be drawn from the nearly identical narratives in 2 Kgs 18–20, although the Isaiah version of the narratives seems to have been modified to enhance the portrayal of Hezekiah's piety and loyalty to YHWH.[27] Major modifications include the removal of 2 Kgs 18:14-16, which presents Hezekiah's surrender to Sennacherib and the stripping of the Temple to pay off the Assyrians; the reorganization of the narrative concerning Hezekiah's illness, including the addition of Hezekiah's thanksgiving psalm to YHWH following his healing; and the reformulation of Hezekiah's statement following his condemnation by Isaiah for receiving the Babylonian embassy. Whereas Hezekiah's question in 2 Kgs 20:19*b* suggests some doubt of YHWH, the reformulation as an assertion in Isa 39:8*b* removes any hint of doubt. Hezekiah emerges in the Isaian version of these narratives as a loyal and faithful servant to YHWH. He therefore serves as a model for readers of the book to emulate.

Although Isa 36–39 is formulated as historical narrative, interpreters have long recognized that it contains a very idealistic account of Sennacherib's siege. The slaying of 185,000 Assyrian troops by the angel of YHWH appears to be influenced by the Exodus tradition of the death of the firstborn. Furthermore, the account of Sennacherib's assassination by his sons appears to be basically accurate, although it took place some twenty years after the siege of Jerusalem had concluded. Indeed, Sennacherib's own account of the siege acknowledges that he left Jerusalem without capturing the city, although he does claim to have taken with him some two hundred thousand captives, a large sum of silver and gold that corresponds in part to the amounts listed in 2 Kgs 18:14-16, and even Hezekiah's own advisor and daughters.[28] Apparently, Sennacherib had to cut short the siege to put down revolt in Babylonia, and he left Hezekiah on the throne in Jerusalem after forcing his capitulation. Both sides were able to claim victory. The biblical account of the siege was apparently adapted from 2 Kgs 18–20 to serve as part of the seventh century Josianic edition of

Isaiah. It thereby illustrates YHWH's protection of Jerusalem and the house of David. In relation to the sixth and fifth century editions of the book, it highlights Hezekiah's piety and points to the Babylonian exile.

ISAIAH 40–54

Most modern interpreters tend to treat Isa 40–55 (or 40–66) as an entirely separate unit from the preceding material in Isa 1–39 based upon the identification of an anonymous prophetic writer from the sixth century as the author of the work.[29] Although such a diachronic conclusion is undoubtedly correct, it has unduly influenced the synchronic literary reading of this material. In addition to treating these chapters as an independent work, interpreters have tended to focus on the short, presumably original textual units that comprise these chapters. And yet such a fragmented reading of this material obscures its larger literary structure and rhetorical character. Isaiah 40–54/66 is designed to be read as a larger literary unit within the book of Isaiah. It is presented to the reader as part of the vision of Isaiah ben Amoz concerning the realization in the early Persian period of earlier prophecies of restoration from the Assyrian period. It is designed to convince its readers that YHWH is acting to restore Zion. As noted in the analysis of the structure of Isaiah outlined above, these chapters are organized to make a progressive series of arguments, that YHWH is creator, that YHWH is master of human events, that YHWH is redeemer of Israel, and that YHWH has appointed Cyrus as king, in order to demonstrate the primary contention that YHWH is acting to restore Zion. Each subunit within this text is identified by a combination of formal and thematic factors, and each has a place in the argumentative structure of the whole.

ISAIAH 40:1-11

Isaiah 40:1-11 is the first component of Isa 40–54. It serves as the introduction to these chapters insofar as it reiterates the prophetic commission to announce YHWH's restoration of Zion. The prophet begins by announcing YHWH's message of comfort to Jerusalem that her term of punishment is over and that the time for restoration is at hand. A variety of voices speak, perhaps from

YHWH's heavenly council (cf. Isa 6; 1 Kgs 22:19-23; Ps 82), to call for the preparation of a new highway in the wilderness to lead the people home. An important element of this section is the assertion that "the word of our G-d will stand forever" (v. 8), which in the context of Isaiah indicates that the prophet's earlier prophecies of restoration are now coming to fruition. The passage concludes in verses 9-11 with a commission to *mebaṣṣeret Ṣion*, "the herald of good tidings to Zion," perhaps a designation for the prophet, to proclaim YHWH's act of restoration.

ISAIAH 40:12-31

The second subunit in the sequence is Isa 40:12-31, which asserts that YHWH is the master of all creation and therefore quite capable of redeeming Jacob/Israel. The text begins with a series of rhetorical questions in verses 12-20 that are designed to assert that only YHWH—and not the idols of the nations—could have set the world in order and established justice in it. A second set of rhetorical questions in verses 21-26 carries the argument further by asserting that the audience for this text, i.e., the people of Israel, should know that this is the case from tradition. Indeed, this assertion is key to understanding the argument, particularly since the prophet draws on past traditions, Noah's and Abraham's covenant, the birth of a son to the barren Sarah and Rachel, Jacob's exile and return, the exodus, the wilderness, and so forth, to make the point that YHWH is acting once again. The concluding section in verses 27-31 employs rhetorical questions once again to assert that YHWH is the everlasting creator of the earth who does not grow weary and whose understanding is unsearchable. The unit concludes with an appeal to accept the contention that YHWH is acting on behalf of Jacob by stating that those who wait for YHWH will themselves not grow weary.

ISAIAH 41:1–42:13

Isaiah 41:1–42:13 then presents the next stage in the sequence of argumentation with an assertion that YHWH is the master of human events who is therefore able to redeem Jacob. This particular subunit employs the rhetorical devices of speech before a court of law to make its case to its audience. The passage begins in Isa 41:1-4 with YHWH's speech to a court comprised of creation and the nations which again employs the technique of rhetorical questions to make its points, i.e., YHWH has brought a victor from the east to subdue nations (Cyrus), and YHWH is the first and the last. YHWH then addresses Israel/Jacob in verses 5-20 to assert that Israel is YHWH's servant and that YHWH will continue to be Israel's G-d. These contentions draw upon the traditions of YHWH's covenant with Abraham (v. 8) and the traditions concerning YHWH's provision of water in the wilderness (vv. 17-20). YHWH addresses the court once again in Isa 41:21–42:4 with demands that the other gods of the nations prove their power by demonstrating their ability to tell the former things and the things to come. Again, this is an appeal to the traditions on which the prophet draws. In the context of the book of Isaiah, such traditions would include the oracles of Isaiah ben Amoz. When the gods are unable to provide such proof, YHWH addresses the servant in Isa 42:5-9 to assert that the servant (Israel) will serve as a covenant people and light to the nations, and thereby open their eyes to YHWH's role in planning and carrying out the restoration of Jacob. A hymn of praise for YHWH concludes the segment in Isa 42:10-13.

ISAIAH 42:14–44:23

Isaiah 42:14–44:23 then turns to the contention that YHWH is the redeemer of Israel. The first part of this subunit in Isa 42:14–43:7 employs a combination of motifs from the wilderness traditions and Isaiah's characterization of Israel as blind and deaf to provide an overview of YHWH's actions, i.e., YHWH brought punishment on Israel for failing to observe YHWH's Torah, and YHWH will restore Israel now that the punishment is complete. Isaiah 43:8–44:22 then shifts back to the language of the courtroom to assert YHWH's role as redeemer of Israel. Again, the speech draws upon the traditions of the exodus and wilderness to assert that YHWH will lead a new exodus from Babylon through the sea and the wilderness. An important component of this section is the contention that the idols are powerless to answer YHWH and the call to look to tradition to see that YHWH acts on behalf of Israel. Once again, the subunit concludes in Isa 44:23 with a hymn that extols YHWH's redemption of Jacob/Israel.

ISAIAH 44:24–48:22

Isaiah 44:24–48:22 then makes the extraordinary assertion that YHWH will employ King Cyrus of Persia for the restoration of Israel. Such an assertion is particularly innovative insofar as it posits that YHWH's agent will be a foreign monarch rather than the expected Davidic king. The subunit begins in Isa 44:24–45:8 with YHWH's explicit identification of Cyrus as the agent for Israel's restoration. The assertions draw upon the imagery of the Babylonian *akitu* or New Year festival in which Cyrus was proclaimed king of Babylon in 539 B.C.E. A series of trial speeches then follows in Isa 45:9–48:19. Isaiah 45:9-25 contends that no one can challenge YHWH's role as creator and redeemer of Israel. Isaiah 46–47 presents evidence for this contention by portraying the bowing and stooping of the Babylonian gods, Bel and Nebo, as they are carried through the streets, and the humiliation of Babylon, metaphorically portrayed as a former mistress of the nations now sitting in the dirt to grind meal. Isaiah 48:1-19 rehearses the earlier arguments of YHWH's knowledge and power to assert that the time of Jacob's redemption has come. The concluding hymn in Isa 48:20-21(22) calls upon Jacob to flee from Babylonian captivity into the wilderness where YHWH will again provide water as in the exodus from Egypt (cf. Exod 17:1-7; Num 20).

ISAIAH 49–54

The climactic subunit of the sequence of argumentation in Isa 40–54 appears in Isa 49:1–54:17, in which the prophet contends that YHWH is restoring Zion. It draws extensively on past tradition in its efforts to reformulate the classical Zion tradition. It focuses especially on the enigmatic servant figure, and it calls for the restoration of Bat Zion, "daughter Zion," at the center of creation without a simultaneous restoration of the Davidic monarchy.[30]

The first component of Isa 49–54 appears in Isa 49:1-13, which announces the role of the servant. The servant himself speaks and employs imagery from Jeremiah's call narrative (Jer 1) to announce his own call by YHWH while still in the womb. The identification of the servant is very problematic, since verse 4 identifies Israel as the servant and verse 6 indicates that the role of the servant is to raise up the tribes of Jacob and to restore the remnant of Israel as a light to the nations. Although Isa 40–55 presupposes throughout that Israel is the servant, interpreters have been unable to offer a fully satisfactory explanation for this characterization. YHWH's speech in verses 7-12 reaffirms the choice of the servant and the servant's role as "a covenant people" (Hebrew, *berit 'am,* literally, "covenant of people"; contra NRSV, "covenant to the people"). YHWH's portrayal of the people's restoration to the land once again draws upon the wilderness traditions. A concluding hymn in verse 13 calls for creation to rejoice at YHWH's comforting of the people.

Although the hymn in Isa 49:13 would normally mark the conclusion of a unit, Isa 49:14–52:12 is clearly joined to Isa 49:1-13 by its introductory conjunctive statement, "But/and Zion said, 'YHWH has forsaken me. . . .'" Such a bond indicates that Isa 49:14–52:12 is designed to elaborate on the significance of the preceding text. In this case, Isa 49:14–52:12 elaborates upon the significance of the servant's role by pointing specifically to YHWH's restoration of Zion. The three components of this text make a series of points to demonstrate this contention. Isaiah 49:14-26 employs the metaphors of mother/child and marriage relationships to argue that YHWH has not forsaken Zion. Isaiah 50:1-11 returns again to the language and rhetorical questions of the courtroom to assert that YHWH has not divorced Zion. YHWH points to the Red Sea tradition as a demonstration of divine power, and once again presents the servant, who asserts YHWH's support through all of the suffering that the servant has endured. The third portion of this text in Isa 51:1–52:12 calls upon the people to look to the traditions of Abraham and Sarah, the Garden of Eden, the slaying of the dragon Rahab, the crossing of the Red Sea, and so on, to assert YHWH's capacity to restore Zion and her children. Again, YHWH personified Zion as a bride, and calls upon her to awaken and to see the messenger who proclaims "peace" to Zion and announces to her that "Your G-d reigns." This segment concludes with a renewed call to depart from captivity and to begin the journey to return to Jerusalem.

The portrayal of the suffering servant in Isa 52:13–53:12 constitutes the third subunit of Isa 49–54. Interpreters have continued to debate the identity of the servant, with suggestions including Israel, Josiah, Jeremiah, Zerubbabel, and others.[31] The appearance of this section immediately following the announcement of YHWH's restoration of Zion in Isa 49:14–52:12 suggests that the servant should be identified as Israel (cf. Isa 49:4, 6). Certainly the portrayal of the servant as one who is marred, despised, rejected, wounded, oppressed, and so forth, fits with the general portrayal of YHWH's plans to punish Israel and then to use Israel as a light or example to the nations to demonstrate YHWH's worldwide sovereignty. The portrayal of the servant draws on the image of sacrifice, particularly in Isa 53:10-12, insofar as sacrifice is made in part to play a role in the expiation of sin. In the context of the book of Isaiah, the portrayal of the suffering servant functions as one means to address the problem of evil or exile by asserting that it was divinely ordained. Although such a conceptualization underlies one portrayal of Jesus in the New Testament, the dangers of such a theology become apparent when it is used to justify the killing of Jews (or other groups) as an act of divine will. The history of persecution of Jews throughout Christian and Muslim history until the present day demonstrates that such a concern is not merely theoretical.

The hymnic portrayal of Zion's restoration in Isa 54 constitutes the concluding component of Isa 49:1–54:17. The unit draws upon traditional portrayals of Zion or Israel as the bride of YHWH (see Zeph 3:14-20; cf. Jer 2; Hos 1–3; Ezek 16) and the traditions of the barren ancestral wife (e.g., Sarah, Rachel) to portray Zion's restoration.[32] She appears first as a mother whose children return to her and as an abandoned wife whose husband has returned to her. The passage draws upon the tradition of YHWH's hidden face in Isa 8:16–9:6 in which Isaiah ben Amoz announces that YHWH will hide the divine face from Israel and that Isaiah's children will serve as signs and portents until YHWH acts to restore Israel with righteous (Davidic) kingship. YHWH's assertions of everlasting love and covenant for Zion also draw upon the tradition of YHWH's eternal covenant with Noah (Gen 9:1-17).

ISAIAH 55–66

The last major subunit of Isa 34–66—and indeed of the book as a whole—appears in Isa 55–66, which constitutes the prophet's exhortation to adhere to YHWH's covenant. Although most modern scholars correctly maintain that Isa 55 was composed to function as the conclusion to the work of the anonymous sixth century prophet, Second Isaiah, a synchronic literary analysis of the book indicates that this chapter functions as an introduction to Isa 56–66. Isaiah 55 is set off from the preceding material by an introductory *hoy*, "woe!" or "Ho!" that calls the reader's attention to the following material. In contrast to chapters 40–54, which are designed to convince the reader that YHWH is acting to restore Zion, Isa 55 asks the reader to come, listen, and seek YHWH, who is making an eternal covenant with them. Insofar as Isa 56–66 is designed to define YHWH's expectations of the people within the context of such a covenant in the restored Jerusalem, Isa 55 signals a new concern with adherence to YHWH's covenant.

ISAIAH 55

Isaiah 55 functions as the basic exhortation to adhere to YHWH's covenant in Isa 56–66. It does not spell what such adherence entails—that is left to Isa 56–66—but it employs a combination of imperative addresses and rhetorical questions to invite the audience of the text to accept YHWH's covenant. Once again there is a reformulation of the Davidic or Zion tradition in this passage insofar as it refers to YHWH's eternal covenant with the people with Davidic language even though no Davidic monarch is envisioned.[33] Essentially, the eternal covenant applied by earlier tradition to the house of David (see 2 Sam 7; Pss 89; 110; 132) is now applied generally to the people of Israel at large. The passage reiterates the themes of YHWH's purpose, incomparability, and power by emphasizing YHWH's higher thoughts and ways in relation to those of human beings. It likewise reiterates the continuity of YHWH's word, which will accomplish what YHWH purposes (v. 11). Again, such a statement is particularly important in pointing to the continuity between the two halves of the book that respectively presuppose the Assyrian and early Persian periods.

ISAIAH 56–66

The major component of this unit then follows in Isa 56–66. The chapters have generally been identified as the work of Trito-Isaiah from the late-sixth or fifth centuries B.C.E.[34] Although early scholars argued that they were the work of a single prophet from this period, the variety of concerns and literary forms within these chapters have prompted later interpreters to argue that they represent the work of multiple writers. Some continue to maintain that Isa 56–66 is a continuation of Second Isaiah, particularly since Isa 60-62 appears to be so closely related to Isa 40–55 in theme, style, and content. Indeed, Isa 60–62 does appear to be the work of Second Isaiah, although the same cannot be said for the differing materials in Isa 56–59 and 63–66.

When read synchronically, however, Isa 56–66 emerges as a literary unit that is fundamentally concerned with defining the expectations of the restored people in Jerusalem. These chapters presuppose that a restoration of the people to Jerusalem is imminent, but that it has not yet been fully accomplished. They presuppose that opponents of YHWH's will remain among the people, and that the restoration will take place as those opponents are removed from the people or convinced to join in observing YHWH's will. The presentation of consequences for the wicked together with restoration for the righteous constitutes a very powerful theme within these chapters that plays an important role in attempting to persuade the readers of Isaiah to count themselves among the righteous by observing YHWH's expectations. A combination of formal and thematic criteria indicates that Isa 56–66 comprises three major components: Isa 56–59; 60–62; and 63–66.

ISAIAH 56–59

Isaiah 56–59 is the first major component of chapters 56–66. It is fundamentally concerned with the proper observance of YHWH's covenant and YHWH's willingness to forgive those who repent. It builds upon the prior exhortation to observe YHWH's covenant in Isa 55, but the introductory prophetic messenger formula identifies the following material as a new section. The passage begins in Isa 56:1-8 with a prophetic oracle that calls upon the people to observe justice and righteousness, the Shabbat, and Temple worship, including both sacrifices and prayer, as the basic elements of YHWH's covenant. The oracle also calls for the acceptance of eunuchs and foreigners who observe YHWH's covenant. Many Jews who were compelled to serve as officers in the Babylonian government were made into eunuchs as an expression of their subservient status and many were also born of intermarriages between Jews and foreigners. Although such persons might not have been accepted in the Temple in the past (cf. Deut 23:1-8), the realities of life in the Babylonian exile called for change. The reference to "a monument and a name" (Hebrew *yad wešem*) indicates that the eunuchs would have a future as part of the people. The expression was employed as the name of modern Israel's museum for the Shoah/Holocaust. Interpreters often overlook the fact that this passage speaks of foreigners who have in essence converted to Judaism in keeping with Exod 12:48-49; Lev 16:29; 19:33-34; 24:22; Num 9:14; 11:14-16; Deut 16:11, 14; 24:17-18; 26:11). It is noteworthy that Ezra and Nehemiah did not expel foreign men from the Temple, presumably because they had become part of the people by observing YHWH's expectations. The second element of this text appears in Isa 56:9–57:21, which emphasizes YHWH's willingness to forgive those who repent. The following text in Isa 58:1-14 calls specifically for such repentance, and indicates that YHWH expects both ritual observance and just behavior (cf. Lev 19). The lamentation in Isa 59:1-21 draws upon earlier Isaian themes of YHWH's hidden face and blindness to express the people's expectation that YHWH will restore Zion and enable justice to be realized.

ISAIAH 60–62

The second major component appears in Isa 60–62, which proclaims YHWH's restoration to Zion. The passage presents alternating statements by the prophet and YHWH concerning what the people might expect. The unit begins in Isa 60:1-9 with an announcement of restoration directed to Zion concerning the return of YHWH's glory and the approach of the nations, who will return Zion's sons and daughters and bring gifts and sacrifices to YHWH's altar. YHWH speaks in Isa 60:10-22 to reiterate the scenario of punishment and restoration articulated throughout the book. YHWH's characterization of Zion's people as "the shoot of my planting" recalls both the vineyard allegory of Isa 5:1-7, in which YHWH metaphorically planted Israel and Judah as a vineyard (Isa 5:2), and the oracle concerning the righteous monarch in Isa 11:1-16, which called for the growth of a righteous Davidic shoot (Isa 11:1) who would ultimately see to the restoration of Israel and Judah from exile among the nations (Isa 11:10-16). The prophet speaks once again in Isa 61:1-7 to proclaim liberty to captives and to declare that they will serve as priests for YHWH

81

among the nations. YHWH's speech in Isa 61:8-9 announces an everlasting covenant with the people. The prophet speaks once again in Isa 61:10–62:12 to rejoice in YHWH's restoration of Jerusalem.

ISAIAH 63–66

The third and final component appears in Isa 63–66, which anticipates the period of violence and struggle that will take place as the remaining wicked are punished prior to the full realization of restoration. The unit begins with a depiction of YHWH's punishment of Edom on the day of YHWH's vengeance, which will fulfill the earlier call for Edom's punishment on the Day of YHWH in Isa 34. Isaiah 63:7–64:11 presents the people's lament in which they appeal to YHWH for mercy at a time when adversaries have trampled the sanctuary. The culmination of the book appears in Isa 65–66 in which YHWH answers the lament by declaring death for the wicked and restoration for the righteous as YHWH's kingship is finally realized. This passage refers repeatedly to earlier Isaian texts, such as Isa 65:25, which recalls the portrayal of the peaceful existence of the wolf and the lamb in Isa 11:6-9, and the role of the nations in restoring the exiles of Israel and Judah in Isa 66:18-24 (see Isa 11:10-16; 60:1-7).[35] Although some understand Isa 66:21 to indicate that YHWH will take some of the nations for priests and Levites, the syntax of the Hebrew requires that it refer to YHWH's taking priests and Levites from among the restored Israelite exiles mentioned in verse 20. The result will be a new creation in which all the world will recognize YHWH in keeping with the ideal expressed in Isa 2:2-4.

In sum, the book of Isaiah constitutes a sustained theological reflection on Jerusalem's and Judah's experience from the time of the Assyrian invasions of the eighth century B.C.E. through the Persian-period restoration of the late-sixth and fifth centuries. It grapples with the theological problem of evil—expressed through the historical realities of Assyrian invasion and Babylonian exile—by positing that such an experience was necessary for the revelation of YHWH's sovereignty to all the world. The message of Isaiah is based consistently in the theological traditions of the royal house of David and the Zion tradition that posited an eternal relationship between YHWH and Jerusalem based on the Davidic monarchy and the presence of the Jerusalem Temple. In the absence of a restored monarchy, the book of Isaiah asserts that YHWH is the true king who restores the people around the Temple in Zion for all the world to see.

SELECTED BIBLIOGRAPHY

Baltzer, Klaus. *Deutero-Isaiah.* Hermeneia. Minneapolis: Fortress, 2001.

Blenkinsopp, Joseph. *Isaiah 1–39.* AnBib 19. New York: Doubleday, 2000.

———. *Isaiah 40–55.* AnBib 19A. New York: Doubleday, 2002.

———. *Isaiah 56–66.* AnBib 19B. New York: Doubleday, 2003.

Broyles, Craig C., and Craig A. Evans, editors. *Writing and Reading the Scroll of Isaiah: Studies of an Interpretive Tradition.* VTSup 70/1-2. Leiden: Brill, 1997.

Childs, Brevard. *Isaiah: A Commentary.* OTL. Louisville: Westminster John Knox, 2001.

Darr, Katheryn Pfisterer. *Isaiah and the Family of G-d.* Louisville: Westminster John Knox, 1994.

Hanson, Paul. *Isaiah 40–66.* Interpretation. Louisville: Westminster John Knox, 1995.

Leclerc, Thomas L. *YHWH Is Exalted in Justice: Solidarity and Conflict in Isaiah.* Minneapolis: Fortress, 2001.

Melugin, Roy F. *The Formation of Isaiah 40–55.* BZAW 141. Berlin: Walter de Gruyter, 1976.

Melugin, Roy F., and Marvin A. Sweeney, editors. *New Visions of Isaiah.* JSOTSup 214. Sheffield: Sheffield Academic Press, 1996.

Seitz, Christopher R. *Isaiah 1–39.* Interpretation. Louisville: Westminster John Knox, 1993.

———. "Isaiah 40–66." Pages 307-552 in vol. 6 of *The New Interpreter's Bible,* edited by L. E. Keck, et al. Nashville: Abingdon, 2001.

Sommer, Benjamin D. *A Prophet Reads Scripture: Allusion in Isaiah 40–66.* Stanford: Stanford University Press, 1998.

Sweeney, Marvin A. *Isaiah 1–4 and the Post-exilic Understanding of the Isaianic Tradition.* BZAW 171. Berlin and New York: Walter de Gruyter, 1988.

———. *Isaiah 1–39, with an Introduction to Prophetic Literature.* FOTL 16. Grand Rapids and Cambridge: Eerdmans, 1996.

Tucker, Gene M. "Isaiah 1–39." Pages 25-305 in vol. 6 of *The New Interpreter's Bible,* edited by L. E. Keck, et al. Nashville: Abingdon, 2001.

Wildberger, Hans. *Isaiah 1–12: A Commentary.* Translated by Thomas Trapp. Continental Commentaries. Minneapolis: Fortress, 1991.

———. *Isaiah 13–27: A Commentary.* Translated by Thomas Trapp. Continental Commentaries. Minneapolis: Fortress, 1997.

———. *Isaiah 28–39: A Commentary.* Translated by Thomas Trapp. Continental Commentaries. Minneapolis: Fortress, 2002.

Willey, Patricia Tull. *Remember the Former Things: The Recollection of Previous Texts in Second Isaiah.* SBLDS 161. Atlanta: Scholars Press, 1997.

Williamson, H. G. M. *The Book Called Isaiah: Deutero-Isaiah's Role in Composition and Redaction.* Oxford: Clarendeon, 1994.

CHAPTER 4

THE BOOK OF JEREMIAH

Jeremiah presents one of the most deeply personalized and emotional accounts of all of the prophetic books. The prophet tells us more about himself and his struggles with his people, YHWH, and the events of his day than any other prophet in the Bible. He lived in Jerusalem during one of the most important and challenging periods in biblical history, i.e., the final years of the kingdom of Judah, from the time when the nation lost its independence following the unexpected death of King Josiah in 609 B.C.E. through the Babylonian destruction of Jerusalem and the exile of much of its surviving population in 587 B.C.E. The book of Jeremiah portrays his attempts to grapple with the tragedy that overtook the entire nation. On the one hand, the prophet argues that the destruction of Jerusalem and the suffering of its people is a consequence of their own failure to abide by YHWH's Torah. On the other hand, he looks forward to the restoration of Israel, Jerusalem, and the Davidic monarchy following a period of seventy years of punishment in which YHWH's Torah will be written upon the hearts of the people in the form of a new covenant. For Jews, Jeremiah represents the necessity of life guided by Torah as the means to overcome evil in the world. For Christians, Jeremiah symbolizes the suffering of Jesus that ultimately results in human redemption.

The book of Jeremiah generally appears as the second book of the Latter Prophets in the Jewish Tanak, although some rabbinic authorities maintain that it should be the first book because like Kings it is concerned with destruction throughout (*b. Baba Batra* 14*b*). It also generally appears as the second book of the Prophets following Isaiah in most versions of the Christian Old Testament. Lamentations follows in the Old Testament because of the tradition that Jeremiah wrote this book, and Roman Catholic Bibles include the deuterocanonical books of Baruch and the Epistle of Jeremiah because of their associations with the prophet. With its 1364 verses, Jeremiah is the longest prophetic book of the Bible.

The superscription for the book of Jeremiah in Jer 1:1-3 identifies it as "the words of Jeremiah son of Hilkiah, of the priests who were in Anathoth in the land of Benjamin, to whom the word of [YHWH] came in the days of King Josiah son of Amon of Judah, in the thirteenth year of his reign. It came also in the days of King Jehoiakim son of Josiah of Judah, and until the end of the eleventh year of King Zedekiah son of Josiah of Judah, until the captivity of Jerusalem in the fifth month." The reader learns several important things from this superscription. First, a quick survey of the book of Jeremiah demonstrates that it contains much more than simply the words of Jeremiah. There is a great deal of narrative material about the prophet, major events in his lifetime, and his oracles. The received form of the book of Jeremiah therefore presents the prophet, his actions, and his words in the book, but the superscription does not indicate that Jeremiah wrote the whole book. Other writers are responsible at least for the superscription and the narratives. Many interpreters point to the scribe, Baruch ben Neriah, who wrote down Jeremiah's words after the prophet was banned from speaking in the Temple (see Jer 36; 45), as the composer of the book.[1] The discovery of the name "Baruch ben Neriah the scribe" on a clay bulla or seal used to sign documents from the time of the Babylonian destruction of Jerusalem demonstrates that Baruch was a historical figure,[2] but interpreters cannot be certain that he was in fact the composer of the book. Nevertheless, the prose portions of Jeremiah have much in common, both with regard to literary style and theological outlook, with the books of the Deuteronomistic History (Joshua; Judges; Samuel; Kings).[3]

Second, Jeremiah is a Levitical priest. Although virtually nothing is known about his father (Hilkiah, the high priest during the reign of Josiah [2 Kgs 22–23; 2 Chr 34–35], is not the same man), Jeremiah's identification as a priest from Anathoth is crucial for understanding the prophet as a representative of the Elide priestly line. According to 1 Kgs 2:26-27, Solomon expelled the high priest Abiathar to Anathoth from Jerusalem, leaving only Zadok to found the Zadokite priestly line. First Samuel 22:2-23 states that Abiathar ben Ahimelech, the great grandson of Eli (cf. 1 Sam 14:3) escaped the slaughter of the priests at Nob, and later served as David's priest (1 Sam 23:6-11; 2 Sam 20:25). Jeremiah later refers to the destruction of his ancestral sanctuary at Shiloh (Jer 7:12-14) and to Samuel, who served at Shiloh (Jer 15:1). This background might help to explain his challenge to the view that the presence of the Jerusalem Temple would ensure the security of the city. Jeremiah's identity as a Levitical priest certainly explains his role as a teacher of YHWH's Torah like Moses (see, e.g., the Levitical sermon in Jer 7:1–8:3, in which Jeremiah quotes from the Ten Commandments; cf. Lev 10:11, which states that the Levites are to teach Israel all the statutes that YHWH gave to them through Moses). It also explains in part the presence of the so-called "confessions" or "laments" of Jeremiah (Jer 11:18-23; 12:1-6; 15:10-21; 17:14-18; 18:18-23; 20:7-13; 20:14-18), in which the prophet expresses his frustration concerning his prophetic task, his relationship with YHWH, and the persecution that he suffers from his opponents. Jeremiah's "confessions" are formulated after the pattern of liturgical psalms.[4] As portrayed in Chronicles, the Levites formed the Temple choirs responsible for the singing of liturgical psalms in worship (1 Chr 16:4-37; cf. the Psalms of Asaph in Pss 50; 70–83 and the Psalms of Korah in Pss 42–49). Indeed, the Levitical theology of the Mosaic covenant tradition, which bases Israel's relationship with YHWH on the observance of divine Torah, defines the basic theological outlook of the book of Jeremiah.

Third, the superscription claims that Jeremiah spoke for forty years, from the thirteenth year of Josiah (627 B.C.E.) through the captivity of Jerusalem in the eleventh year of Zedekiah (587 B.C.E.). The superscription notes the reigns of Josiah (640–609

B.C.E.), Jehoiakim (609–598 B.C.E.), and Zedekiah (597–587 B.C.E.).
It omits the brief reigns of Jehoahaz (609 B.C.E.), who was exiled
by the Egyptians, and Jehoiachin (597 B.C.E.), who was exiled by
the Babylonians. This was a crucial period in Judah's history. The
Assyrian monarch who controlled Judah, Assurbanipal, had died
by 627, which enabled Josiah to begin a program of religious and
national restoration in his twelfth year (see 2 Chr 34:3).
Following Josiah's tragic death at the hands of the Egyptians in
609 B.C.E., Judah was subjugated first to Egypt and then to
Babylon in 605 B.C.E. Following Jehoiakim's unsuccessful revolt
against Babylon and his death in 598, the Babylonians deported
his son Jehoiachin and other leading Judeans to Babylon. When
Jehoiakim's brother, Zedekiah, whom the Babylonians had
placed on the throne, failed to prevent a second revolt, the
Babylonian king Nebuchadnezzar destroyed Jerusalem and the
Temple in 587 B.C.E., and deported thousands more to Babylon. A
third revolt in 582 B.C.E., in which Gedaliah ben Ahikam, the
Babylonian-appointed governor of Judah was assassinated, was
put down before the Babylonian army arrived. Unfortunately, a
survey of the book indicates little evidence of oracles spoken during the reign of King Josiah (see Jer 3:6; cf. Jer 22:11-19, esp. v.
15), but it does demonstrate that Jeremiah continued to speak in
Egypt after the assassination of Gedaliah in 582 B.C.E. (see Jer
41–45). This would suggest that the superscription idealizes the
span of Jeremiah's career in an effort to make a theological point
by comparing Jeremiah to Moses, i.e., whereas Moses spent forty
years leading Israel from Egypt to the promised land, Jeremiah's
forty years saw Israel/Judah exiled from the land and Jeremiah
ultimately in Egypt.[5]

Study of the book of Jeremiah is both complicated and
enhanced by the existence of two distinct and yet interrelated versions of the book in the Masoretic Hebrew and Septuagint Greek
traditions. Although both versions contain much of the same
material, the Masoretic Text (MT) is about one eighth longer
than the Septuagint text (LXX). Many scholars maintain that the
MT appears to be an expanded version of the Hebrew text underlying the Greek LXX, although some evidence in the texts suggests the possibility that both texts have undergone extensive
editing since the times of their respective origins.[6] The earliest
complete manuscripts of the LXX text are Codex Vaticanus and

Codex Sinaiticus, both of which are early Christian manuscripts that date to the fourth century B.C.E. Most scholars maintain that the shorter LXX version of the text must be the earlier version of the text that was composed in the Jewish community of Egypt, sometime during the third or second century B.C.E., although the Hebrew text underlying this version likely dates to a much earlier time in the Second Temple period. The earliest masoretic manuscripts, Leningrad Codex of the Bible (1009 C.E.), the Aleppo Codex of the Bible (925 C.E.), and the Cairo Codex of the Prophets (896 C.E.), presuppose a version of the book produced in the Jewish community of Babylonia at some point during the Second Temple period.

Examples of both versions of the text have been discovered among the four fragmentary Jeremiah manuscripts found by the Dead Sea at Qumran Caves 4 and 2.[7] The oldest Qumran manuscript is 4QJer[a], which dates to 225–175 B.C.E., and includes Jer 7:1-2, 15-19; 7:28–9:2 (minus 7:30–8:8); 9:7-15; 10:9-23; 11:3-20; 12:3-16; 12:17–13:7; 13:27–14:8; 15:1-2; 17:8-26; 18:15–19:1; 20:15-18; 22:3-16; and 26:10. This manuscript corresponds to the MT, although it contains many corrections. 4QJer[b] dates to the mid-second century B.C.E., and it includes Jer 9:22–10:18; 43:3-9; and 50:4-6. The text of the first fragment corresponds to the shorter text of the LXX version of this passage, which indicates that 4QJer[b] represents the Hebrew text that underlies the LXX text. 4QJer[c] dates to the Herodian era (30–1 B.C.E.), and it contains a proto-MT version of Jer 4:5, 13-16; 8:1-3; 8:20–9:5; 10:12-13; 19:8-9; 20:2-5, 7-8, 14-15; 21:6-10; 22:4-6, 10-28; 25:7-8, 15-17, 24-26; 26:10-13; 27:1-3, 14-15; 30:6–31:14; 31:16-26; and 33:16-20. Finally, 2QJer dates to the first century C.E., and contains a proto-MT version (with some variations) of Jer 42:7-11, 14; 43:8-11; 44:1-3, 12-14; 46:27–47:7; 48:7, 25-39, 43-45; and 49:10.

Apart from the expanded form of the MT, both versions are substantially the same through Jer 25:13a, but they differ markedly after this point. The MT form of the text includes the largely oracular material in chapters 1–25; the largely narrative material about the prophet in chapters 26–45; the oracles concerning the nations in chapters 46–51; and the historical narrative concerning the Babylonian siege and destruction of Jerusalem, which appears to be drawn from 2 Kgs 25, in Jer 52. The LXX version, however, begins with Jeremiah's oracular material in LXXJer 1:1–25:13a, and continues with the oracles concerning the nations in LXX Jer 25:14–31:14 (= MTJer 46–51); the narrative materials concerning the prophet in LXXJer 32–51 (= MTJer 25:13*b*–45:5); and it concludes once again with the narrative concerning the fall of Jerusalem in LXXJer 52 (= MTJer 52). For the most part, scholars have been unable to determine the significance of the differences in this arrangement. Some have argued that the LXX structure represents a common tripartite pattern in the organization of prophetic books that announce judgment against Israel, judgment against the nations, and restoration for both Israel and the nations.[8] But such a pattern is not well represented in the prophetic books, and it appears to be a pattern derived from Christian systematic theology that is imposed upon the reading of the prophetic books with insufficient justification. Of course, the proposed tripartite pattern does little to explain the structure of the masoretic version of Jeremiah.

We must note that past attempts to explain the structure of both versions of the book of Jeremiah have been largely unsuccessful because they employ diachronic criteria, which are better suited to explaining the history of the literary growth of the text than its final literary structure. Because both the LXX and MT versions of the book begin with a very similar structure in chapters 1–25, most interpreters presuppose that they represent the first major unit within the literary structure of the book. And yet such a view overlooks the role of the superscriptions as the most fundamental markers of literary structure within both versions of the book. Superscriptions appear throughout the book to introduce and characterize the individual blocks of material that comprise both versions of the book of Jeremiah.[9] As noted above, the book of Jeremiah begins with the superscription in Jer 1:1-3, which identifies the contents of the book as "the words of Jeremiah ben Hilkiah. . . ." It is noteworthy that a standard version of this formula, "the word that came to Jeremiah from YHWH," and slight variations appear at the beginning of textual subunits in Jer 7:1; 11:1; 14:1; 18:1; 21:1; 25:1; 30:1; 32:1; 34:1; 34:8; 35:1; 40:1; 44:1; 45:1; 46:1; 46:13; 47:1; 50:1; and 51:59 in the MT version of the book. In addition, a number of examples of this formula begin with the conjunction, "and," which indicates that they introduce sections that are subsumed structurally into the preceding material. The result is a general statement of the superscription of the book as "the words of Jeremiah" in Jer 1:1 followed by a succession of individual words given by YHWH to the prophet throughout the balance of the book. The narrative concerning the fall of Jerusalem in Jer 52 stands outside of this structure as a concluding appendix. A similar phenomenon may be observed in the LXX form of the book, which likewise begins with the phrase, "the word of G-d, which came to Jeremiah the son of Hilkiah," in LXXJer 1:1, and continues with individual examples in LXXJer 1:4; 1:11; 11:1; 14:1; 18:1; 21:1; 25:1; 37:1; 39:1; 41:1; 41:8; 42:1; 47:1; 50:8; 51:5. Again, the narrative in LXXJer 52 concerning the fall of Jerusalem stands outside of this structure as an appendix.

The sequence of superscriptions cuts through the major blocks of material, including the oracles concerning Judah and Israel in MTJer 1–25, the narratives in MTJer 26–45, and the oracles concerning the nations in MTJer 46–51. They likewise cut through the oracles concerning Israel and Judah in LXXJer 1–25 and the narratives in LXXJer 37–51, but the oracles concerning the nations in LXXJer 25–36 appear together with the narratives concerning Jeremiah's warnings to submit to Babylon (= MTJer 26–29) as a single block of text within the structure of the book. Both versions present a sequence of events in the prophet's career, but the differences in the respective sequences indicate a substantive difference in the overall historical and theological perspective of each.

The structure of LXXJeremiah indicates an interest in presenting YHWH's plans for Israel/Judah and the nations, followed by a depiction of the consequences for Jerusalem for failing to abide by YHWH's will. The LXX sequence includes oracles that call upon Israel and Judah to observe YHWH's will in chapters 1–25 and a block of oracles that announce YHWH's judgment against the nations together with Jeremiah's warnings to submit to Babylon in LXXJer 26–36. The following sequence in LXXJer 3–51; 52 then presents a scenario for future restoration followed by a sequence of subunits that recount Jerusalem's destruction and its aftermath in LXXJer 37–52. Such a structure indicates a retrospective perspective to the book, insofar as it is designed to explain the destruction of Jerusalem as a consequence of the people's failure to heed the prophet's warnings. The structure of LXXJeremiah appears as follows:

THE WORDS OF JEREMIAH SON OF HILKIAH
CONCERNING YHWH'S JUDGMENT
AGAINST JERUSALEM

The structure of the Masoretic version of Jeremiah demonstrates a different concern. It, too, begins with a sequence in MT Jer 1–25 in which the prophet warns Israel and Judah to abide by YHWH's will, and it presents the consequences for the people's failure to do so together with a portrayal of future restoration in the narrative sequence of MTJer 26–45. The placement of the individual oracles concerning the nations, in which the oracle concerning Babylon concludes the sequence, in MTJer 46–51 points to a concern to demonstrate the future realization of YHWH's plans to bring about the downfall of the nations, culminating in Babylon. Such a structure indicates a prospective, hopeful interest in the book, insofar as it is designed to point to the rise of the Persian Empire as the agent of YHWH's restoration for Jerusalem and punishment against Babylon and the nations that oppressed Judah. The structure of the Masoretic version of Jeremiah appears as follows:

THE WORDS OF JEREMIAH BEN HILKIAH CONCERNING THE RESTORATION OF JERUSALEM AND THE DOWNFALL OF BABYLON

The diachronic dimensions of the book of Jeremiah must also be considered. The synchronic analysis of the respective forms of both versions of the book points to their distinctive theological perspectives. Both are concerned with the issue of theodicy because both attempt to argue that the destruction of Jerusalem was caused by the failure of the people to observe YHWH's Torah. Both also point to future restoration in which YHWH's Torah will be inscribed upon the hearts of the people. But the retrospective perspective of the LXX form of the book places greater weight on explaining the destruction of Jerusalem as an act of YHWH as part of a more general pattern of divine punishment for the nations. The LXX version likewise gives greater emphasis to comparing Jerusalem's fate to that of the northern kingdom of Israel (see esp. LXXJer 2–6; 11; 37–38 [= MTJer 30–31]), and the inclusion of only one royal oracle together with the prophet's diatribe against false prophets (LXXJer 23) indicates that it places less emphasis on the restoration of Davidic kingship. Such concerns would be typical of those of the early Persian period in which books such as Isaiah and Ezra–Nehemiah would call for the restoration of Judah under the authority of the Persian Empire. The Masoretic version of Jeremiah, however, places much more emphasis on the downfall of the nations, particularly Babylon, after the destruction of Jerusalem is complete. It also places far greater emphasis on the restoration of righteous Davidic kingship by including a second oracle concerning the restoration of the Davidic king that is not qualified by its proximity to a concern with false prophecy (Jer 33). Indeed, it appears together with the narrative concerning Jeremiah's attempt to redeem land in Anathoth (Jer 32), and it follows upon Jeremiah's oracles of restoration (Jer 30–31). Such a perspective has far more in common with the Book of the Twelve Prophets, which frequently challenges Isaiah's notions of submission to the nations by positing the downfall of the oppressor and the rise of a new Davidic king. Such sentiments were known in the Persian period (see Haggai), but did not achieve their realization until the rise of the Hasmonean state in the second century B.C.E.

Both versions point to an interest in shaping the books of Jeremiah, including the extensive material that appears to go back to the prophet himself, in order to serve competing interests in the Persian period and perhaps also in the Hellenistic period.

And yet there are also diachronic factors to be considered within the traditions attributed to Jeremiah himself. Although the book lacks clear indications of the prophet's oracles from the reign of Jeremiah, the oracular material in Jer 2–6 and 30–31 shows signs of editing in which oracles concerned with the restoration of the northern kingdom of Israel to Davidic rule have been reworked to consider the downfall of Jerusalem as well. This suggests that the prophet was an early supporter of Josiah's reform, but reconsidered his views and reworked his oracles following Josiah's unexpected death in 609 B.C.E.[10]

The balance of the discussion will examine the various subunits of the Masoretic form of the book of Jeremiah in relation to their synchronic roles in both versions of the book as well as their diachronic dimensions.

JEREMIAH 1–6

The first major textual block of the book of Jeremiah appears in Jer 1–6. It serves as an introduction to the basic concerns of the book of Jeremiah by pointing to the impending punishment of both Israel/Judah and the nations as well as the restoration of both. The block is defined by the superscription in Jer 1:1-3, which introduces both Jer 1–6 and the book as a whole as "the words of Jeremiah ben Hilkiah. . . ." As noted above, the superscription also identifies Jeremiah as a priest from Anathoth, and it sets his prophetic activity from the thirteenth year (627 B.C.E.) of the reign of Josiah (640–609 B.C.E.), through the reign of Jehoiakim (609–598 B.C.E.), and through the eleventh and final year of the reign of Zedekiah (597–587 B.C.E.) when the Babylonians destroyed Jerusalem. Examples of the formula, "and/now the word of YHWH came to me, saying . . . ," in Jer 1:4, 11 and 2:1 are joined together by their introductory conjunctions, "and/now," to introduce each of the following three subunits of chapters 1–6. Although the third-person formulation of the superscription indicates that it is the work of the book's final editor, the first-person formulation of the following subunits indicates that they are autobiographical. They include an account of the prophet's commission to serve as a prophet in Jer 1:4-10; and account of the signs given by YHWH to Jeremiah to indicate YHWH's purpose in Jer 1:11-19; and a lengthy block of oracles in

Jer 2–6 that is formulated as the prophet's call for Israel and Judah to return to YHWH. The formula, "the word of YHWH that came to Jeremiah from YHWH," in Jer 7:1 lacks a conjunction. It therefore stands as a syntactically independent statement that introduces the next major unit in the Masoretic version of Jeremiah.

Jeremiah 1:4-10 presents Jeremiah's account of his commissioning as a prophet. YHWH's claims to have formed Jeremiah in the womb and to have consecrated him as a prophet to the nations before birth frequently prompt interpreters to posit that Jeremiah must have considered his birth to be the beginning of his prophetic career. This would suggest that the prophet was born in 627 B.C.E., and that he would have been eighteen years old in 609 when Josiah was killed and the Egyptians placed Jehoiakim on the throne.[11] Unfortunately, there is no evidence for such a claim. The reference to Jeremiah's birth is important, however, because of his identity as a Levitical priest. Priestly identity is hereditary. Like Moses (cf. Exod 3:1–4:17), Jeremiah attempts to persuade YHWH that he is inadequate for his role by claiming that he is only a boy. But YHWH places the words in his mouth and reassures him with the statement, "Do not fear them, for I am with you to deliver you" (cf. Exod 3:12; Isa 6:6-7; Ezek 3:1-3). As a Levitical priest, he is born to this role and cannot escape it (cf. Jer 20:7-18). Because a sanctuary such as the Jerusalem Temple was considered to be the focal point of creation,[12] Jeremiah's role as a Levitical priest as well as a prophet would have an impact on the nations as well. YHWH's commission of the prophet employs six verbs, four of destruction ("to pluck up and to pull down, to destroy and to overthrow") and two of restoration ("to build and to plant") to express the basic themes of judgment and restoration that appear throughout the book (see also Jer 12:14-17; 18:5-9; 24:5-7; 31:27-30, 38-40; 42:7-12; 45:2-4).

The prophet's account of the two signs from YHWH in Jer 1:11-19 again indicate YHWH's intentions to bring judgment and to stand by the prophet. Both signs likewise presuppose Jeremiah's identity as a Levitical priest. Symbolic visions frequently presuppose a vision of a common phenomenon or event (cf. the vision of locusts in Amos 7:1-3 or the four horns of the Temple altar in Zech 2:1-4). The first sign appears in verses 11-12, and follows a standard form for the presentation of a symbolic vision to a prophet (cf. Amos 7:7-9; 8:1-14; Zech 4:1-13; 5:1-4). The sign depends upon a verbal pun, i.e., Jeremiah's vision of an almond branch (Hebrew *maqal šaqed*) indicates that YHWH is watching *(šoqed)* over the divine word to carry it out. The almond branch symbolizes the Levitical staff carried by the Levites to indicate their roles as Levitical priests. According to Num 17, the tribe of Levi was chosen as the priestly tribe and Aaron was chosen as high priest when their staffs sprouted with blossoms. The second sign appears in verses 13-19 in the form of a boiling pot tilted away from the north. This symbolizes the gathering of tribes and nations from the north who will attack Jerusalem and in turn be judged themselves. Although Babylon is situated to the east of Jerusalem, the presence of the Arabian Desert requires that Mesopotamian armies march through the fertile crescent in Syria to approach Jerusalem from the north. Likewise, biblical Jerusalem was protected on the east, west, and south by valleys leaving the north, where the Temple was located, as the weakest point. Jeremiah's oracles concerning the enemy from the north appear in Jer 4:5–6:30 and 8:4–10:25. As a Levitical priest, Jeremiah would have been responsible for food preparation, including the boiling of sacrificial meat in pots (cf. 1 Sam 2:12-17; Ezek 24:1-14). The vision apparently presupposes this role, and signals the difficulties that Jeremiah will face.

The final subunit of Jer 2–6 is the prophet's account of YHWH's call for Israel and Judah to repent.[13] Most of this material appears in oracular form, but it is organized by three prose statements in 2:1; 3:6; and 3:11 in which the prophet recounts YHWH's instructions to him to proclaim the following oracles to the people. These statements introduce the three major components of this oracle complex.

The first appear in Jer 2:1–3:5. This material employs the metaphor of marriage between YHWH and Israel to recount YHWH's dissatisfaction with the people. The use of the marriage metaphor to express the covenant relationship between YHWH and Israel appears frequently in the prophets (see Isa 54; Ezek 6; Hos 1–3; Zeph 3:14-20). In contrast to the Pentateuch's presentation of continuous tension between Israel and YHWH in the wilderness (see e.g., Exod 32–34; Num 14), YHWH here alludes to the wilderness period in verses 2-3 as an ideal time when Israel first became YHWH's bride. But YHWH's tone changes markedly in Jer 2:4–3:5 as YHWH calls for a divorce by claiming that Israel has pursued other lovers. Following a call to attention in verse 4, YHWH outlines Israel's negligence of YHWH in verses 5-11. YHWH's specific accusations of abandonment appear in verses 12-28. Although they include the charge of following other gods, they also entail Israel's alliances with Egypt and Assyria, from whom King Josiah sought independence in the latter part of the seventh century B.C.E. The subunit concludes in Jer 2:29–3:5 with YHWH's claims that Israel has no grounds to challenge the accusations. The emphasis on Israel and its relationship with Egypt and Assyria is very interesting from a diachronic or historical perspective, because it indicates that the prophet supports Josiah's efforts to sever Israel's relationship with Egypt and Assyria and to return to its own G-d, YHWH (cf. 2 Kgs 22–23).

The second subunit in Jer 3:6-10 employs the metaphor of sisters to compare Judah's abandonment of YHWH to that of Israel. The passage is formulated as a retrospective look back to the days of Josiah, which of course presupposes that this text was composed after Josiah's death when the king's reform was abandoned as Judah was subjugated to Egypt. In the synchronic or final literary form of the text, such a claim merely entails that the prophet is concerned with judgment against Judah. But this is also very important from a diachronic perspective because it indicates that the prophet ultimately reconsidered his early support for Josiah's program to conclude that Judah would suffer YHWH's judgment just as the northern kingdom of Israel had suffered during the earlier Assyrian period. This suggests that Jeremiah's early oracles concerning Israel in Jer 2:2–3:5; 3:11-14, 19–4:2 have been updated and expanded following Josiah's death to account for judgment against Judah as well.

The third subunit in Jer 3:11–6:30 gets to the main point of these chapters by portraying YHWH's call for Israel's and Judah's repentance. Overall, Jer 2–6 is formulated rhetorically as an attempt to persuade the prophet's audience to change their course of action. It thereby builds upon the previous accusations of faithlessness to make the case that YHWH is justified in bringing punishment, and then it portrays the punishment as a threat of attack by the enemy from the north to be realized if the people do not heed YHWH's call for return. YHWH's formal call for repentance appears in Jer 3:11-17. Although it is not very specific about what constitutes repentance, it emphasizes Israel's return to Zion in keeping with

Josiah's program of restoring northern Israel to Judean/Davidic rule. The following material in Jer 3:18–6:30 emphasizes an idyllic future in which Israel and Judah are joined together again (Jer 3:18-25); the benefits of repentance and the costs of a failure to repent are outlined in true parenetic fashion (Jer 4:1-4); and the scenario of judgment by an enemy from the north is laid out in great detail should the people not respond to YHWH's and Jeremiah's call (Jer 4:5–6:30). It is also noteworthy that the prophet cites continuously from the Isaiah tradition. Jeremiah 5:15-17 and 6:19, 22-23 draw heavily on Isaiah's portrayal of the advancing enemy army in Isa 5:25-30; Jer 6:12 recalls Isaiah's repeated statement of YHWH's "outstretched hand" in Isa 5:25-30 and 9:7–10:5; and Jer 5:20-21 and 6:10 reiterate Isaiah's depiction of the people as blind and deaf in Isa 6. Such citations suggest that Jeremiah was very aware of the earlier Isaian tradition; indeed, his later confrontation with Hananiah in Jer 27–28 indicates that he ultimately rejected Isaiah's claims that YHWH would protect Jerusalem against Mesopotamian powers, i.e., Jeremiah apparently concluded that just as YHWH had brought judgment against Israel with Assyria, so YHWH would bring judgment against Jerusalem with Babylon. In keeping with Isaiah, Jerusalem would ultimately be restored, but a period of judgment would be realized first if Judah did not submit to Babylon.[14]

JEREMIAH 7–10

The second major textual block of the book of Jeremiah appears in Jer 7–10, which presents an account of YHWH's instructions to the prophet to deliver his famous Temple sermon. An account of Jeremiah's delivery of this sermon and his subsequent trial for sedition appears in Jer 26. By presenting the sermon in the context of YHWH's instructions to the prophet, the narrative lends authority to Jeremiah's words by attempting to demonstrate that they come directly from YHWH. Such a formulation would thereby aid in answering charges, such as those outlined in Jer 26, that Jeremiah deserved to die because he had misrepresented the will of YHWH by stating that the Temple and the city of Jerusalem would suffer destruction.

YHWH's instructions call upon Jeremiah to deliver a typical Levitical sermon, like that spoken by Moses to the people of Israel in Detueronomy as they stood on the banks of the Jordan River prior to their entry into the promised land.[15] As a Levitical priest, one of Jeremiah's primary tasks is to teach YHWH's Torah to the people (see Lev 10:11). By standing in the gate of the Temple, he stands at the position of the Levitical gatekeepers who ensure the sanctity of the Temple by admitting those who had sanctified themselves for divine service (1 Chr 9:17-27). As the so-called entrance liturgies in Pss 15 and 24 indicate,[16] such preparation included the observance of YHWH's ritual and moral commands. Jeremiah's sermon will focus specifically on calling the people to amend their ways by observing YHWH's Torah. This is a particularly crucial issue because of the prevailing view, represented in the Zion/Davidic tradition of Isaiah and many of the Psalms, that the presence of YHWH's Temple would ensure the security of Jerusalem, the Davidic monarchy, and the people at large. Jeremiah, however, represents the Mosaic understanding of the covenant that security also depends upon the people's observance of YHWH's holy Torah. He cites elements of the Ten Commandments, demanding to know whether people can steal, murder, commit adultery, swear falsely, and serve other gods, and then declare that they are safe as they stand in the Temple. The prophet cites the fate of his ancestral sanctuary at Shiloh, where Samuel originally served under the supervision of the high priest Eli (see 1 Sam 1-3). Although the traditions concerning the Philistine defeat of Israel in 1 Sam 4 make no mention of destruction, Jeremiah's reference to Shiloh's destruction helps to demonstrate that if YHWH's sanctuary at Shiloh could be destroyed, so too could YHWH's sanctuary at Jerusalem suffer the same fate. The emphasis on lamentation and YHWH's stated intention to make Jerusalem a heap of ruins and the towns of Judah a desolation (see esp. Jer 9:11) point explicitly to Jerusalem's destruction.

Interpreters disagree concerning the full extent of Jeremiah's original sermon, particularly since various elements of the narrative anticipate that the people will in fact suffer punishment when they decline to follow the prophet's instruction.[17] Readers must recognize that the present form of the narrative is clearly retrospective, and its purpose is not simply an attempt to record Jeremiah's speech; rather, it is designed to reflect upon the significance of the speech and the subsequent destruction of

Jerusalem. Because it argues that the people did not observe YHWH's instruction and emphasizes YHWH's own struggle with Jerusalem's destruction, the narrative serves as a form of theodicy that attempts to demonstrate YHWH's righteousness while placing the responsibility for Jerusalem's destruction on the people themselves. Such a contention represents an attempt to explain the problem of evil, although modern theologians (and ancient theologians such as the writer of Job) point to severe moral problems with attempts to blame the victims for their own suffering.

JEREMIAH 11–13

The third major component of the book of Jeremiah appears in Jer 11–13, which presents Jeremiah's oracles concerning Israel's and Judah's breaking of their covenant with YHWH. Again, the narrative framework for this section presents these oracles within the context of YHWH's instructions to the prophet. As in Jer 7–10, such a rhetorical strategy aids in establishing the authenticity of Jeremiah's oracles concerning punishment for Israel and Judah, especially since the book is so concerned with the issue of false prophecy (see Jer 23:9-39; 27–29).

The present unit builds upon the concern of the preceding section with proper observance of YHWH's Torah by emphasizing that the people broke their covenant with YHWH (see esp. Jer 11:10). The passage therefore plays a key role in the prophet's debate with the Zion/Davidic tradition and its representatives. By maintaining that the covenant could be broken, the prophet calls into question the notion of an eternal covenant with Jerusalem and the house of David (see 2 Sam 7; Pss 89; 110; 132; cf. Gen 15). This lays the foundation for Jeremiah's earlier contention that Jerusalem and the Temple could be destroyed.

The initial charge in Jer 11:1-17 that the people had broken their covenant introduces a series of additional passages that prompt the reader to reflect on the significance of the prophet's contention. The first are two examples of Jeremiah's so-called complaints or laments in Jer 11:18-23 and 12:1-6. Both are formulated after the model of liturgical complaint psalms in which the prophet raises questions concerning suffering in an attempt to request intervention and redress by YHWH.[18] The first refers to threats against Jeremiah made by the people of his own hometown in Anathoth who apparently sought to silence the prophet. Jeremiah appears to be one of the few Levites outside of Jerusalem who responded to Josiah's call to serve in the Jerusalem Temple (see 2 Kgs 23:8-9, which states that none came to Jerusalem). Such a move on his part would likely be opposed by his family members and colleagues in Anathoth. The second lament demands to know why YHWH allows the wicked to prosper in the expectation that YHWH's righteousness will ultimately prompt action against them.

YHWH in turn expresses sorrow in a lament in Jer 12:7-13 much like the prophet. The lament expresses the struggles that both YHWH and Judean society undergo in the aftermath of the death of Josiah and the subsequent failure of his reforms. These reverses point to impending punishment and suffering for the nation rather than to the restoration that was expected during Josiah's reign. The prophet's own struggle with the Isaian tradition emerges with references to Isaiah's vineyard parable (Isa 5:1-7) and the birds of prey that threaten Jerusalem (Isa 31). A series of oracles then addresses the fate of the nations around Israel and Judah (Jer 12:14-17); a symbolic act involving Jeremiah's loincloth, a linen garment worn by priests while serving in the Temple (Jer 13:1-11); a symbolic act involving a jar filled with wine (Jer 13:12-14); and a concluding oracle that draws upon Isaiah's oracle of gloom and darkness (Isa 8:23–9:6) to anticipate YHWH's punishment of Jerusalem.

JEREMIAH 14–17

The fourth major section of the book in Jer 14–17 takes up two major themes, drought and marriage, that symbolize YHWH's decision to bring punishment against Jerusalem. The introductory statement in Jer 16:1, "and the word of YHWH came to me," simultaneously marks the transition between the two concerns while joining them with its initial conjunction. Both themes draw upon traditional metaphors to express YHWH's relationship with Israel. As author of creation, YHWH brings rain to the land to ensure fertility and the life of the people in the land (see esp. Deut 28–30), and the relationship between YHWH and Israel is frequently expressed through the metaphor of marriage between

YHWH the husband and Israel the bride (see Isa 54; Jer 2; Ezek 16; Hos 1–3; Zeph 3:14-20).

The theme of drought appears in Jer 14:1–15:21. The initial oracle in Jer 14:1-9 emphasizes the mourning that engulfs the land when the rains fail and the land withers for lack of water. Such a lament is particularly pertinent at the fall festival of Sukkot (Tabernacles, Booths), which commemorates both the onset of the rainy season in Israel and the tradition of wilderness wandering when YHWH and Israel were "married." Here the lack of rain points to YHWH's decision to punish the people for wandering after other gods (14:10). YHWH's decision prompts an exchange with the prophet concerning false prophecy for peace. While the prophet pleads for mercy, YHWH draws upon the Levitical tradition to assert that neither Moses nor Samuel could avert the punishment. Jeremiah's third lament in Jer 15:10-21 expresses regret over his birth and prophetic vocation, but it prompts YHWH's reassurance that Jeremiah's return to YHWH will be accepted and that his words to the people will result in their return as well.

Jeremiah's own marital situation becomes a symbol for the upcoming punishment of the people in Jer 16:1–17:27. Although the first commandment in Judaism is to "be fruitful and multiply" (Gen 1:28), i.e., have children to carry on the tradition, YHWH commands Jeremiah not to marry in order to symbolize the death and mourning that will overtake the land. As a priest, Jeremiah likewise is forbidden to offer laments in the Temple on the people's behalf or to celebrate with them. The passage does not presuppose a full end, however, but looks to restoration when the punishment is over in order to teach the world about YHWH's power. This introduces material that reflects upon the significance of punishment and exile. On the one hand, it presents Israel as the guilty party; on the other it presents YHWH's role as the hope of the people. Jeremiah's fourth lament in Jer 17:14-18 calls upon YHWH for healing and defense. A concluding oracle in Jer 17:19-27 calls for the observance of Shabbat as a basis for Jerusalem's restoration.

JEREMIAH 18–20

The fifth segment of the book of Jeremiah appears in Jer 18–20, which presents the prophet's condemnation of Jerusalem and

Judah based upon his symbolic actions concerning the potter and the shattered pot. Following upon the preceding segment concerned with YHWH's punishment of Jerusalem and Judah as symbolized by drought and Jeremiah's failure to marry, this section represents YHWH's decision to "break" the people of Jerusalem and Judah much as one breaks a pot. It therefore serves as counterpoint to Jer 11–13, which portrays the people's rejection of their covenant with YHWH. The segment includes the final two laments by the prophet as he calls for the punishment of those who persecute him and expresses his frustration over the role that YHWH has assigned to him.

The first subunit of this segment is the account in Jer 18:1-17 of Jeremiah's oracles against Judah and Jerusalem based upon his observation of a potter at work. The making of pottery serves as a particularly instructive representation for the prophet's oracles, particularly since the word employed for "potter" (Hebrew *yoṣer*, "one who forms, fashions") is used frequently both for the making of pottery (Isa 29:16; 41:25; Lam 4:2) and for YHWH's fashioning of human beings (Gen 2:7, 8), animals, and birds (Gen 2:19), the nation Israel (Isa 27:11; 43:1; 44:21; 45:9), and even Jeremiah himself (Jer 1:5). As Jeremiah observes the potter fashioning and then refashioning pots as he makes mistakes and corrects them, the prophet concludes that this represents YHWH's relationship with the people of Jerusalem and Judah, i.e., YHWH had fashioned the people, but the work had gone wrong and needed to be redone. This provides the opportunity to repeat a basic theme of the book, viz., YHWH calls for repentance, but will bring judgment if the people do not change their ways. Because Jeremiah is concerned with theodicy, the oracle in verses 13-17 charges the people with apostasy as a rationale for their upcoming punishment.

The experience prompts Jeremiah's fifth lament in Jer 18:18-23. The prophet relates the words of his enemies, who attempt to silence him. We are not told who they might be, although the prophet's strong support for submission to Babylon suggests that his opponents are those who call for revolt against the Babylonians (see Jer 27–29; 32). The reference to the pit dug for the prophet anticipates Jeremiah's imprisonment in a pit during the siege of Jerusalem (see Jer 38).

JEREMIAH 19–20

The material that follows in Jer 19–20 then illustrates Jeremiah's persecution. Following upon the earlier account of the potter, Jeremiah purchases an earthenware jug and gathers some of the priests and elders for a symbolic action that will illustrate YHWH's condemnation of the people. The prophet takes them to the valley of Hinnom (Topheth) by the Potsherd Gate. The exact location of the gate is unknown, but Topheth or the Valley of Hinnom is located along the southwestern edges of the eighth–seventh century site of Jerusalem as expanded by King Hezekiah. The site was used for the burning of waste, and it apparently was also used for pagan rites of human sacrifice (cf. Jer 7:30-34; 2 Kgs 23:10).[19] Because of its reputation, the valley of Hinnom provides a suitable location for Jeremiah's symbolic action in which he shatters the earthenware jug to symbolize YHWH's decision to shatter Jerusalem and Judah. Jeremiah's action prompts his arrest by the priest, Pashhur ben Immer, who placed the prophet in stocks. Jeremiah's final laments then follow in Jer 20:7-13 and 20:14-18 in which he denounces YHWH for having forced him to condemn his own people. He employs the language of rape, "you enticed me, . . . you have overpowered me, and you have prevailed," to describe how YHWH forced him to speak. As he suffers, he calls for retribution against his persecutors. Jeremiah's final lament bitterly curses the day of his birth, because of the grim task of condemnation that YHWH requires of the prophet.

JEREMIAH 21–24

The sixth major segment of the book of Jeremiah appears in Jer 21–24, which presents the prophet's oracles against Jerusalem and the house of David. Having taken up the condemnation of the nation as a whole in the preceding segments, the present section focuses specifically on the leadership of the nation. In doing so, it directly challenges the Davidic/Zion tradition of YHWH's protection of the city of Jerusalem and the house of David.

The initial episode of the segment takes the reader forward to the reign of Zedekiah (597–587 B.C.E.) and the imminent Babylonian siege of Jerusalem in 588–587 B.C.E. in an effort to present the prophet's earlier condemnation of the Davidic kings.

In this manner, Nebuchadnezzar's siege of Jerusalem appears to be the outcome of the prophet's earlier statements as presented in this textual block. The narrative in Jer 21:1-14 presents the prophet's response to the king's inquiry concerning Nebuchadnezzar's impending attack. Jeremiah states unequivocally that YHWH will fight against Zedekiah and Jerusalem and support the Babylonians in their efforts to take the city. He calls upon the people and the king to submit to Babylon, stating that only those who do so will survive.

Jeremiah 22:1-30 then presents a series of oracles in which Jeremiah condemns the kings Jehoiakim and Jehoiachin. The sequence begins with YHWH's calls for justice on the part of the Davidic monarchs, as righteous rule will ensure their continued rule in Jerusalem and presence in the Jerusalem Temple. The oracle shows signs of having been delivered originally at the death of Josiah and the Egyptian deportation of his son Jehoahaz, apparently nicknamed Shallum, when Pharaoh Neco placed Jehoiakim on the throne (see 2 Kgs 23:28-35). The prophet accuses Jehoiakim of looking to his own needs by building a large palace while ignoring the needs of his people—Jehoiakim, after all was a loyal supporter of Egypt throughout his reign, and was responsible for Judah's policy of confrontation against the Babylonians. When Jehoiakim died during Judah's first revolt against Babylon in 598–597 B.C.E., the Babylonians deported his son, Jehoiachin, and placed his brother Zedekiah on the throne to rule as a Babylonian puppet (see 2 Kgs 24:1-19). The prophet's oracle points to Jehoiachin's (Coniah's) deportation to Babylon. Jeremiah's oracle concerning the house of David begins with a condemnation of the dynasty, here portrayed metaphorically as shepherds who have misguided their people. Jeremiah looks forward to the rule of a righteous Davidic monarch, whom he calls the "branch," apparently presupposing the imagery employed in Isa 11:1-16 to describe the righteous "shoot" of Jesse or David who will preside over a restored Israel and Judah. The placement of Jeremiah's oracle against the false prophets in Jer 23:9-40 immediately after his oracle concerning the house of David is particularly striking. Many maintain that the prophet was opposed to the monarchy altogether, although his comments concerning Josiah's righteousness (see Jer 22:15-16) indicate that this is not the case. Although MTJer 33:14-26 also calls for a righteous Davidic monarch, a Davidic king never again sat on the throne in Jerusalem after the Babylonian destruction of the city. Elsewhere, the prophet declares those prophets who speak of Jerusalem's deliverance from Babylon as false (see Jer 27–29).

The concluding oracle of this segment, Jer 24:1-10, employs the metaphor of two baskets of figs to argue that those who go into captivity, for example, Jehoiachin, will provide the basis for Jerusalem's and Judah's restoration, whereas those who remain, for example, Zedekiah, are condemned.

JEREMIAH 25–29

The seventh major segment of the book of Jeremiah appears in Jer 25–29, which present narratives concerning Jeremiah's warnings to submit to Babylon. Overall, this unit anticipates a period of exile that will last for seventy years, which happens to correspond to the period from the destruction of Jerusalem and the Temple in 587 B.C.E. until 520–515 B.C.E., when the Temple was rebuilt in the early Persian period. The retrospective narrative viewpoint of this section suggests that it has been edited and organized to point to just such a period as the fulfillment of the prophet's words. Although the LXX version of Jeremiah likewise points to a period of seventy years, this material is organized very differently with the oracles concerning the nations placed between Jer 25:1-13a and 25:13b–29:32 (= LXXJer 32–36). This indicates that the LXX version of Jeremiah looked back on a scenario of judgment that engulfed both Jerusalem and the nations, whereas the MT version of the book focuses more specifically on judgment against Jerusalem and its anticipated restoration.

The MT version of the segment begins in Jer 25 with a retrospective view of Jeremiah's words to the people of Jerusalem and Judah from the thirteenth year of Josiah (627 B.C.E.) until the fourth year of Jehoiakim (605 B.C.E.) when the Babylonians took control of Jerusalem from Egypt. The prophet contends that the people did not listen to his warnings, and that the time of judgment when the nation must submit to Babylon has now begun. Once the seventy years is complete, YHWH will then bring punishment against Babylon and the nations that supported her. Many contend that the seventy years of judgment is based in a Levitical reckoning of time like that of the Jubilee year, based on a system of seven-year periods of time (see Lev 25), but no equivalent period of time appears in priestly tradition. The present form of the text points to a period of divine sovereignty following the fall of Jerusalem and the nations. Isaiah 40–66 equates YHWH's worldwide sovereignty with the rise of the Persian Empire, which may be the case here as well.

The text then turns to a retrospective look at Jeremiah's trial for sedition at the beginning of Jehoiakim's reign. The prophet was charged as a result of his statements in his famous Temple sermon (see Jer 7–10) that Jerusalem would be destroyed. Insofar as the unit as a whole is set in the fourth year of Jehoiakim when Babylon took control of Jerusalem, the placement of the text here aids in vindicating the prophet's message that Jerusalem and Judah would suffer punishment. The prophet Micah, who also announced Jerusalem's destruction (Mic 3:12), is cited in Jeremiah's defense, particularly since his words are said to have prompted Hezekiah to turn to YHWH so that the city was saved from the Assyrians (but see Isa 26–27; 2 Kgs 18–19, which identify Isaiah as the prophet). But Jeremiah's accusers cite the case of an otherwise unknown prophet named Uriah, who was hunted down and executed by King Jehoiakim for his statements that Jerusalem would be destroyed. Interestingly, Jeremiah is saved only when Ahikam ben Shaphan intervenes. Although we may be prone to think of Jeremiah as a lonely figure, he has considerable support from the Shaphan family. Shaphan ben Azaliah ben Meshullam was an officer in Josiah's court who played a role in the discovery of the Torah scroll that prompted the king's reform (2 Kgs 22). Ahikam himself was part of the delegation sent by Josiah to consult the prophetess Huldah. Josiah's pro-Bablyonian policy apparently was followed by Shaphan's descendants who supported Jeremiah, i.e., Ahikam saved Jeremiah from execution; Elasah ben Shaphan delivered Jeremiah's letter to the exiles (Jer 29:3); Jeremiah's scroll was taken to the house of Gemariah ben Shaphan before it was read to the king (Jer 36); and Gedaliah ben Ahikam ben Shaphan, the soon to be assassinated governor of Judah, was appointed by the Babylonians and gave his support to the prophet (Jer 40–41).[20]

The chronology of the next episode, Jeremiah's confrontation with the prophet Hananiah (Jer 27–28), is uncertain because Jer 27:1 places it at the beginning of Jehoiakim's reign while

Jer 28:1 places it at the beginning of Zedekiah's reign. It should likely be placed at the beginning of Zedekiah's reign (see esp. Jer 27:12) since the text of Jer 27:1 may have been influenced by the retrospective presentations of the previous chapters. Jeremiah engages in a symbolic action, appearing in the city wearing a yoke that is designed to illustrate his contention that Jerusalem and Judah must submit to Babylon.[21] He is challenged by the prophet Hananiah, who breaks Jeremiah's yoke to proclaim that the exiles taken to Babylon with Jehoiachin would be returned within two years. But Jeremiah returns with an iron yoke that could not be broken to reinforce his call for submission to Babylon and his contention that Hananiah was a false prophet (cf. Jer 23:9-40) who would soon die. Notably, Hananiah's message of deliverance for Jerusalem echoes Isaiah's similar message to Ahaz a century before (see Isa 7). Of course, Hananiah's death confirms Jeremiah's message.

The final episode of this segment concerning Jeremiah's letter to the exiles taken with Jehoiachin in 597 B.C.E. (Jer 29) reiterates the prophet's call for submission to Babylon for a period of seventy years. He was apparently responding to statements and letters by prophets like Hananiah who proclaimed their impending deliverance by YHWH. He reiterates his contention that YHWH would restore the exiles, but only after the seventy year period of exile was completed.

JEREMIAH 30–31

The eighth major unit of the book of Jeremiah appears in Jer 30–31, which presents the prophet's oracles of restoration for Israel and Judah. This section is more commonly known as "the book of consolation." From the early days of modern critical scholarship, it has frequently been viewed as a later addition to the book because of its focus on restoration rather than judgment. A significant number of scholars have noted, however, that Jeremiah's focus on the restoration of both Israel and Judah signals the concerns of the premonarchic period when King Josiah of Judah attempted to reunite the former northern kingdom of Israel with Judah. Indeed, it is noteworthy that the segments of this text introduced by the formula, "behold the days are coming," speak about the restoration of Israel and Judah, whereas those introduced by the prophetic messenger formula, "thus says YHWH," focus on the return of Jacob or northern Israel to Zion. This suggests that the unit represents an early cycle of oracles by the prophet that supported Josiah's efforts to restore northern Israel to Davidic rule, but that the passage was updated after Josiah's death to account for the restoration of both Israel and Judah.[22]

The theme of punishment followed by restoration is correlated with Jeremiah's call narrative as well as in Jer 31:27-28 by the appearance of the key words used to describe YHWH's punishment, i.e., "to pluck up, break down, overthrow, destroy, bring evil," and those used for restoration, "to build, plant" (cf. Jer 1:10; see also 1:11, which mentions YHWH's "watching"). The book signals its interest in restoration from the outset, and the present unit represents one of the primary expressions of this interest in the book (but see also the Temple sermon in Jer 7–10). Such a concern with restoration is inherent in the Levitical worldview, which calls for human beings to restore their relationships with YHWH and with their own people after having committed some wrong. The priestly sacrificial system is based in part on the need for human beings to maintain their relationships with YHWH by proper conduct and to symbolize that relationship through the sacrificial system (see, e.g., Lev 4:1–5:13, which stipulates the presentation of a sin offering as part of the means to atone for wrongdoing and thereby to play a role in restoring one's relationship with YHWH). Although Deuteronomy calls for punishments such as exile from the land in the case of wrongdoing, it also calls for restoration once the punishment is complete (see Deut 28–30).

The present passage begins with an introduction in Jer 30:1-3, 4, which calls upon Jeremiah to write the following words of restoration for Israel and Judah. They follow in sequence, each introduced by the messenger formula. Jeremiah 30:5-11 employs the imagery of gender reversal (can a man bear a child?) to express Jacob's distress, but it also points to YHWH's action to deliver Jacob from captivity so the people might serve YHWH and David their king.[23] Jeremiah 30:12-17 employs the metaphor of wounds and healing to state that YHWH has brought punishment on Jacob because of its sins, but that YHWH will restore Jacob now that the punishment is complete. Jeremiah 30:18–31:1 states that YHWH draws upon the language of Balaam's blessing for

Israel (see Num 22–24, esp. 24:5) to rebuild Jacob's cities and citadels. It employs the standard covenant formula in verse 22, "and you shall be my people, and I will be your G-d," to express the restoration of the covenant relationship (see Jer 7:23; 11:4; Gen 17:7-8; Exod 6:3; Deut 26:17-19).[24] Jeremiah 31:2-14 combines two oracles that draw upon the traditions of Israel as a bride in the wilderness (cf. Jer 2; Hos 1–3) to express Israel's return to YHWH and to Jerusalem with singing and dancing like that of Miriam and the women at the Sea (Exod 15:20-21). Jeremiah 31:15 recalls the image of Rachel, who weeps for her lost children, as a means to depict Israel bereft of its exiled people. Jeremiah 31:16-22 then depicts the return of the children and the maiden Israel. Jeremiah 31:25-34 portrays the return to Zion, and calls for a new covenant in which YHWH's Torah will be inscribed on the people's hearts. Jeremiah 31:35-36 ties this covenant to creation, and Jer 31:37-40 continues this motif with a depiction of the restored city of Jerusalem. Such a motif presupposes the priestly covenant with creation (Gen 9:1-17; Exod 31:12-17) and the eternal covenant of the priestly line from Phineas ben Eleazar ben Aaron (Num 25:10-13).

JEREMIAH 32–33

The ninth major section of the book of Jeremiah appears in Jer 32–33, which relates Jeremiah's oracles based upon his attempt to redeem family property during a lull in the Babylonian siege of Jerusalem in 588 B.C.E. Jeremiah 37:11-21 states that the prophet was arrested as a traitor when he tried to leave the city at the time of the Babylonian withdrawal. The present block of material apparently represents Jeremiah's explanation for his act. The prophet here lays out his understanding of the relationship between punishment and restoration in YHWH's plans.

The narrative is set at the time of Jeremiah's arrest, when King Zedekiah demanded to know why the prophet had stated that Nebuchadnezzar would capture Jerusalem and take Zedekiah to Babylon. The prophet explains his statements in relation to his attempt to redeem family property in his hometown of Anathoth. In cases when a family member used land as collateral for a debt, priestly law requires that the land be redeemed by a family member (Lev 25:25-28). The prophet describes the transaction in

111

detail, and states that he redeemed the land at YHWH's instruction. The purpose of the transaction was to symbolize YHWH's intentions to redeem Jerusalem after it had been punished for its apostasy. At the time of Jerusalem's redemption, fields would be bought once again.

The second portion of the narrative in Jer 33 continues the motif of YHWH's intentions to restore Jerusalem following its punishment, but it focuses specifically on YHWH's intentions to restore a righteous Davidic monarch, here designated as the "branch" (cf. Jer 23:1-7; Isa 11:1-16). Just as Jerusalem's restoration is tied to creation in Jer 30–31, so is the house of David (cf. Pss 89; 110). It is noteworthy that the covenant with the house of David includes the Levitical priests as well (Jer 33:17-18). This text draws heavily on the language and imagery of Jer 23:1-7, and it appears only in the MT version of Jeremiah.[25] This indicates greater interest in the restoration of the Davidic line on the part of its editors. The LXX version of the book is more equivocal about restoration, particularly of the house of David.

JEREMIAH 34:1-7

The tenth major unit of the book of Jeremiah appears in the very brief passage, Jer 34:1-7, which presents Jeremiah's condemnation of King Zedekiah. The prophet reiterates his message that the Babylonians will take Jerusalem. He states that Zedekiah will not be killed, but will be taken to Babylon where he will die in peace. This is a very ironic prophecy insofar as it resembles Huldah's prophecy to Zedekiah's father Josiah that he would die in peace before the destruction of Jerusalem (2 Kgs 22:14-20).

JEREMIAH 34:8-22

In the eleventh unit of the book, Jer 34:8-22, the prophet condemns Zedekiah for reneging on his promise to release the slaves in the city of Jerusalem. Biblical law indicates that people may become slaves to pay a debt, but they are to be released after six years of service (Exod 21:1-11; Deut 15:1-18; Lev 25:39-55). The motives for the release are unclear; perhaps it would allow the slaves to participate in the defense of Jerusalem or perhaps it was done to gain YHWH's favor. Many argue that the reenslavement took place when the Babylonian army left Jerusalem to fight an

Egyptian relief force. In any case, Zedekiah is condemned for this action, and the prophet reiterates his claims that YHWH will deliver Jerusalem and Zedekiah into the hands of the Babylonians.

JEREMIAH 35–39

The twelfth major unit of the book of Jeremiah appears in Jer 35–39, which relates Jeremiah's experiences at the fall of Jerusalem. The narrative provides an overview of the prophet's actions and message from the time of Jehoiakim's reign through the fall of the city during the reign of Zedekiah. It thereby provides a brief overview of the reasons for the city's conquest with a special focus on the actions of Kings Jehoiakim and Zedekiah. Although many interpreters claim that Jeremiah is anti-monarchic, these narratives are designed to demonstrate that Kings Jehoiakim and Zedekiah do not match the standards for righteous Davidic kingship as portrayed in Jer 23:1-7 and 33:14-26 (see also Jer 22:15-16).

The narrative begins with an account of Jeremiah's use of the Rechabites to illustrate loyalty to YHWH. The narrative is set in the reign of Jehoiakim in order to demonstrate that the reasons for the destruction of the city are rooted in the earlier monarch's reign (contra 2 Kgs 21, which attributes the city's destruction to Manasseh's actions). The Rechabites were a group founded by Jonadab ben Rechab, who is described as zealous for YHWH and who supported Jehu's revolt against the house of Omri in which he destroyed the Omride supporters of Baal (see 2 Kgs 9–10). Biblical tradition identifies the Rechabites as Kenites (1 Chr 2:55), who were descended from Moses' father-in-law, Jethro (Judg 1:16; Exod 3:1; 18:1), and ultimately from Cain after whom the Kenites are named (Gen 4:1-16). The prophet offers them wine, which the Rechabites refuse because of their vows to avoid wine and to live in tents in keeping with their understanding of YHWH's expectations (cf. the Nazirite vow in Num 6:1-21; N.B., Levitical priests do not drink wine when in the Temple [Lev 10:9; Ezek 44:21], and they do not possess land [see Num 18]). He then contrasts the loyal Rechabites with the people of Judah and Jerusalem, whom he maintains have not shown such loyalty to YHWH.

The second narrative in the sequence points to Jehoiakim's contempt for YHWH and Jeremiah following Jeremiah's Temple sermon (see Jer 7–10; 26). The narrative is set in the fourth year of Jehoiakim (605 B.C.E.) when the Babylonians took control of Jerusalem. Presumably, the prophet's message included a call for submission to Babylon in accordance with YHWH's will (see Jer 27–28). The prophet apparently had been banned from speaking in the Temple, but he simply had the scribe Baruch ben Neriah write a scroll with his words so that Baruch could read them in the Temple in Jeremiah's place. After Baruch read the scroll, it was taken to the home of Gemariah ben Shaphan, a highly placed member of the Shaphan family that supported the prophet,[26] for discussion among the scribes as to how to proceed. When it was taken to the king, he burned each column after it was read to show his contempt for Jeremiah and his message. Within the context of the book, such an act also shows the king's contempt for YHWH. The prophet dictates another scroll, which condemns Jehoiakim. Many interpreters argue that this episode provides a model for the composition of the book, and that the scroll is represented in the oracles of Jer 1–20 or 1–25.

The final segment of this unit appears in Jer 37–39, which focuses on Jeremiah's imprisonment by Zedekiah during the Babylonian siege of Jerusalem. Zedekiah ben Josiah was the brother of Jehoiakim who was placed on the throne by the Babylonians as a puppet to control the population following the death of his brother and the exile of his nephew, Jehoiachin. The narrative portrays him as a very weak figure—he was not after all the true king of Judah—who was unable to control the pro-Egyptian forces loyal to Jehoiakim who called for revolt. Because of his statements that Judah must submit to Babylon, Jeremiah was imprisoned as a traitor when he attempted to leave the city to redeem land in Anathoth at the time when the Babylonians lifted their siege to fight an Egyptian relief force (see Jer 32–33).

Zedekiah had Jeremiah imprisoned, although he continued to consult the prophet. When the prophet continued to speak out for submission to Babylon, several officials called for Jeremiah to be cast into a cistern where he would be left to die without food. The apparently weak Zedekiah complied, but an Ethiopian slave, identified only as Ebed-Melech, "servant of the king," pulled Jeremiah out of the pit and placed him back in the court of the guard. This was done apparently at Zedekiah's command, as the king continued to consult the prophet, who repeated his claims that YHWH would give Jerusalem and the king to the Babylonians.

Finally, Jer 39 describes the Babylonian conquest of Jerusalem, the killing of Zedekiah's sons before his eyes, and the blinding and deportation of the king. The Babylonians' treatment of Jeremiah is noteworthy, apparently because they were aware of his calls for submission to Babylon. He is released from prison and placed in the care of Gedaliah ben Ahikam ben Shaphan, a member of the pro-Babylonian Shaphan family, who was appointed by the Babylonians as governor of Judah. The passage concludes with Jeremiah's statement that Ebed-Melech's life would be spared.

JEREMIAH 40-43

The thirteenth major segment of the book of Jeremiah appears in Jer 40–43, which presents narratives concerning Jeremiah's decision to remain in Judah following the Babylonian destruction of Jerusalem and his subsequent move to Egypt following the assassination of Gedaliah ben Ahikam. This section is particularly important within the narrative sequence of Jeremiah because it points to Jeremiah's removal to Egypt—against his will—at the end of his forty year prophetic career, and thereby plays a crucial role in presenting him as an antithetical character to Moses, whose forty year period of leadership led to Israel's journey from Egyptian bondage to the land of Israel.[27]

The narrative relates the circumstances of Jeremiah's removal to Egypt by focusing on the assassination of Gedaliah ben Ahikam, whom the Babylonians appointed as governor of Judah following the destruction of Jerusalem and the deportation of a large number of its surviving population. It begins in Jer 40:1-6 with a portrayal of Jeremiah's decision to remain in the land of Judah. Although he was initially among those whom the Babylonians planned to exile, apparently because of his standing as a Levitical priest, Nebuzaradan, the captain of the guard, decided to release him. We may speculate that Nebuzaradan made this decision based on Jeremiah's consistent calls for submission to Babylonia. Perhaps Nebuzaradan saw Jeremiah as a Babylonian loyalist—certainly many in Judah viewed him as a traitor—and he offered to make sure that the prophet was well cared for in Babylon. When Jeremiah declined the offer Nebuzaradan gave him provisions, and Jeremiah chose to remain with Gedaliah.

The assassination of Gedaliah is a key element in Jeremiah's story. As noted before, Gedaliah was a member of the Shaphan family that had served the royal court as officers under King Josiah and later continued to advocate Josiah's policy of alliance with Babylon even after the pro-Egyptian Jehoiakim was placed on the throne. Members of the Shaphan family were among Jeremiah's key supporters. Although Gedaliah would have been associated with the royal house of David, he was not of the Davidic line. It therefore made eminent sense for the Babylonians to appoint him as governor, since they had removed Zedekiah and killed his sons as punishment for revolt. The narrative portrays Gedaliah as a capable administrator who is able to convince many Judeans who had fled the country to return and to begin the process of rebuilding. Johanan ben Kareah, described as leader of the military forces left in the field, provides support for Gedaliah, and warns him of assassination plots. In the aftermath of the lost war, such plots would emerge by those who might attempt to seize power for themselves or who would attempt to reestablish the house of David.

Although Gedaliah was warned of assassination plots, he brushed the warnings aside. Unfortunately, the plot by Ishmael ben Nethaniah ben Elishama would succeed. Ishmael is described as a member of the royal house of David who had apparently fled to Ammon. In the absence of the sons of Zedekiah or Jehoiachin, he would then be in a position to claim the Judean throne. His assassination of Gedaliah following dinner is portrayed as an act of treachery, and his murder of the mourners who came from Shechem also raises questions about his character. By portraying Ishmael in this manner, the narrative makes sure to inform the reader that Ishmael does not constitute Jeremiah's image of the righteous Davidic monarch (Jer 23:1-7; 33:14-26). Ishmael's defeat by Johanan at the Gibeon pool is also significant, because it was David's victory over the forces of Ish-bosheth that paved the way for him to become king over all Israel (2 Sam 3–5). Even Ishmael's association with the Ammonites and his flight to Ammon after his defeat is significant. When Absalom revolted against David, David's flight to Ammon enabled him to reorganize, defeat Absalom, and reclaim the throne of Israel and Judah (2 Sam 15–19). By portraying Ishmael in relation to these traditions, the narrator attempts to demonstrate that the house of David—at least this branch of the royal house—will not return to power in Judah.

The assassination of Gedaliah and the defeat of Ishmael set up the circumstances in which Jeremiah is taken to Egypt against his will. Although Johanan ben Kareah has defeated Ishmael, he is justifiably concerned about what might happen if the Babylonian army were to return. After two invasions of Judah in 598–597 and 588–587 B.C.E., the assassination of Gedaliah would likely provoke a return of the army with potentially brutal consequences. Jeremiah consults YHWH to determine what to do, and YHWH's oracular reply reiterates Jeremiah's initial call to build and to plant now that the punishment is over (cf. Jer 1:10). Jeremiah's confidence in the Babylonians is consistent with his pro-Babylonian position throughout his career, but Johanan's rejection of the prophet's position is consistent with the portrayal of Judah's rejection of YHWH. The narrative does not tell us why Johanan and his supporters believed that Jeremiah lied; perhaps there were lingering suspicions that Jeremiah was a traitor. Although the prophet condemns the proposal to go to Egypt in the harshest possible terms, the group decides to go to Egypt anyway and they take Jeremiah and Baruch ben Neriah with them.

The final episode of this segment in Jer 43:8-13 begins with its own introduction that is tied to the preceding material with a conjunction, "and the word of YHWH came to Jeremiah in Tahpanhes." It portrays the prophet in the city of Tahpanhes, identified with the site of Tel Hisn, about seven miles northeast of modern Cairo,[28] where he engages in symbolic actions and delivers oracles to demonstrate that Babylon would conquer Egypt as well. Babylon never conquered Egypt, but the Persians took Egypt in 525 B.C.E.

JEREMIAH 44

The fourteenth segment of the book of Jeremiah appears in Jer 44, which presents Jeremiah's oracles against the Judeans who had fled to Egypt to escape the Babylonians. Excavations at the island of Elephantine near Aswan reveal the existence of a Jewish military colony, with its own Temple, that was established in the sixth century B.C.E.[29] Aramaic texts found at the site indicate a wide variety of deities and heavenly figures. Jeremiah charges the people with apostasy and idolatry much as 2 Kgs 17 explains the demise of the northern kingdom of Israel with similar charges. The people respond that they worship the Queen of Heaven because they lack food, which is an interesting reflection of the wilderness traditions in which YHWH provided food for Israel in the wilderness (Exod 17; Num 11). Indeed, the experience of invasion and exile in Judah would hardly promote confidence in YHWH among the exiles, but Jeremiah charges that abandonment of YHWH prompts the punishment.

JEREMIAH 45

The fifteenth section of the book of Jeremiah appears in the very brief narrative in Jer 45, which presents Jeremiah's oracle to his scribe, Baruch ben Neriah, who had so loyally supported him and went with him to exile in Egypt. In response to Baruch's own laments, Jeremiah promises that YHWH will spare his life despite the destruction. The initial reference to Baruch's recording of Jeremiah's words prompts many to maintain that Baruch played a major role in writing the book of Jeremiah (see also Jer 36).[30]

JEREMIAH 46:1-12

The sixteenth segment of the book of Jeremiah appears in Jer 46:1-12, which presents Jeremiah's first oracle against Egypt. The initial superscription in Jer 46:1 functions as an introduction to all of the oracles concerning the nations, but the appearance of superscriptions in Jer 46:14; 47:1; and 50:1 indicates separate groupings of the oracles within the present form of the oracles concerning the nations in Jeremiah.

The oracle in Jer 46:2-12 is addressed specifically to Pharaoh Neco of Egypt. Neco II took control of Egypt in 609 B.C.E. following the death of his father Psamtek (664–609 B.C.E.).[31] Neco was initially an ally of the Assyrians, who killed King Josiah of Judah at Megiddo in 609. Following the Babylonian defeat of Assyria in 609, Neco took control of Judah. He deposed Jehoahaz ben Josiah, apparently because he would follow his father's pro-Babylonian policy, and replaced him with his older brother Jehoiakim ben Josiah, who apparently favored the Egyptians. Following the Babylonian defeat of Egypt at Carchemish in 605 B.C.E. (the fourth year of Jehoiakim), the Egyptians were forced to relinquish Judah to Babylonian control, which set in motion a chain of events that ultimately led to the unsuccessful Judean revolts against Babylon. Jeremiah's oracle clearly reflects his own pro-Babylonian views. He draws on the Day of YHWH tradition, which is well known in Isaiah (Isa 2; 13; 34) and other prophets (Amos 5:18-20; Obadiah; Joel; Zephaniah) as a day when YHWH would punish enemies. He also draws upon the imagery of the rising Nile River to depict Egypt's arrogance, but his portrayal of the Babylonian defeat of Egypt recalls elements of the Song of the Sea (Exod 15) in which the Egyptian horses and chariots are destroyed with the rising waters of the Nile by the river Euphrates in Mesopotamia. The placement of this oracle at the head of the oracles concerning the nations in MTJeremiah makes eminent sense in the book of a prophet who is also a Levitical priest. Egypt is the quintessential enemy of YHWH in the Pentateuchal tradition. The Septuagint version of Jeremiah, however, begins with Elam, a nation that was incorporated into the Persian Empire from an early period.

JEREMIAH 46:13-28

The seventeenth segment of the book of Jeremiah appears in Jer 46:13-28, which presents Jeremiah's second oracle against Egypt. This oracle differs from the first insofar as it anticipates Nebuchadnezzar's conquest of Egypt. Although Nebuchadnezzar invaded Egypt in 601–600 B.C.E., he did not succeed in conquering the nation. The prophet employs the motif of the enemy from the north that he had previously employed against Judah (see Jer 1:14-19; 4-6). He concludes the oracle with assurances to Jacob that Jacob/Israel would suffer punishment, but Jacob would ultimately be delivered from captivity.

JEREMIAH 47–49

The eighteenth segment of the book of Jeremiah appears in Jer 47–49, which presents the prophet's oracles against the

Philistines, Moab, the Ammonites, Edom, Damascus, Kedar, and Elam. This section takes up the smaller nations that, with the exception of Elam, bordered Israel and Judah or stood in close proximity. In the masoretic version of Jeremiah, they are gathered together between the major powers of Egypt (Jer 46) and Babylon (Jer 50–51). In the LXX, Elam heads the list, probably because it was a part of the Persian Empire. The major powers of Egypt and Babylon are next, followed by the remaining smaller nations.

The first oracle against the Philistines appears in Jer 47:1-7. The passage again employs the image of rising waters to depict the threat posed to Philistia by Egypt, but the reference to the north suggests that the oracle may have been modified to account for the threat from Babylon. The Philistines are located along Mediterranean seacoast, which would be the usual route of any Egyptian advance into western Asia. This would explain the reference to Sidon and Tyre, the two major Phoenician cities located along the coast to the north of Philistia and Israel. Pharaoh Neco made such an advance in 609 B.C.E. when he killed Josiah. Herodotus reports that Neco also subjugated Ashdod, one of the major Philistine cities.[32] The Babylonians ultimately took control of the region following their defeat of Egypt in 605.

The oracle against Moab appears in Jer 48:1-47. The initial depiction of threat in verses 1-10 draws heavily on the language and imagery from the oracle against Moab in Isa 15–16. This would suggest once again that Jeremiah was familiar with the Isaiah traditions, and drew upon them in his work.[33] Isaiah depicts a threat posed by Assyria and then applies it to Babylon, and Jeremiah apparently sees the Babylonian threat as a fulfillment of Isaiah's oracles. Although the Moabites survived by submitting to the Assyrians in the eighth century, the Babylonians destroyed Moab in the sixth century. Later statements also apparently draw on the work of other prophets, such as the references to Moab's arrogance in verses 29-30, 42, which recall Zeph 2:8-11. Verses 45-46 apparently draw upon Num 21:28-29. Isaiah 24:17-18 apparently reworks the statement in verses 43-44.

The oracle against the Ammonites appears in Jer 49:1-6. Ammon served as refuge for Judeans who fled the Babylonian assault, including Ishmael ben Nethaniah, the Davidic figure who assassinated Gedaliah ben Ahikam (see Jer 40–43). The

Babylonians later destroyed the Ammonites along with Moab in the sixth century.

The oracle against the Edomites appears in Jer 49:7-22. Various texts in the Bible indicate that the Edomites assisted the Babylonians in the destruction of the Temple and the city of Jerusalem (see Ps 137:7; Lam 4:21-22; Obad 10-16). Following the destruction of Jerusalem, the Edomites moved westward into the Judean Negeb Desert, and took control of the city of Hebron. The Edomites, later known as Idumeans, survived the Babylonian period, although they were eventually displaced by the Nabateans.

The oracle against Damascus appears in Jer 49:23-27. The city had been destroyed by the Assyrians in 734-732 B.C.E., and later functioned as an administrative center. Verse 27 quotes Amos 1:4 to indicate judgment against the city that is now fulfilled.

The oracle against Kedar in Jer 49:28-33 is directed against the Arab tribes that inhabited the north Arabian Desert. The ancient Arabs gave extensive support to the Babylonians in their campaigns against Assyria and later against southwestern Asia.

Finally, the oracle against Elam in Jer 49:34-39 focuses on a nation that was subdued by Assyria, Babylon, and finally Persia.

JEREMIAH 50:1–51:58

The nineteenth major section of the book of Jeremiah is the lengthy oracle against Babylon in Jer 50:1–51:58. This oracle forms the climactic conclusion to the oracles concerning the nations in the masoretic form of the book of Jeremiah, which indicates the book's fundamental concern with the downfall of Babylon in the aftermath of Jerusalem's and Judah's exile. The oracle's appearance in LXXJer 27–28 as the third of the oracles concerning the nations following Elam and Egypt suggests that it is included in a sequence of major powers that will fall together with Judah in a judgment that will engulf the entire world. Both scenarios suggest YHWH's identification with the rise of the Persian Empire as the agent of divine punishment and restoration (cf. Isa 44:28; 45:1).

The oracle itself is concerned with Babylon's impending downfall, and it portrays Babylon's fall as the opportunity for exiled Jews to depart from Babylon and return to their homeland. The oracle ironically employs the same motif of an enemy from the north (Jer 50:3) that will carry out the punishment, much as earlier material in Jer 4–6 made the same claims for the punishment of Judah. Like Isaiah, the oracle envisions the nations' recognition of YHWH and their efforts to join with Judah to return to Jerusalem under the auspices of an eternal covenant (cf. Isa 2:2-4; 11:1-16; 56:1-8; 60–62; 66:18-24). The portrayal of Israel as lost sheep (Jer 50:6-7) echoes Ezek 34 and Mic 2:12-13, and the command to flee from Babylon (Jer 50:8-10) echoes Isa 48:20-21. The descriptions of the army that threatens Babylon may well presuppose the Persian King Cyrus's advance against Babylon in 545–539 B.C.E. and perhaps even his defeat of the Babylonian army in the field, but the lurid descriptions of Babylon's destruction never came to pass, since the priests of Marduk submitted to Cyrus, declared him to be Marduk's chosen monarch, and opened the gates of the city to allow him and his army to enter peacefully. This suggests that the oracle—or at least parts of it—was written prior to Cyrus's entry into the city in 539 B.C.E.

The oracle makes an effort to establish an analogy between the punishment of Assyria and the punishment of Babylon, much like Isaiah (see Isa 10:5–11:16; 13:1–14:27). As part of the general scenario of destruction depicted throughout this oracle, the passage makes a special effort to point to the Medes, one of the primary nations incorporated into the Persian Empire, as the agents of YHWH's judgment (Jer 51:11, 28). Indeed, the following statements concerning a raised standard against Babylon recalls motifs from Isa 11:10-16, and the depiction of YHWH's power as creator recalls Isa 41:12-31. The depiction of the rising waters that inundate Babylon (Jer 51:42) reverse the motif of the Babylonian creation epic in which Marduk, the city god of Babylon, establishes order in creation by defeating the sea goddess, Tiamat. The motif also recalls the defeat of the Egyptians at the Red Sea (Exod 15). The final call for the exiles to go out from Babylon (Jer 51:45) and to remember YHWH and Jerusalem (Jer 51:50) likewise recalls motifs that appear throughout Isa 40–66.

JEREMIAH 51:59-64

The twentieth major component of the book of Jeremiah appears in Jer 51:59-64, which presents Jeremiah's instructions to

Seraiah ben Neriah ben Mahseiah to engage in a symbolic act concerning the punishment of Babylon. Seraiah is the brother of Baruch ben Neriah, Jeremiah's scribe. Seraiah is to accompany Zedekiah to Babylon in Zedekiah's fourth year (ca. 593 B.C.E.), apparently to present tribute to the Babylonian king. Jeremiah instructs him to take a scroll with his oracles concerning Babylon, read them in the city (much as Baruch read Jeremiah's scroll during the reign of Jehoiakim in Jer 36) and to sink the scroll in the Euphrates River. Such an act would symbolize the fact that Babylon would sink, to rise no more, and thus fulfill the oracle of judgment against the city. The concluding statement, "thus far are the words of Jeremiah," apparently signals the conclusion of the prophet's oracles prior to the following historical appendix.

JEREMIAH 52

The final segment of the book of Jeremiah appears in Jer 52, which portrays the Babylonian destruction of Jerusalem, the exile of much of its surviving population, and the release of Jehoiachin from prison by King Evil-Merodach of Babylon. This material is drawn from 2 Kgs 25. Evil-Merodach is identified with Amel Marduk, the son of Nebuchadnezzar, who ruled for only two years (562–560 B.C.E.) before he died. Although this material is clearly appended to Jeremiah's oracles (note Jer 51:64 above), it is apparently placed here to confirm Jeremiah's oracles of judgment against Judah and Jerusalem. The concluding notice concerning Jehoiachin's release also suggests that Jeremiah's oracles of restoration would come to pass.

In sum, the book of Jeremiah portrays the struggle of the prophet to discern divine will in relation to the decline and ultimately the collapse of Judah in the late-seventh and early-sixth centuries B.C.E. as the nation witnessed King Josiah's attempts at religious reform and national restoration following the collapse of the Assyrian Empire, Josiah's unexpected death at the hands of Pharaoh Neco of Egypt in 609 B.C.E., the subsequent subjugation of Judah first to Egypt and then to Babylon, the invasions of Judah by the Babylonians in 597, 588, and 582 B.C.E., and ultimately the destruction of Jerusalem and the Temple in 587–586 B.C.E. and the exile of much of the surviving population. Throughout the book, Jeremiah appears as a prophet and Levitical priest who attempts to interpret the events of his day in relation to earlier traditions extant in his time, including early forms of Mosaic Torah and Isaian prophecy. In the end, the book of Jeremiah portrays a reversal of the Exodus tradition, as Israel returns to Egypt and Babylon at the conclusion of Jeremiah's forty-year career. Nevertheless, Jeremiah anticipates restoration of the nation following its period of judgment (cf. Deut 28–30).

SELECTED BIBLIOGRAPHY

Bright, John. *Jeremiah.* AB 21. Garden City: Doubleday, 1965.

Carroll, Robert. *Jeremiah: A Commentary.* OTL. Philadelphia: Westminster, 1986.

Clements, Ronald E. *Jeremiah.* Interpretation. Atlanta: John Knox, 1988.

Diamond, A. R. Pete. *The Confessions of Jeremiah in Context: Scenes of a Prophetic Drama.* JSOTSup 45. Sheffield: JSOT Press, 1987.

Diamond, A. R. Pete, Kathleen O'Connor, and Louis Stulman, editors. *Troubling Jeremiah.* JSOTSup 260. Sheffield: Sheffield Academic Press, 1999.

Holladay, William L. *Jeremiah: A Commentary on the Book of the Prophet Jeremiah.* 2 vols. Hermeneia. Philadelphia: Fortress, 1986; Minneapolis: Fortress, 1989.

Janzen, J. Gerald. *Studies in the Text of Jeremiah.* HSM 6. Cambridge: Harvard University Press, 1973.

Jones, Douglas Rawlinson. *Jeremiah.* NCB Commentary. London: Marshall Pickering; Grand Rapids: Eerdmans, 1992.

King, Philip J. *Jeremiah: An Archaeological Companion.* Louisville: Westminster John Knox, 1993.

Lundbom, Jack. *Jeremiah 1–20.* AB 21A. New York: Doubleday, 1999.

McKane, William. *A Critical and Exegetical Commentary on Jeremiah.* 2 vols. ICC. Edinburgh: T & T Clark, 1986, 1996.

Miller, Patrick. "Jeremiah." Pages 553-926 in vol. 6 of *The New Interpreter's Bible,* edited by Leander Keck, et al. Nashville: Abingdon, 2001.

Nicholson, E. W. *Preaching to the Exiles: A Study of the Prose Tradition in the Book of Jeremiah.* New York: Schocken, 1971.

O'Connor, Kathleen. *The Confessions of Jeremiah: Their Interpretation and Role in Chapters 1–25*. SBLDS 94. Atlanta: Scholars Press, 1988.

Perdue, Leo, and Brian Kovacs, editors. *A Prophet to the Nations: Essays in Jeremiah Studies*. Winona Lake: Eisenbrauns, 1984.

Seitz, Christopher R. *Theology in Conflict: Reactions to the Exile in the Book of Jeremiah*. BZAW 176. Berlin and New York: Walter de Gruyter, 1989.

Stulman, Louis. *Order amid Chaos: Jeremiah as Symbolic Tapestry*. BibSem 57. Sheffield: Sheffield Academic Press, 1998.

CHAPTER 5

THE BOOK OF EZEKIEL

The book of Ezekiel presents some of the most difficult, dynamic, and bizarre material among the prophets of the Hebrew Bible. Ezekiel is a Zadokite priest, who would have served in the Jerusalem Temple had he not been among the exiles taken by Nebuchadnezzar with King Jehoiachin of Judah to Babylonia in 597 B.C.E. As a priest in exile, Ezekiel was compelled to apply his highly mythologized worldview of the holiness of YHWH and creation in his attempts to grapple with the meaning and significance of the exile, the destruction of Jerusalem and the Temple, and his expectations of a return to the holy center of creation in Jerusalem. Because early modern critical scholarship viewed the priesthood and priestly literature with suspicion, the study of Ezekiel lagged behind the study of other prophetic books, such as Isaiah and Jeremiah, until relatively recent times. Modern interpreters are now discovering in Ezekiel some of the most profound and challenging theological literature of the entire Bible.[1] For Jews, Ezekiel represents an important figure in the foundation of the Jewish mystical tradition, with its emphasis on the manifestation and recognition of the holy divine presence within the world, and a key proponent for the restoration of Israel around the Temple in Jerusalem. For Christians, Ezekiel is especially important for defining the concept of resurrection together with the reconstitution of creation, and thereby serves as an important witness to the role of Jesus as the Christ figure.

The book of Ezekiel generally appears immediately after Jeremiah as the third book of the Latter Prophets in the Tanakh, although some authorities consider it to be the second book because Isaiah is sometimes placed in the third position (*b. Baba Batra* 14b). Rabbinic tradition raises questions about the canonical status of Ezekiel, however, since the book frequently conflicts with halakhic statements found in the Torah. Talmudic tradition states that Rabbi Hanina ben Hezekiah burned three hundred barrels of oil working at night to reconcile the differences so that Ezekiel might be accepted as sacred scripture (*b. Shabbat* 13b; *b. Haggigah* 13a; *b. Menahot* 45a). Ezekiel also appears as the third book of the Prophets in most versions of the Christian Old Testament, where it follows Jeremiah/Lamentations in the Protestant canon and the deuterocanonical literature associated with Jeremiah, viz., Epistle of Jeremiah and Baruch, in the Roman Catholic canon.

The superscription for the book in Ezek 1:1-3 presents a mixed introduction which combines a first-person autobiographical statement, purportedly by the prophet, with third-person descriptive statements apparently made by an editor of the book. The initial autobiographical statement in verse 1 places the prophet among the exiles by the river Chebar, in the thirtieth year, on the fourth day of the fifth month, when he began to see visions of G-d. The third-person statements in verses 2-3 specify that it was the fifth year of King Jehoiachin's reign when the word of YHWH came to Ezekiel ben Buzi by the river Chebar in the land of the Chaldeans. The term *Chaldeans* refers to the Neo-Babylonian Empire established in 627 B.C.E. by Nabopolassar, the father of Nebuchadnezzar. The fifth year of Jehoiachin's exile would be 593–592 B.C.E., and the fifth day of the fourth month would be 5 Tammuz in the ancient Jewish and Babylonian calendars, approximately late June or early July. The river Chebar is a known canal that ran by the ancient city of Nippur.[2] Ezekiel's later reference to a city called Tel Aviv (Ezek 3:15), after which the modern Israeli city was named in 1909 to signify the restoration of modern Israel, apparently corresponds to the site of a town called *til abūbi,* located along the Chebar canal.[3] The records of a fifth century Babylonian trading house run by Murashu and his sons indicate that exiled Jews were known to have been settled in this region.[4]

The significance of Ezekiel's initial reference in Ezek 1:1 to the thirtieth year, however, is not entirely clear, which has prompted considerable speculation. Some posit that it refers to the thirtieth year since King Josiah's reform began in 627 B.C.E.; others posit that it refers to Ezekiel's initial call.[5] It seems most likely, however, that it refers to the prophet's age at the time of his initial visions.[6] As a Zadokite priest, Ezekiel would have assumed his priestly duties at the age of thirty, and he would have continued service until the age of fifty (see Num 4:3, 23, 30, which specify that the lines of Kohath, the ancestor of the high priest Aaron, Gershom, and Merari would begin their specialized service in relation to the tent of meeting at the age of thirty; cf. Num 8:23-25, which specifies twenty-five, Ezekiel's age at the time of his exile, as the initial year of service for Levites in general). As the chronology of the book indicates, all but one of the prophet's oracles are placed from Ezekiel's initial vision in the fifth year of Jehoiachin's exile through the twenty-fifth year when Ezekiel saw the vision of the restored Temple (see Ezek 40:1). The result is a twenty (or twenty-five) year chronological framework for Ezekiel's oracles that would take him from the age of thirty (or twenty-five) through the age of fifty, the years of active service normally expected of a Zadokite priest. Only the reference to the twenty-seventh year in Ezek 29:17, which introduces a brief oracle concerning Nebuchadnezzar's campaign against Tyre, stands outside of this framework. Interpreters have noted, however, that this oracle was updated and its date likely changed to account for the actual circumstances and timing of Nebuchadnezzar's conquest of Tyre following a thirteen-year siege that finally concluded in 572 B.C.E. Some have speculated that Ezekiel himself may have made the correction.[7]

Interpreters have generally employed thematic criteria to determine the structure of the book. The destruction of Jerusalem by the Babylonians in 587 B.C.E. looms very large in this respect, particularly since Ezek 24 indicates that the prophet learned of the destruction of Jerusalem at the time of the death of his wife.

Chapter 24 is a key element in the book of Ezekiel because it concludes a lengthy sequence of chapters in Ezek 1–24 that anticipates the destruction of the city, whereas Ezek 25–32 constitutes a segment of the book devoted to the presentation of Ezekiel's oracles concerning the nations (cf. Isa 13–23; Jer 46–51; Zeph 2:4-15; Nahum; Obadiah). Chapters 33–48 then focus on the anticipated restoration of Jerusalem and creation at large now that the destruction of the city is completed. Because of these thematic indicators and because the material is presented in a generally chronological sequence, interpreters tend to maintain that the structure of the book of Ezekiel follows a general tripartite sequence of punishment against Jerusalem (or Israel) in Ezek 1–24; punishment against the nations in Ezek 25–32; and restoration for Israel and the nations in Ezek 33–48.

Although many take this tripartite sequence as the general pattern for the organization of prophetic books, the pattern appears to be the product of systematic theology rather than a close reading of biblical texts. Indeed, the pattern only appears to hold up decisively for the Septuagint version of the book of Jeremiah, but even there the sequence of prophetic word formulas constitutes the basic pattern for the organization of the book. As for Ezekiel, it appears to hold some possibilities, although it must be noted that the nations play only a very indirect role in Ezek 33–48 as witnesses to divine action. It may be that the tripartite pattern plays an underlying conceptual role in the organization of Ezekiel, but it does not account for the surface structure of the text. Instead, Ezekiel's structure is evident in the sequence of chronological statements that introduce the major components of the book. These appear in Ezek 1:1-3 (cf. Ezek 3:6), which introduces the initial account of Ezekiel's visions in the fifth year of Jehoiachin's exile; Ezek 8:1, which describes YHWH's departure from the Temple in the sixth year, sixth month, fifth day; Ezek 20:1, which introduces a sequence of oracles concerned with the punishment of Israel in the seventh year, fifth month, tenth day; Ezek 24:1, which introduces oracles concerned with the fall of Jerusalem and the nations in ninth year, tenth month, tenth day; Ezek 26:1, which introduces the initial oracle against Tyre in the eleventh year on the first day of an unspecified month; Ezek 29:1, which introduces the first oracle against Egypt in tenth year, tenth month, twelfth day; Ezek 29:17, which introduces the second block of oracles concerned with Egypt in the twenty-seventh year, first month, first day; Ezek 30:20, which introduces the first oracle against Pharaoh on eleventh year, first month, seventh day; Ezek 31:1, which introduces the second oracle concerning Pharaoh in the eleventh year, first month, seventh day; Ezek 32:1, which introduces an oracle concerning Pharaoh and Egypt in the twelfth year, twelfth month, first day; Ezek 32:17, which introduces an oracle sequence concerning the nations and Ezekiel role as watchman in the twelfth year and the first day of an unspecified month; Ezek 33:21, which introduces a sequence of oracles concerned with the restoration of Israel in twelfth year, tenth month, fifth day; and Ezek 40:1, which introduces Ezekiel's vision of the restored Temple in the twenty-fifth year, on the tenth day of the beginning of the year (Rosh Ha-Shanah, presumably the seventh month). The prevalence of the chronological formulas in relation to the oracles against the nations suggests that they were formulated originally in association with these oracles, and were only later employed to organize the entire book. Nevertheless, they function synchronically to signal the literary structure of the received form of the book. Insofar as the sequence envisions a process of punishment, restoration, and purging that extends from the destruction of Jerusalem to its reestablishment, the book as a whole may be characterized as Ezekiel's visions concerning the purging of Jerusalem. That structure is represented as follows:

EZEKIEL'S VISIONS CONCERNING THE PURGING OF JERUSALEM

EZEKIEL AS PRIEST AND PROPHET

Such a reading of the book must take into account Ezekiel's identity as a Zadokite priest.[8] Although early modern critical scholarship sought to differentiate the authentic material of the prophet Ezekiel from the later additions of the book's priestly editors, it is becoming increasingly clear that such a distinction can no longer be maintained as Ezekiel functions simultaneously as both prophet and Zadokite priest. Indeed, prophets in the ancient Near East frequently served in priestly or quasi-priestly roles as oracle diviners who were closely associated with temples of local deities. As noted above, a number of Israelite prophets combine prophetic and priestly roles, such as Moses, a Levitical priest and prophet (Exod 2:1-10; Num 26:58-59; Deut 18:15; 34:10), who functions as an oracle diviner in the tent of meeting (Exod 33:7; 34:29-35; Num 7:89); Samuel, the first born of Hannah, who was raised in the Shiloh sanctuary to serve as a priest and prophet under the supervision of the high priest Eli (1 Sam 1–3; cf. Num 3:11-13, 40-43; 8:14-19, which indicate that the Levites were designated to serve as priests in place of the firstborn of Israel); Jeremiah, a Levitical priest and prophet to whom an entire prophetic book is ascribed; and Zechariah, a Zadokite priest who also served as a visionary prophet (Zech 1:1; Ezra 5:1; 6:14; Neh 12:16). The placement of Moses and Samuel before the ark in the holy of holies points to the later role of the high priest before the ark in the Jerusalem Temple who would ecstatically experience the presence of YHWH on behalf of the people (see Lev 9–10; 16).

Ezekiel's language, use of visual imagery, and theological concepts indicate an attempt to combine the traditional perspectives and worldview of a Zadokite priest with the very new circum-

stances of life in Babylonian exile.[9] Ezekiel was raised in the cir-
cumscribed holy precincts of the Jerusalem Temple for a life of
service within the sanctuary. Although the Temple functioned as
the holy center of creation in Zadokite priestly thought, Babylonia
was a foreign land that stood outside of the Temple compound. As
such, it was impure, although the Zadokite worldview would ultimately call for its sanctification as well. Thus Ezekiel's visions,
oracles, and symbolic actions indicate an effort to recognize the
manifestation of YHWH in creation at large and to adapt the usual
practices and perspectives of life in the holy Temple to account for
YHWH's presence throughout all of creation and to explain the
significance of YHWH's destruction of Jerusalem and the Temple
itself.

Fundamental to Ezekiel's attempts to portray the manifestation
of divine presence is his use of the expression, "the glory of
YHWH" (Hebrew *kebod yhwh*), which is employed throughout the
biblical tradition to describe YHWH's presence among the people
(Exod 16:7, 10-12), in the Tabernacle (Exod 40:34-38), and in the
Temple (1 Kgs 8:10-11; 2 Chr 7:1-3; cf. 1 Sam 4:21-22). The expression appears throughout Ezekiel's visions to describe YHWH's
presence in relation to the destruction of Jerusalem and the
Temple in Ezek 1–11 and the reestablishment of the Temple at the
center of creation in Ezek 40–48. Ezekiel's portrayal of the glory
of YHWH in Ezek 1:4-28 presupposes the imagery of the ark of the
covenant located in the Holy of Holies of the Jerusalem Temple.
As a priest, Ezekiel would be well familiar with such imagery as
part of his preparation for divine service in the sanctuary. His
description of YHWH's glory as a cloud from the north would take
up a combination of elements from priestly tradition and from the
general ancient Near Eastern cultural environment. On the one
hand, the ten incense stands would fill the great hall of the
Temple with clouds of smoke to symbolize the divine presence at
times of worship. Likewise, both biblical and ancient Near
Eastern traditions portrayed YHWH, the Ugaritic/Canaanite god
Baal, and the Assyrian Assur as divine figures who rode through
the clouds on a chariot or other suitable vehicle to symbolize their
power and mastery in the world of creation (see 2 Sam 22:7-20;
Pss 18:6-19; 68:17-20, 32-35; Hab 3). The four living creatures or
cherubim that bear the glory of YHWH through the heavens correspond to the two cherubim that are constructed on top of the

ark of the covenant and the two cherubim that are constructed in the Holy of Holies of the Temple (Exod 25:1-22; 37:1-9; 1 Kgs 6:23-28; 2 Chr 3:10-14). Such figures typically appear beside the thrones of kings in the ancient Near East and at the gates of cities.

Other elements of the vision likewise reflect Temple imagery. The gleaming bronze recalls the description of the ark as overlaid with gold, and perhaps reflects the realities of the ark after the gold was stripped from the Temple by foreign invaders and replaced with bronze (1 Kgs 14:25-28; cf. 2 Kgs 18:14-16). The burning coals of fire apparently presuppose the burning incense altars within the great hall of the Temple or perhaps even the sacrificial altars themselves. The wheel within the wheel likely presupposes the four rings used with poles to convey the ark through the wilderness (Exod 25:12-15) or perhaps the wheels of the cart later used to carry the ark from Kiriath Jearim to Jerusalem (2 Sam 6:3; 1 Chr 13:7). The firmament that shines like crystal above the heads of the creatures that bear the glory of YHWH apparently symbolizes the mercy seat of the ark (Exod 25:17) or the clear pavement underneath the throne of YHWH at the time when Moses, Aaron, Nadab, Abihu, and the seventy elders of Israel ascend Mount Sinai to engage in a banquet with YHWH (Exod 24:9-11). Of course, such a banquet represents the sacrificial meals eaten at the Temple on holy festivals. The final image of the bow in the clouds (Ezek 1:28) of course represents the bow that appeared in relation to YHWH's covenant with Noah (Gen 9:8-17). Such a bow would also represent the promise of rain that would follow upon the Temple festival of Sukkot (Booths, Tabernacles) that would inaugurate the rainy season in the land of Israel.

Other images from the vision reflect Ezekiel's priestly role and practice. YHWH's designation of Ezekiel as "Mortal," literally, "Son of Man/Adam," reflects the belief that the high priest in the Temple was the descendant of Adam, the first human being, who represented all humanity before YHWH. The portrayal of his eating the scroll presented to him by YHWH (Ezek 2:8–3:3) reflects the priestly role for learning Torah and teaching it to the people, most notably in public readings of the Torah at the Temple (Lev 10:11; Deut 31:9-13; cf. Hag 2:10-19). Ezekiel's role as watchman or sentinel who warns the people of YHWH words so that they might avoid wrongdoing (Ezek 3:16-21; 33:1-20) appears to presuppose the role of the Levitical Temple gatekeepers, who would ensure the sanctity of the Temple by permitting only those who were properly prepared for Temple worship to enter the Temple grounds (see 1 Chr 9:17-27; 26:1-19; cf. Pss 15, 24; 2 Chr 23).

Other elements and images in the book likewise point to Ezekiel's priestly identity.[10] Ezekiel's sitting in silence for seven days (Ezek 3:15) reflects the seven-day period of seclusion when priests are first ordained for service at the altar (Lev 8:33). Ezekiel bears the guilt of his people (Ezek 4:4-8) in keeping with the priestly task to bear the guilt of the people (Lev 9:1-21; Num 18:1). His portrayal of the destruction of Jerusalem as a sort of purging sacrifice reflects the presentation of sin offerings at the Temple (Lev 4:1–5:19) and the scapegoat sacrifice for Yom Kippur (Lev 16). His discussion of individual moral responsibility (Ezek 18) draws heavily on the teachings of the Holiness Code in Lev 17–26, which define holy, righteous life in ancient Israel. His concern with the profanation of YHWH's holy name (Ezek 20; 33) reflects the priestly concern with YHWH's holiness in general. The portrayal of besieged Jerusalem as a sacrificial cauldron that must be cleansed (Ezek 24:1-14) draws upon the fundamental priestly duty to prepare sacrifices for consumption in the Temple. His portrayal of YHWH's lack of mourning at the fall of Jerusalem in relation to the death of his own wife (Ezek 24:15-27) draws upon the extensive tradition of Israel as the bride of YHWH (Jer 2; Hos 1–3; Zeph 3:14-20; Ezek 16; Isa 54) and the prohibition of mourning for priests except for blood relatives (Lev 21). The portrayal of the cleansing of the land through the resurrection of the dead (Ezek 37) and the burning of enemy corpses (Ezek 38–39) presupposes the priestly concern with death as the ultimate form of impurity (Lev 21). Even the vision of the restored Temple employs the fundamental image for a pure and stable creation, viz., the Temple itself (Ezek 40–48).

Although the book portrays Ezekiel as a prophet, the priestly elements are inherent in his identity and cannot be separated as the work of later redactors. Overall, much of the book of Ezekiel appears to represent the work of the prophet himself, although it has been lightly edited.[11] Insofar as Ezekiel's vision of the restored Temple was never achieved—our representations of the Second Temple built in 520–515 B.C.E. appear to differ markedly from Ezekiel's portrayal—the book must be dated to the period of the

Babylonian exile before the restoration of the early Persian period. As such, it presents a programmatic rationale for the restoration of the land and people of Israel centered at the Temple in Jerusalem.

THE BOOK OF EZEKIEL

The remaining portion of this chapter will examine each of the major components of the book of Ezekiel, in order to understand their role and function within the sequence of the book as a whole.

EZEKIEL 1-7

The initial segment of the book of Ezekiel appears in Ezek 1-7, which is set in Ezekiel's thirtieth year, the fifth year of Jehoiachin's exile (593-592 B.C.E.). As noted above, this segment begins with Ezekiel's initial vision of YHWH by the banks of the river Chebar in Babylonia. Following the account of Ezekiel's vision in Ezek 1:4-3:15, the appearance of the formula, "the word of YHWH came to me," in Ezek 3:16; 6:1; and 7:1 marks the other subunits of this section. Overall, Ezek 1-7 presents YHWH's commission of Ezekiel to act as a prophet and Ezekiel's initial activity to convey YHWH's message concerning the upcoming destruction of Jerusalem to his fellow exiles.

As noted above, Ezekiel's initial vision of YHWH is based largely on the imagery of the ark of the covenant in the Holy of Holies of the Jerusalem Temple. The image has been modified, however, to account for YHWH's mobility and manifestation in the world of creation outside of the Jerusalem Temple. Such an image may well depend in part on the above-mentioned representations of YHWH flying through the heavens in a divine chariot or pagan representations of deities such as Baal, who is portrayed in Ugaritic texts as the rider of clouds,[12] or Assur, who is depicted in Assyrian art in relation to a winged solar disk who appears at the head of the Assyrian armies as well as in other contexts.[13] Although Ezekiel is a priest, raised to serve in the Jerusalem Temple, his unexpected presence as an exile in a foreign land obviously influences his view of the world, and his visions and actions reflect his adaptation to the circumstances and culture in which he finds himself. The Temple is conceived as the holy center of creation in Zadokite thought. Ezekiel finds himself outside of that holy center in the world of creation itself. He never gives up his identity as a Zadokite priest, but instead he finds the means to serve as a priest outside of the sanctuary in which he would normally have spent his life.

Coming in his thirtieth year, the time when he would normally begin his service in the Temple itself, Ezekiel's initial vision of YHWH appears to reflect an adaptation of the priestly ordination in which young priests would commence their holy service. According to Lev 8 (see also Exod 28), the priestly ordination ceremony calls for a seven-day period of incubation in which the priest remains in the sanctuary (tent of meeting) as daily sacrifices are made in order to consecrate him for holy service (see esp. Lev 8:31-36; Exod 28:35-37).[14] Insofar as the priest remains in the sanctuary, he is located before the Holy of Holies and the ark of the covenant, which represents the divine presence in the Temple. The presence of the cherubim with the ark contribute markedly to the image. Although they are called living creatures here, Ezek 10 refers to them as cherubim. Presumably, the incense altars and *menorot* (candelabra) add smoke and light to the imagery of divine presence. Moses' experience in the tent of meeting (Exod 33:7; 34:29-35; Num 7:89), Samuel's experience before the ark in Shiloh (1 Sam 3), and Zechariah's experience at the ordination of the high priest Joshua ben Jehozadak (Zech 3) suggest that visions of the divine presence could well be a part of the ordination process. Of course, Ezekiel is not able to go to the Temple, but the ark comes to him. He receives his commission to act from YHWH in the form of specific instructions to speak YHWH's words to the people of Israel and a scroll that he is to eat in order to internalize the divine message (Ezek 2:1–3:11). Such a commission, of course, recalls the priestly task to teach YHWH's Torah to the people (Lev 10:10-11). He sits stunned among the exiles at Tel Aviv for a period of seven days (Ezek 3:15), and it is only at the end of his seven days of silence among his fellow exiles that he begins to carry out the divine commission (Ezek 3:16), much as a newly ordained priest begins his service at the altar on the eighth day immediately following his ordination (Lev 9, esp. v. 1).

Ezekiel 3:16–5:17 presents a series of divine commands to the prophet/priest that will define his role and message in relation to the exiled people. YHWH begins by informing him that he will serve as a sentinel for the people to warn them of their wicked-ness. As noted above, this role appears to represent an adaptation of the priestly gatekeepers who were to ensure that only those who were properly prepared could enter the holy precincts of the Temple. Ezekiel's task is to inform the people of wrongdoing so that they might correct themselves and not die or otherwise suf-fer punishment. Should Ezekiel fail in his task, he is held account-able just as the priest is expected to bear the sins of Israel or the Temple (Num 18:1). It is noteworthy that Ezek 3:22-27 specifies that Ezekiel is to remain silent in his house and to speak only when YHWH commands him to deliver an oracle to the people. Such a role appears to conform to that of Moses as oracle diviner in the tent of meeting (see Exod 33:7-11; 34:29-35; Num 11). It also appears to reflect priestly service at the altar, insofar as the priests carry out the sacrifice without speaking.[15] Speech apparently is left to the Levitical choirs, whose singing constitutes a form of prophetic speech that corresponds to the singing of the angelic choirs of the heavenly Temple (see 1 Chr 15–16). Ezekiel cannot serve at the altar or in the Temple, but his service in Babylonia appears to reflect an adaptation of his expected Temple role.

YHWH's instructions include several symbolic acts that repre-sent the profanation or punishment of Israel. In the first instance, YHWH commands Ezekiel to construct a model of the city of Jerusalem under siege and to lie on his side to symbolize the time of the punishment of Israel and Judah. He is to lie on his left side for three hundred and ninety days to symbolize the years of the punishment of Israel and on his right side for forty days to sym-bolize the years of the punishment of Judah. The significance of these periods of time is uncertain. They are noteworthy, however, because forty years corresponds to the time from Josiah's reform in 627 B.C.E. until the destruction of the Temple in 587 B.C.E. The three hundred and ninety years would then correspond roughly to the time from Saul's kingship (ca. 1020 B.C.E.; see 1 Sam 13:1) or David's establishment of Jerusalem as the site for the Temple ca. 1000 B.C.E. to the beginning of Josiah's reform. Such a chronology accepts biblical claims that the northern kingdom of Israel was punished for idolatry (2 Kgs 17) and that Josiah attempted to atone for past wrongdoing through his reform (2 Kgs 22–23). His early death, however, signaled the end of his reform and led ulti-mately to Jerusalem's destruction by the Babylonians.

This action is to be accompanied by the preparation of impure food, which Ezekiel is to eat while lying on his side for the specified periods of time. The mixed grains perhaps symbolize the privation of the people in exile since they must scrounge for food and use whatever is available. It is impure because it is cooked over a fire fueled by human dung. As a priest, Ezekiel was enjoined to eat only food that had been sanctified for presentation at the altar and prepared for consumption in the holy Temple (Lev 7; 10–11; Num 18; Deut 14). Human dung was obviously inappropriate for the preparation of food to be consumed by the priests. When Ezekiel protests to YHWH, he is allowed to use cow dung instead. Although still unclean, it is apparently not as bad as human dung. Such an act symbolizes Ezekiel's own profanation as a priest who is forced to live outside of the sanctuary.

The second symbolic action calls for Ezekiel to cut his hair and divide it into thirds so that each third will represent the fate of a segment of Jerusalem's population; one third will be burned, one third will be stricken with the sword, and one third will be scattered to the wind. Such an act likewise symbolizes Ezekiel's loss of sanctity as a priest. Although the priests were to cut their hair, they were not to shave it off entirely as Canaanite or Egyptian priests apparently did (Lev 21:5; 19:27).

Ezekiel 6 presents YHWH's instruction for Ezekiel to prophesy against the hills of Israel. The oracle continues the themes of the symbolic acts in Ezek 4–5, but it adds references to the profanation of the land of Israel by the presence of unauthorized cultic high places and altars. As the holy center of creation and the land of Israel[16] the Jerusalem Temple was to serve as the only sanctuary in the land. With the profanation of Jerusalem and the Temple—and even Ezekiel himself—the land itself becomes unclean and subject to punishment.

The concluding subunit appears in Ezek 7, which presents a prophecy of judgment against the entire nation. The oracle draws upon the Day of YHWH traditions in the Hebrew Bible (e.g., Amos 5:18-20; 8:1-14; Isa 2:6-13; 13; 34; Zeph 1:7-18), which appear frequently to announce YHWH's judgment against either the nations or Israel and Judah. The references to sword, pestilence, and famine recall Ezekiel's statements in chapters 5–6, and the budding rod of judgment recalls the budding of Aaron's rod, which designates Levi as the priestly tribe (Num 17), or Jeremiah's sign of punishment (Jer 1:11-12). In the present instance, the oracle concludes the first section of the book, and therefore prepares the reader for the scenario of Jerusalem's destruction that begins in Ezek 8–11.

EZEKIEL 8–19

The second major segment of the book of Ezekiel is Ezek 8–19, which presents Ezekiel's vision of the departure of the glory of YHWH from Jerusalem in Ezek 8:1–11:13 together with a series of oracles that take up the significance of this event. Each of the following oracles is introduced with the phrase, "and the word of YHWH came to me, saying. . . ." The first appears in Ezek 11:14, which introduces an oracle in verses 14-24, which state YHWH's intentions to restore Israel with a new heart following the conclusion of the exile. Successive prophetic word formulas, each of which introduces a new oracle in the sequence, appear in Ezek 12:1; 12:17; 12:21; 13:1; 14:1-2; 15:1; 16:1; 17:1; 17:11; and 18:1. Although these oracles take up the coming punishment of the people, Ezek 11:14-24 defines Israel's restoration as the ultimate goal of the punishment articulated throughout this section.

The introductory date formula in Ezek 8:1 places the sequence in relation to the fifth day of the sixth month (5 Elul, late August or early September) in 592–591 B.C.E. This would likely correspond to the period when sentiment for a revolt against Babylon began to rise in Jerusalem and Judah. King Zedekiah, the brother of Jehoiakim and uncle of Jehoiachin, had been placed on the throne by the Babylonians as a puppet to keep the country under control. Because the exiled Jehoiachin would have been regarded as the true king, Zedekiah was ultimately unable to quell sentiment for a revolt. Although Nebuchadnezzar's attack began in Zedekiah's ninth year (ca. 589 B.C.E.), the notice in Jer 27:2 that Zedekiah had gathered the kings of Edom, Moab, Ammon, Tyre, and Sidon, presumably to discuss their situation under the newly imposed Babylonian rule. As noted in the discussion of Jer 27–29, Jeremiah unsuccessfully called for submission to Babylon. Although Ezekiel was already in Babylonian exile, the debate over the future course of Jerusalem and Judah would have provoked discussion among the exiles and influenced Ezekiel as well. His vision concerning YHWH's departure from the Temple suggests that the prophet had already concluded that revolt and the subsequent punishment of Jerusalem by the Babylonians was inevitable.

Ezekiel's portrayal of YHWH's departure from the Temple draws heavily from priestly notions of purification or expiation in an effort to interpret the anticipated destruction of the Temple as an attempt to purge the Temple and Jerusalem of impurity.[17] Various biblical narratives portray attempts at Temple purification during the reigns of Hezekiah (2 Kgs 18:1-8; 2 Chr 29–31), Josiah (2 Kgs 23:1-25), and Judah the Maccabee (1 Macc 4:36-51). Such purges represent attempts to resanctify the Temple following periods when it was employed for foreign worship or was otherwise compromised. Portrayals of attempts to purge the people of Israel appear in the golden calf episode in the wilderness (Exod 32), the narrative concerning the deaths of Korah, Dathan, and Abiram for conducting improper worship in the wilderness (Num 16), and the narrative concerning Achan's theft of booty during the conquest of Canaan (Josh 7). As in the Temple purges, these incidents suggest attempts to purge wrongdoers by removing them and their sins from the midst of the people. The expiatory *ḥaṭṭa't*, "sin offering" and *'ašam*, "guilt offering" (Lev 4:1–5:26; 6:17–7:10) are offerings that accompany attempts to purge the Temple or the people of the impurity of sin.[18]

Ezekiel begins with a description of a heavenly or angelic figure who transports him to the Temple. He portrays the Temple as a sanctuary that has been corrupted by foreign worship, where he describes the presence of "an image of jealousy" (NRSV) or "an infuriating image" (*TANAKH*). We do not know what he means by this term, but it clearly suggests something improper, as do the references to abominations, creeping things, loathsome animals, idols, and so on., that appear within the Temple. The reference to the elders of Israel and Jaazniah ben Shaphan deserves our attention, since the elders were an important authoritative body in Israel, and Jaazniah is a member of the Shaphan family that gave its support to Jeremiah. Interpreters frequently take Ezekiel's description as an account of true idolatry in the Temple, but his perspective as an exiled Zadokite priest must be considered. If the Babylonians had taken Zadokite priests like Ezekiel from the Temple, those who were left behind to serve in the Temple might have been viewed as somehow inadequate to maintain Temple sanctity. Although Jeremiah was a priest, he was an Elide Levite who would not have been qualified to offer sacrifice at the altar as the Zadokites were. Ezekiel's vision need not depict people who were deliberately committing sins, but only reflect his understanding of the compromised sanctity of the Temple following the removal of key Zadokite priests. Late-summer mourning rituals that call for rain are easily cast as worship of the Babylonian fertility god, Tammuz, and morning prayer directed to the east is easily cast as worship of the sun. In any case, Ezekiel's description represents his attempt to explain the destruction of the Temple by claiming that its sanctity had been compromised.

The portrayal of the executioners is particularly important for its use of priestly imagery. Ezekiel describes six men with weapons in hand supervised by a man dressed in white linen with a writing case at his side. White linen is the characteristic dress of the priests while serving in the Temple (Exod 28:29) and of the angels who represent the heavenly counterparts of the priests (Dan 10:5). Later rabbinic literature notes that a priestly officer typically supervised other priests during times of sacrifice (m. Tamid 1:2; 3:1-9). Although interpreters generally attempt to claim that the executioners are to destroy the guilty,[19] there is little indication that "those who sigh or groan over all the abominations that are committed in it" are guilty of sighing or groaning in support of the abomination or in disgust at them. The following command to show no pity in cutting down old men, women, and children likewise suggests little interest in determining guilt or innocence. Insofar as the entire city has been judged to be guilty, it seems that guilt or innocence is not the determining factor in who is to die and who is to survive—the entire city is guilty in Ezekiel's estimation. In this respect, we may recall the scapegoat ritual of Yom Kippur (Day of Atonement) in which two goats are employed as sin offerings for the people (Lev 16). One is sacrificed at the altar, and the other is sent out to the wilderness to carry away the sins of the people. Insofar as Ezekiel later claims that those who survive are to be sent into exile to be judged, whereas those who died are likened to meat in a sacrificial pot (Ezek 11:5-12), it would appear that Ezekiel's understanding of the destruction of Jerusalem is heavily influenced by the scapegoat ritual in which the people are purged in part by the sacrifice of the one goat and the expulsion of the other.

Indeed, the destruction of the city represents a form of sacrifice. YHWH, portrayed once again in relation to the ark or throne imagery of chapter 1, commands the man in white linen to take coals from among the cherubim and scatter them over the city to ignite it. Such an image represents the procedure of sacrifice, and the portrayal of smoke and brightness would represent the incense altars and sacrificial altar in operation during worship. The rise of the cherubim who bear the presence of YHWH represents the departure of the glory of YHWH from the Temple in contrast to the descent of the glory of YHWH into the wilderness tabernacle portrayed in Exod 40:33-38 (cf. 1 Kgs 8:1-13).

Following Ezekiel's description of YHWH's departure from Jerusalem and the destruction of the city, a sequence of oracles follows that attempt to explain the significance of the catastrophe. As noted above, the initial oracle in the sequence, Ezek 11:14-24, portrays the destruction as an act of purification and states YHWH's intentions to restore Jerusalem and the people once the process purification is complete. YHWH pledges to serve as a "little sanctuary" for the people and to give them a new heart and spirit to observe divine expectations. Many interpreters see in this statement the beginnings of diaspora: Jewish organization and worship that lead ultimately to the emergence of the synagogue, as exiled Jews attempted to establish community religious life outside of the land of Israel.[20]

The remaining oracles of this section, each introduced by the formula, "and the word of YHWH came to me, saying . . ." reflect on the message of judgment and restoration laid out in Ezekiel's vision. Ezekiel 12:1-16 presents YHWH's call for Ezekiel to carry out a symbolic act to represent the exile of the people. He is to carry his baggage, dig through the wall, cover his face, and then explain to the people that this act serves as a sign to represent YHWH's intentions to exile the people among the nations. Such a portrayal draws upon the observance of Pesaḥ (Passover) in the Temple, in which the people are dressed for travel as they eat the sacrificial offering in the Temple (see Exod 12–13, esp. 12:11). Ezekiel 12:17-20 likewise draws upon the Passover tradition by calling on the people to drink water and eat bread in fear, much like the slaves of the Exodus tradition, as they go out into the wilderness away from the land of Israel rather than toward it. Ezekiel 12:21-25 emphasizes that the realization of Ezekiel's vision is near, which would dispel any notions that judgment is far off. Ezekiel's language draws upon the Day of YHWH tradition, which frequently states that YHWH's day of judgment is near (see Isa 13:6; Obad 15; Joel 1:15; 2:1; Zeph 1:7, 14; cf. Ezek 30:3). Ezekiel 12:26-28 envisions a long period of fulfillment before the entire process of exile and restoration is complete.

Ezekiel 13 takes up the issue of false prophecy, which so frequently emerges as a concern in biblical tradition (see Deut 18:9-22; 1 Kgs 13; 22; Jer 23:9-40; 27–29). One of the major hermeneutical questions of biblical prophecy is whether it is true or false, which entails that a prophecy cannot be considered true until it is fulfilled (see Deut 18:9-22).[21] When the issue is placed before the people in ancient Israel and Judah, for example, when Jeremiah challenges Hananiah's claims that Jerusalem would be freed from Babylon in two years' time (Jer 27–28), the problems associated with the issue become very apparent, i. e., how does one decide between two competing claims? Modern readers have an advantage in knowing the later events of the biblical period and the definition of a biblical canon which the ancients lacked, but even then modern readers have recognized that not all biblical prophecy was fulfilled as stated (e.g., Ezek 40–48, which is considered in Jewish tradition to be a portrayal of the third Temple of the future). Ezekiel agrees with Jeremiah in claiming that those prophets who announce peace must be false. From Ezekiel's perspective, judgment followed by restoration is inevitable.

Ezekiel 14:1-11 takes up the question of repentance, insofar as YHWH calls upon the people to change, but justifies judgment by charging that the people have turned to idols and thereby defiled themselves. Ezekiel 14:12-23 argues that even the presence of righteous figures, such as Noah, Daniel, and Job, could not save the lives of those who had acted against YHWH (cf. Jer 15:1, who cites Moses and Samuel for similar reasons). The choice of figures is noteworthy, since Noah is known in the priestly tradition as the righteous man who saved a remnant of humanity and the animals from the flood and Job is known for saving the lives of his friends after demanding that YHWH act righteously. Daniel poses a problem, however, not only because Daniel appears to be written in the Hellenistic period, but also because he does not save the lives of his friends. Instead, he merely serves as an example for others. Ezekiel appears to presuppose the Canaanite figure, Dan-El (note the Hebrew spelling of the name corresponds to the Canaanite Dan-El rather than the biblical Daniel). According to the Ugaritic Aqhat legend, Dan-El was a righteous man who saved the life of his son Aqhat and thereby inaugurated the seasonal pattern of a dry summer and a rainy winter.[22] These examples support Ezekiel's argument that individuals are responsible for their own fate (cf. Ezek 18).

Ezekiel 15 presents an allegory in which the prophet compares the wood of vine to the people of Israel. Just as the twisted wood of the vine is useless for anything but burning, so YHWH will give up Israel to burning (cf. Judg 9:7-21). Such an analogy is typical of the wisdom tradition (see the examples in Prov 30), although prophets frequently make use of wisdom perspectives (see Isa 5:1-7; 28:23-29; Amos 2:13; 3:3-8).

Ezekiel 16:1-63 represents another example of the use of the marriage metaphor to portray the relationship between YHWH and Jerusalem as husband and bride (cf. Hos 1–3; Jer 2; Isa 54; Zeph 3:14-20).[23] Although the northern prophets, such as Hosea and Jeremiah, portray the wilderness period as an ideal "honeymoon" period in which YHWH and Israel were first wed, the tradition frequently presents Israel as a cheating wife in an effort to charge the people with having abandoned YHWH.[24] Ezekiel's portrayal is particularly harsh, insofar as he presents Jerusalem as an abandoned baby girl, whom YHWH takes in, clothes, raises to maturity, and then marries, only to be abandoned when the grown-up girl goes off with other lovers. The metaphor is not to be understood strictly in religious terms. The designation of Egypt, the Assyrians, and the Chaldeans/Babylonians, indicates that the prophet has in mind Jerusalem's history of alliances with foreign nations that brought the nation into the international arena and frequently resulted in its defeat or conquest. The charge that Jerusalem's mother was a Hittite and her mother an Amorite calls to mind Jerusalem's background as a Jebusite city, whose population was never destroyed when David took control (2 Sam 5). The portrayal of the fate of the sisters, Samaria and Sodom, is apparently intended to demonstrate that Jerusalem had ample warning in the fate of the northern kingdom of Israel (2 Kgs 17) and in the portrayal of Sodom's destruction in the ancestral period (Gen 18–19). The concluding portrayal of Jerusalem's restoration, like that of Samaria and Sodom, draws upon the Zadokite concept of an eternal covenant with creation in which the Temple and its practices (Gen 9:8-17; Exod 31:12-17), the priesthood (Num 18:23; 25:10-13), and the house of David (2 Sam 7; 23:1-7; Pss 89; 110) are rooted. It is not a new covenant as in Jeremiah (Jer 31:31-34), but an eternal covenant that YHWH remembers.

Ezekiel 17:1-10 presents an allegory about two great eagles. The first came to Lebanon to break off the top shoot of a cedar. It placed the shoot in a land of merchants where it sprouted and flourished. When a second eagle came, the vine reached out again, but YHWH raises questions whether it will thrive after it is pulled up. Ezekiel 17:11-24 then explains the allegory, which draws upon earlier prophetic tradition that portrays the Davidic monarchy as a shoot or vine (Isa 11:1-9; Jer 23:1-8). The first eagle refers to Nebuchadnezzar, the king of Babylon, who took the Judean king Jehoiachin into exile and placed his uncle Zedekiah on the throne. The second refers to the Egyptian Pharaoh Psamtek II, with whom Judah allied in its futile attempt to revolt against Babylon. The oracle clearly envisions the failure of such an attempt, and concludes by stating that only YHWH will ultimately see to the rise of a righteous Davidic monarch in keeping with the above noted oracle from Isaiah and Jeremiah.

The concluding subunit of this section appears in Ezek 18:1–19:14, which calls for the repentance of the current generation as it laments the downfall of the Davidic monarchy. The two subunits of this section, Ezek 18:1-32 and 19:1-14, are linked together by their concern with the deterioration of Judah's position following the deportation of Jehoiachin and others (including Ezekiel). In view of the growing sentiment for renewed revolt against Babylon following the deportation, the prophet apparently hopes to convince people to change their course before it is too late. The first part of this subunit in Ezek 18:1-32 focuses on the question of moral responsibility.[25] Although many see this text as a statement of Ezekiel's view of the moral responsibility of the individual human being, the choice of examples indicates that it focuses on the individual generation. In this respect, it is designed to answer a popular proverb that contends that the current reverses suffered by Jerusalem and Judah are punishments for the sins of past generations (cf. Jer 31:29-30, which quotes the same proverb). Ezekiel responds with a disputation speech that is designed to demonstrate that only the current generation must be held accountable for its own suffering and that, by repentance and change, it has the capacity to change its fate.[26] Ezekiel's contention conflicts with the Decalogue (Exod 20:5; Deut 5:9; cf. Exod 34:7), which states that YHWH holds sinners accountable to the third and fourth generation. The prophet presents four cases of moral action that draw upon the commandments of the Pentateuch, particularly the Holiness Code of Lev 17–26. The first case describes a man who is righteous, and declares that he will live because he is innocent of any crime. The second describes the actions of his wicked son, and declares that he will die because he is culpable. The third case describes the actions of the grandson, who refrains from the sins of his father and therefore lives. Nevertheless, the father is still culpable because the righteousness of the son does atone for the sins of the father. Finally, Ezekiel describes the cases of a wicked man who repents and lives and a righteous man who turns to crime and therefore becomes culpable. Both examples indicate the human capacity to change together with the human responsibility to choose the righteous moral course. Ezekiel concludes his illustration with a call for his generation to repent and live.

The second subunit of this section appears in Ezek 19:1-14 in which the prophet illustrates the preceding principles by lamenting the downfall of the princes of Israel, namely, the royal house of David. The laments employ the typical Qinah (lament) 3/2 metrical pattern. The first lament employs the metaphor of the lion, the symbol of Judah and the house of David (Gen 49:8-12), and her cubs. The first cub is caught and taken to Egypt to symbolize the Egyptians' removal of King Jehoahaz ben Josiah from the throne in 609 B.C.E. (2 Kgs 23:31-34; 2 Chr 36:1-4). The second cub is caught and taken to Babylon to symbolize Nebuchadnezzar's deportation of Jehoiachin (2 Kgs 24:8-17; 2 Chr 36:9-10). The second lament employs the imagery of the vine (see Isa 11:1-9; Jer 23:1-8; Ezek 17:1-24) to depict the demise of a vine that is transplanted to the desert. Although the specific referent is uncertain, it likely refers to Zedekiah, the son of Josiah and uncle of Jehoiachin, who was placed on the throne by the Babylonians following Jehoiachin's exile. By employing laments for lost monarchs in this manner, Ezekiel apparently warns the people that a weak monarch such as Zedekiah offers little chance for successful resistance against the Babylonians. Again, the prophet's goal is to avert an impending disaster.

EZEKIEL 20–23

The next major segment of the book of Ezekiel appears in Ezek 20–23, which presents Ezekiel's oracles concerning the punishment of all Israel. The segment is dated to the tenth day of the fifth month of the seventh year of Jehoiachin's exile, namely, 10 Av (late July or early August), 591–590 B.C.E. This would place the oracles in the period when tensions were rising in Judah and building for a revolt against Babylon. The section employs elements of past tradition to reiterate the sins of the people that will lead to judgment and YHWH's intention to restore them after the punishment is complete.

Ezekiel 20:1-44 draws upon the wilderness traditions to provide an assessment of Israel's past and future. As a priest, Ezekiel's responsibilities include the teaching of YHWH's Torah, both to remember the past and to give direction to the future. The oracle rehearses the traditions of Israel's rebellion in the wilderness and YHWH's efforts to punish them (see esp. Exod 32–34; Num 14). The discourse draws a deliberate analogy between Israel's rebellion in the wilderness and the charge that Israel has rebelled against YHWH in the land to justify YHWH's decision to punish the nation once again. YHWH's statement, "I acted for the sake of my name," and the focus on Shabbat both emphasize the priestly concern with the holiness of YHWH. The oracle concludes with a portrayal of Israel's redemption from foreign lands and service of YHWH on YHWH's holy mountain. Such claims indicate a renewed Exodus and restoration of the Temple that will call for the recognition of YHWH.

The brief oracle in Ezek 21:1-5 (NRSV 20:45-49) against the Negeb Desert employs the imagery of seasonal fires in the late summer to indicate that this region will suffer punishment as well.

Ezekiel 21:6-12 (NRSV 21:1-7) is the first of three oracles concerning YHWH's drawn sword against Jerusalem. The oracles may have accompanied a symbolic act by the prophet. The statement that the sword will cut off both righteous and wicked appears to support the claims in Ezek 9–11 that YHWH will act against all the inhabitants of Jerusalem. The second oracle in Ezek 21:13-22 (NRSV 21:8-17) employs the image of a polished and sharpened sword that strikes its victims. The third oracle in Ezek 21:23-37 (NRSV 21:18-32) makes it clear that the sword will be used by the king of Babylon against the king of Israel and against the Ammonites.

Ezekiel 22:1-16 is the first of three oracles that draw upon the imagery of Isa 1:2-31 to express YHWH's judgment against Jerusalem. The focus on bloodshed both emphasizes the concerns with bleeding wounds, sacrifice, and hands stained with blood from Isa 1:6, 10-17, 18-20 and also the priestly concern with the proper treatment of blood (Lev 17). The crimes of incest, bribery, extortion, and contempt for parents appear throughout Lev 18–20 in the Holiness Code. The second oracle in Ezek 22:17-22 draws upon the smelting imagery of Isa 1:21-26 to portray YHWH's purification of Jerusalem much as one smelts metal to remove its dross or impurities. The third oracle in Ezek 22:23-31 draws upon Isa 1:10, 23, and 26 to charge Jerusalem's leadership, including the prophets, priests, officials, and people of the land with failure to exercise proper leadership for the people at large as they attempt to serve their own interests instead. Altogether, Ezekiel's use of the oracle from Isa 1 indicates his priestly responsibility to teach (Lev 10:10-11).

Ezekiel 23:1-49 concludes this segment with a metaphorical portrayal of Samaria and Jerusalem as the sisters Oholah and Oholibah.[27] The word *Oholah* employed for Samaria means "her tent," and apparently refers to YHWH's presence in the northern kingdom of Israel since YHWH is portrayed as dwelling in a tent or wilderness tabernacle. The term *Oholibah* employed for Jerusalem means "my tent is in her," which alludes to the presence of YHWH's Temple in Jerusalem. The passage presupposes the traditional relationship between the two biblical nations of Israel and Judah, and uses the marriage metaphor as a basis to portray each nation's abandonment of YHWH (cf. Hos 1–3; Jer 2; Ezek 16). The portrayal of Judah as a harlotous sister who is even worse than Israel appears also in Jer 3:6-10, 11. The passage focuses on Israel's and Judah's relationships in the international sphere with Egypt, Assyria, and Babylonia. Ezekiel's charges of Oholah's (Israel's) relationships with Assyria and Egypt apparently refer to Israel's alliance with the Assyrians under the reign of the

Jehu Dynasty, when monarchs such as Jehu (842–815 B.C.E.) and his grandson Joash (802–786 B.C.E.) were known to have allied with Assyria. As indicated in Hosea, the alliance established a relationship with Egypt as well (see Hos 12:1). The breakdown of this alliance following the death of Jeroboam ben Joash in 746 B.C.E. ultimately resulted in the Assyrian invasions of Israel. Judah's relationship with Assyria began during the reign of the Israelite Jehu Dynasty, and continued when King Ahaz called for Assyrian assistance during the Syro-Ephraimite War in 734–732 B.C.E. Following the death of Josiah in 609 B.C.E., Egypt took control of Judah, and Babylon took control after defeating the Egyptians in 605 B.C.E. From Ezekiel's perspective, such alliances defile YHWH's sanctuary, insofar as YHWH protects Judah. The prophet apparently intends to condemn current attempts at alliance with Egypt that might lead to a second revolt against Babylon.

EZEKIEL 24–25

The fourth major segment of the book of Ezekiel appears in Ezek 24–25, which presents the prophet's symbolic actions and oracles concerning the impending fall of Jerusalem and the neighboring nations of Ammon, Moab, Edom, and Philistia. The unit is dated to the tenth day of the tenth month of the ninth year, i.e., 10 Tevet (late January or early February), 589 or 588 B.C.E. According to 2 Kgs 25:1; Jer 52:4 (cf. Zech 8:19), this was the day that Nebuchadnezzar first laid siege to Jerusalem. Although Ezek 25 presents the first of Ezekiel's oracles concerning the nations in Ezek 25–32, these oracles are grouped together with his oracles concerning the onset of the Babylonian siege of Jerusalem because they are charged with various past acts against Israel and Judah and supporting the Babylonians in their efforts to take the city. Each subunit within this text is introduced by the customary formula, "and the word of YHWH came to me, saying. . . ."

The first subunit, Ezek 24:1-14, presents Ezekiel's allegory of the pot. As a Zadokite priest in the Jerusalem Temple, Ezekiel's duties would have included carrying out the sacrifices at the altar and preparing the sacrificial meet for consumption by the priests and other worshipers. References to the thigh and shoulder indicate the choice offerings that are presented to the priests for their service in the Temple (see Num 18:12; Exod 29:26-28; Lev 7:28-36; 10:12-18; Num 18:18; Gen 32:32). Ezekiel focuses on the images of blood and rust or sludge at the bottom of the pot to characterize Jerusalem as the "bloody city" that must be purified. In priestly thought, blood is holy and must be covered when shed (Lev 17:13-16; Gen 9:1-7). Ezekiel proposes to clean the pot by burning it with fire until the sludge at the bottom of the pot is burned away. Of course, such an image compares to the burning of Jerusalem by the Babylonians.

The second symbolic action appears in Ezek 24:15-27, in which YHWH commands Ezekiel to refrain from mourning for his dead wife to symbolize YHWH's attitude at the destruction of Jerusalem and the Temple. Many condemn Ezekiel's actions, but such condemnations fail to account for the reason why Ezekiel acts as he does. As a Zadokite priest, he is forbidden to come into contact with the dead, with the exception of his own blood relatives, and the high priest is forbidden even to mourn (Lev 21:1-12; cf. Lev 10:1-7). Leviticus 21:4 specifically prohibits a priest from mourning for his wife. The reason for these commands is because death represents the ultimate impurity in priestly thought; because of the priests' holy status before YHWH, they are therefore forbidden to come into contact with death except as indicated above. Again, Ezekiel merely draws upon his own experience and expectations as a Zadokite priest to illustrate YHWH's lack of remorse at the fall of Jerusalem and the Temple, symbolically portrayed once again as YHWH's bride (cf. Isa 54; Hos 1–3; Jer 2; Zeph 3:14-20; Ezek 16). He is to remain silent until receiving news that the Temple is destroyed. As a priest, he remains silent while serving at the altar, but the demise of the Temple would preclude such silence.

The section of oracles against Judah's immediate neighbors in Ezek 25:1-17 includes YHWH's instructions for Ezekiel to speak out against Ammon, Moab, Edom, and Philistia. The passage presupposes that each of these nations somehow assisted or supported Babylonia in its attack against Jerusalem. The oracle concerning the Ammonites, located to the east of the Jordan River around the site of modern Amman, in verses 1-7 seems to be somewhat retrospective, insofar as it charges that the Ammonites lauded the profaning of the Jerusalem Temple as well as the destruction of Israel and the exile of Judah. These statements likely refer to events earlier than the Babylonian destruction of Jerusalem. According to 2 Kgs 24:1-2, the Ammonites were among the groups that harassed Jerusalem at the time of Jehoiakim's revolt against Nebuchadnezzar, and Zephaniah condemns them for having seized territory from Gad (Zeph 2:8-11). During the reign of Zedekiah, Jer 27:3 claims that they joined Judah in an anti-Babylonian coalition, but Jer 40:1 indicates that they instigated the assassination of Gedaliah ben Ahikam ben Shaphan, the Babylonian appointed governor of Judah. The oracle concerning the Moabites in verses 8-11, located to the east of the Dead Sea, targets a nation that also harassed Jerusalem during Nebuchadnezzar's campaign against Jehoiakim (2 Kgs 24:2). Zephaniah condemned Moab together with Ammon for attempting to extend its borders at Israel's expense (Zeph 2:8-11). The Moabites later joined the Judean-based anti-Babylonian coalition (Jer 27:1). The oracle concerning Edom, located east of the Negeb and south of the Dead Sea, in verses 12-14 focuses on a nation that is charged in other traditions (see Ps 137:7; Lam 4:21-22; Obad 1-14) with assisting the Babylonians in the destruction of Jerusalem. Curiously, they are not listed among the groups that harassed Judah at the time of Jehoiakim's revolt (2 Kgs 24:2), and Zephaniah says nothing about them. The Philistines, located to the west of Judah along the Mediterranean coast, were occupied by the Assyrians throughout the eighth and seventh centuries, and were condemned by Zephaniah (Zeph 2:4, 5-7). Control of Philistia was essential to the Babylonians to block any intervention from Egypt (see Jer 37).

EZEKIEL 26–28

The fifth major segment of the book of Ezekiel appears in Ezek 26–28, which presents Ezekiel's oracles concerning Tyre and its rulers. The section is dated to the first day of the month of the eleventh year, which presumably refers to the first day of the seventh month, i.e., New Year's Day (1 Tishri or Rosh ha-Shanah, late September or early October) 587 or 586 B.C.E. This would be close to the time of the fall of Jerusalem in the fourth and fifth months of the eleventh year (see 2 Kgs 25; Jer 52). Tyre joined Jerusalem in revolt against the Babylonians (see Jer 27:3). The city was one of the preeminent maritime powers of the day. It was an island until Alexander's conquest of the city in 332 B.C.E. when he built a land bridge to facilitate his assault. Shortly after the conquest of Jerusalem, Nebuchadnezzar laid siege to Tyre. Although he was never able to conquer the city, he did force its capitulation. The lament concerning Tyre in Ezek 27 employs the 3/2 Qinah ("Lamentation") meter, and portrays Tyre's importance as a maritime trading power. The oracles against the king of Tyre in Ezek 28:1-19 draw on Canaanite mythology, particularly the legend of Aqhat, which portrays the descent of Aqhat, son of the wise man Dan-El, to the underworld, and the Garden of Eden tradition. The oracle concerning Sidon targets Tyre's primary ally, which also joined the revolt against Babylon (Jer 27:3). The final verses envision the restoration of Israel.

EZEKIEL 29:1-16; 29:17–30:19; 30:20-26; 31:1-18; 32:1-16

A series of short segments concerned with Egypt or the Pharaoh, each with its own date formula, constitute the sixth through tenth segments of the book of Ezekiel in Ezek 29:1-16; 29:17–30:19; 30:20-26; 31:1-18; and 32:1-16. The relatively small size of the oracles, their common focus on Egypt, and their disruption of the chronological pattern of the book suggest that they were an early collection of oracles that provided the model for the organization of the final form of the book. In their present position and configuration, they give great attention to Egypt, which apparently played a major role in instigating Judah's revolt against the Babylonians, undoubtedly to regain the control over Judah that was lost to Babylon in 605 B.C.E. Egypt also attempted unsuccessfully to relieve the Babylonian siege of Jerusalem (Jer 37).

EZEKIEL 29:1-16

The sixth section in Ezek 29:1-16 is dated to the twelfth day of the tenth month of the tenth year, 12 Tevet (late January or early February), 588–587 B.C.E. The date is about a year earlier than the previous section, although interpreters have noted that Nebuchadnezzar was never able to conquer Egypt. That was left to the Persian king Cambyses, the son of Cyrus and successor to the Babylonian kings, who finally conquered Egypt in 525 B.C.E. The portrayal of Egypt as a great dragon that will be hooked and

153

drawn from the Nile draws upon the images of fishermen who populated its banks and earlier mythological portrayals of Egypt as a sea monster that would be defeated by YHWH (Isa 11:11-16; cf. Exod 15).

EZEKIEL 29:17–30:19

The seventh section in Ezek 29:17–30:19 includes a block of material concerning Egypt that is dated to the first day of the twenty-seventh year, presumably 1 Tishri (late September or early October), 571–570 B.C.E. As noted above, this date disrupts the twenty-year chronological pattern of the book, but apparently represents a later attempt, perhaps by Ezekiel himself, to revise the oracle to account for the actual fall of Tyre. The failure to enter Tyre cost his soldiers the chance to take booty from the conquered city. Following the conclusion of his siege against Tyre in 573 B.C.E., Nebuchadnezzar launched an invasion of Egypt in 668 B.C.E., but failed to conquer the country. Because Tyre controlled the Mediterranean coast leading to Egypt, it was an important step in his campaign against Egypt. The oracle employs the Day of YHWH tradition in Ezek 30:3 (cf. Isa 2; 13; 34; Zeph 1; Obadiah; Joel) to describe the projected fall of Egypt to Nebuchadnezzar.

EZEKIEL 30:20-26

The eighth segment appears in Ezek 30:20-26, which focuses specifically on Pharaoh. The oracle is dated to the seventh day of the first month of the eleventh year, 1 Tishri, 7 Nisan (late March or early April), 587–586 B.C.E., shortly before the destruction of Jerusalem. The oracle apparently refers to Nebuchadnezzar's defeat of Pharaoh Hophra, who sent an army against Nebuchadnezzar in an unsuccessful attempt to relieve the siege of Jerusalem (Jer 37).

EZEKIEL 31:1-18

The ninth segment of the book appears in Ezekiel 31, which presents a second oracle concerning Pharaoh. It is dated to first day of the third month of the eleventh year (1 Sivan, late May or early June), 587–586 B.C.E. The oracle draws heavily on Isaiah's depiction of the downfall of the king of Assyria in Isa 10:5-34 and the downfall of the king of Babylon in Isa 14:3-23. Whereas the former portrays the king of Assyria as a tree that will be chopped down, the latter portrays the king's descent into the world of the dead.

EZEKIEL 32:1-16

The tenth segment of the book in Ezek 32:1-16 presents another oracle concerning Egypt and Pharaoh. It is dated to the first day of the twelfth month of the twelfth year, 1 Kislev (late November or early December), 586–585 B.C.E., shortly after the fall of Jerusalem. Again, the lament employs the 3/2 Qinah (Lamentation) meter and depicts Egypt mythologically as the slain dragon Leviathan (see Isa 11:15; 27:1; Pss 74:12-17; 104:7-9; Job 38:8-11; cf. Exod 15).

EZEKIEL 32:17–33:20

The eleventh major segment of the book of Ezekiel appears in Ezek 32:17–33:20, which takes up the prophet's final oracles concerning the nations and an oracle concerning Ezekiel's role as "sentry" or "watchman" for Israel. The subunit is dated to the fifteenth day of an unspecified month in the twelfth year. Many presuppose that this is a reference to the first month. The date would therefore be 1 Nisan (late March or early April), 586–585 B.C.E., which would place these oracles in the aftermath of the destruction of Jerusalem, when the prophet would then turn to the potential restoration of the people. The oracle in Ezek 32:17-32 concerning Egypt and the other nations lists a succession of nations that have fallen to the Babylonians. Although Egypt was not conquered by Babylon, the fall of Jerusalem would have signaled to Ezekiel that Egypt, too, would succumb. The following oracle in Ezek 33:1-20 returns to the theme of Ezekiel's role as watchman for the people. As noted in the discussion of this motif in Ezek 3:16-21, this role is based upon the roles of the Levitical gatekeepers whose task is to ensure the sanctity of all who enter the holy Temple precincts (see 1 Chr 9:17-27; 26:1-19; cf. Pss 15; 24; 2 Chr 23). It also draws upon the discussion of moral culpability and repentance in Ezek 18, in which the prophet argues that only those who actually commit evil are liable for punishment and that those who repent may be spared punishment. Although his audience apparently questions this principle, it lays the foundation for the following sections devoted to the restoration of the land, people, and Temple. It is unlikely that these oracles were originally composed to form a single block, but their placement together signals Israel's restoration by pointing to the downfall of her major enemies and the possibility of repentance on the part of Israel that will lead to restoration. Such a concern would anticipate the following units in Ezek 33:21–39:29 and 40:1–48:35, which are explicitly concerned with restoration.

EZEKIEL 33:21–39:29

The twelfth major section of the book of Ezekiel appears in Ezek 33:21–39:29, which presents the prophet's oracles concerning the restoration of Israel.[28] The section is dated to the fifth day of the tenth month of the twelfth year, 15 Tevet (late December or early January), 586–585 B.C.E., which would be nearly a year and a half after the fall of Jerusalem. The passage notes that this is when Ezekiel receives word of the fall of the city. With the destruction of Jerusalem now complete, the prophet can now turn to the restoration of Jerusalem, the Temple, and the people. The introductory prophetic word formulas in Ezek 33:23; 34:1; 35:1; 36:15; 37:15; and 38:1 mark the beginning of each subunit in this text. The first subunit of these in Ezek 33:23-29 sets the theme for the prophet's contentions throughout the rest of the unit, i.e., that YHWH is legitimately punishing the people for defiling themselves and that Ezekiel is YHWH's prophet. His assertions come in answer to the claim that the surviving people of the land will inherit the land. In keeping with his earlier claims that all the people would be punished (see Ezek 8–11), Ezekiel maintains that they too will be punished because they have not observed YHWH's requirements (cf. Ezek 18; Lev 16–26). Such contentions provide the foundation for the prophet's later claims in this unit that YHWH will restore the people and the land.

Ezekiel 34:1-31 presents Ezekiel's oracle against the leaders of the nation. He employs the metaphor of a shepherd, which appears very commonly throughout biblical and ancient Near Eastern tradition to portray kings and other leading figures (see, e.g., David in 1 Sam 16:11; 17). His basic charge is that the nation's leaders have failed in their responsibility to care for the people as they served their own interests. In keeping with Davidic ideology, which maintains that YHWH is the true king and the Davidic monarch is YHWH's son or agent (see Ps 2), Ezekiel argues that YHWH will function as the true shepherd for the people. Ezekiel's oracle draws upon Isa 11:1-16 in arguing that YHWH will establish a righteous Davidic monarch (cf. Jer 23:1-8; 33:14-26). The portrayal of the monarch here and in Ezek 40–48 emphasizes his subordination to YHWH and to the priesthood.

Ezekiel 35:1–36:15 presents the prophet's contrasting oracles concerning Edom and Israel. The term Mount Seir, which defines the border between Edom and Israel in the Aravah to the south of the Dead Sea, personifies Edom. Ezekiel apparently condemns Edom because of its support for Babylon in the destruction of Jerusalem and the Temple (cf. Obad 11-14; Ps 137:7-9). The reference to an ancient enmity (v. 5) perhaps refers to the traditions of conflict between Esau, the ancestor of Edom, and Jacob, the ancestor of Israel (see Gen 25–33). In contrast to Edom, which was displaced by Arab Nabatean people in the Second Temple period, Israel will be restored.

Ezekiel 36:16–37:14 focuses on the purification and restoration of Israel. Although Ezek 36:16-38 and 37:1-14 appear to be entirely different oracles, both appear here because they take up the question of purification. Ezekiel 36:16-38 employs the imagery of menstrual purification to portray the restoration of Israel, which has been defiled by the blood shed upon the land. In priestly tradition, blood was a defiling agent and a woman needed to purify herself from the effects of blood following her menstrual period (see Lev 15:19-30; N.B., men are defiled by an emission of semen, Lev 15:1-18). The imagery of blood shed also conveys the presence of idolatry (see Ps 104:38). The impurity of the land defiles the holy name of YHWH, and thereby compromises YHWH's holy standing among the nations and throughout creation. The menstrual imagery continues with the metaphorical portrayal of the cleansing of the land through pure water. Both women and men immerse themselves in pure water to purify themselves (Lev 11:36), and a priest must purify himself before he serves in the Temple (Lev 8). Ezekiel understands that such purification will include a new heart for the people that will enable them to observe YHWH's requirements (see Ezek 11:19; 18:31; Jer 31:31-34). The second element of this section in Ezek 37:1-14 takes up the famous vision of dry bones, in which the prophet sees the bones of Israel's dead return to life. Death is the epitome of defilement in priestly thought, and the Babylonian conquest of Jerusalem and the Temple left many dead, whose corpses defiled the city and the site of the Temple. Ezekiel's vision therefore conveys a very powerful image of YHWH's intent to restore Israel and to purify it from the defilement of death.

Ezekiel 37:15-28 presents Ezekiel's symbolic action concerning the two sticks. Ezekiel's visions of restoration invariably involve the ideal of all Israel, i.e., both the northern kingdom of Israel and the southern kingdom of Judah arrayed around the Jerusalem Temple as in the days of Solomon (1 Kgs 6–8). In the present instance, the prophet writes the names of Judah and Joseph (father of the tribe of Ephraim, the key tribe of Israel) on two sticks and then joins them together to symbolize the reunification of all the people of Israel. To complete the restoration, Ezekiel also includes the restored Davidic monarch (2 Sam 7; Pss 89; 132) in the eternal "covenant of peace" granted to the priest Phineas ben Eliezer, the grandson of Aaron (Num 25:10-13; cf. Ezek 34:25).

Finally, Ezek 38:1–39:29 concludes this segment of the book of Ezekiel with the prophet's oracles concerning Gog of Magog. This section is generally considered to be an apocalyptic text that is read apart from its immediate literary context.[29] Nevertheless, it functions as an integral part of the book of Ezekiel that portrays the purification of the land from the defilement of corpses in preparation for the restoration of the holy Temple in chapters 40–48. There has been much speculation concerning the identity of Gog of Magog; some identify him with Gyges, a seventh century ruler of Lydia in Asia Minor.[30] According to Gen 10:2, Magog is a son of Japhet, who is associated with Europe and Asia beyond the Middle East. Although the identity of Gog must remain uncertain, he clearly functions as an evil threat against Israel in the present context. Such a threat is key to the Zion tradition, which presents YHWH as the protector of Zion from threats by the nations (Pss 2; 46–48). His defeat is portrayed as the fulfillment of prophetic tradition with cosmic consequences for all of creation. Most important, it demonstrates the holy name of YHWH. In the aftermath of Gog's defeat, the land is filled with corpses that leave it defiled. The land must be purified by the fires that burn for seven years and the burial of the corpses of Gog and his army. The sacrificial feast by the birds and wild animals removes the meat and the blood of the dead that mimics the sacrificial feast of the Temple. The result of this defeat of enemies and cleansing of the land is the worldwide recognition of YHWH and the purposes of the exile of Israel. Now that the punishment is complete, YHWH will no longer hide the divine face from Israel (cf. Isa 8:19). YHWH's glory may be restored to the land together with the exiled people of Israel.

EZEKIEL 40-48

The thirteenth and concluding segment of the book of Ezekiel is the prophet's vision of the restored Temple in Ezek 40–48. Many modern scholars argue that this section is a late addition to the book of Ezekiel, but such a contention is based largely on the view that prophets and priests are diametrically opposed to each other.[31] Insofar as Ezekiel combines both identities, like his colleagues Jeremiah and Zechariah, a vision of the restored Temple makes a great deal of sense as the culmination of his book, in which the prophet contends that the destruction of Jerusalem must be viewed as part of a process of purification and the restoration of holiness at the site of the Temple. The portrayal of the structure and dimensions of the Temple and its courts in these chapters does not correspond to the Wilderness Tabernacle (Exod 25–30; 35–40), Solomon's Temple (1 Kgs 6–7; 2 Chr 3–4), or the Second Temple that was built shortly following the exile (*m. Middot* 5; cf. Ezra 3–6; Zech 1–8). It was because of these differences and others throughout the book that later rabbinical authorities raised questions about the status of Ezekiel as sacred scripture. According to tradition, Rabbi Hananiah ben Hezekiah burned three hundred barrels of oil working at night to explain the discrepancies between Ezekiel and the rest of scripture (*b. Shabbat* 13b). Medieval commentators on Ezekiel, such as Rashi and David Kimḥ, came to regard Ezekiel's vision as a description of the third Temple that would be built in the days of the Messiah.

It is noteworthy that the vision is dated to the tenth day of the month at the beginning of the year (Rosh ha-Shanah) of the twenty-fifth year of exile. This would place the vision on 10 Tishri (late September or early October), 573 B.C.E. The tenth of Tishri is Yom Kippur, the Day of Atonement, when the high priest would enter the Holy of Holies of the Temple to experience the presence of YHWH as part of the observance of the day (Lev 16; *m. Yoma* 3:8; see also Lev 23:26-32; Num 29:7-11). Yom Kippur marks the day when the people would ask forgiveness from YHWH for wrongdoing throughout the prior year. In Ezekiel's case, the twenty-fifth year of exile would mark the twentieth year from the time of his initial vision of YHWH as presented in Ezek 1–7. If he was indeed thirty years old at the time of his initial vision (see Ezek 1:1), he would be fifty years old in the twenty-fifth year. According to Num 4:3; 8:23-25, fifty is the age of retirement for the priests, which suggests that Ezekiel's vision of the restored Temple came at the time that he would have retired from active priestly service had he remained in the Jerusalem Temple. Because he is in exile, the vision expresses his expectation that YHWH would act to restore the Temple and the people of Israel around it, and thereby restore the newly purified holy center of all creation.

Ezekiel's vision of the Temple includes three major subunits, each of which focuses on a different aspect of the envisioned Temple: Ezek 40:1–43:12 provides instruction for the building of the Temple and the return of YHWH's glory; Ezek 43:13–47:12 provides instruction for building the associated structures and activities of the larger Temple complex; and Ezek 47:13–48:35 provides instruction for the reestablishment of the land and people of Israel around the Temple together with the renewal of creation. Because the prophet's vision is formulated as instruction, it represents an attempt to fulfill one of the basic tasks of the priesthood, i.e., to instruct the people in what is holy (Lev 10:10-11).

Ezekiel 40:1–43:12 claims that the prophet is transported supernaturally to Israel to receive instructions for the building of the Temple. The site is apparently Mount Zion where the Temple was situated, since the biblical city of Jerusalem lay immediately to the south of the Temple Mount. His guide is described as a man whose appearance shone like bronze, much like the four living creatures or cherubim who bore the presence of YHWH through the heavens in Ezekiel's earlier visions (Ezek 1–3; 8–11). The man is clearly an angelic figure, who carries measuring instruments to carry out his task.

The guide begins in Ezek 40:5-47 by instructing Ezekiel in the dimensions of the Temple walls, gates, and courtyards. The reed or long cubit is six handbreadths long (one standard cubit equals five handbreadths), which equals 518 millimeters or 20.68 inches. The man begins with the main outer wall of the Temple and enters through the eastern gate. This gate faces east toward the sun, and is therefore considered to be the main entry gate of the Temple. It is built in the standard pattern of the Solomonic gate, with three recesses on either side for the four sets of doors that are placed within the gate. He then proceeds to provide full dimensions for the gates and buildings of both the outer court, identified as the women's court in later tradition (*m. Middot* 2:5), and the inner court, later identified as the Israelite's court (*m. Middot* 2:6). The descriptions of these courts in the Mishnah differ considerably (see *m. Middot*).

Ezekiel 40:48–41:26 then presents instruction concerning the building of the Temple itself. The Temple is constructed according to the three-room pattern of Solomon's Temple with a vestibule or porch (Hebrew *'ulam*), a nave or main hall (Hebrew *heykal*), and the Holy of Holies (Hebrew *qodeš haqodešim*; *debir*). Indeed, this three-room pattern is typical of Temple construction in ancient Israel, Canaan, and Syria. It is modeled on the pattern of royal palaces in which the Holy of Holies corresponds to the throne room, consistent with the portrayal of deities as kings (cf. the portrayal of YHWH in Ezek 1; Isa 6; 1 Kgs 22).[32] The vestibule is an entry hall or reception room. The nave or main hall is where the Temple furnishings are placed, such as the lamp stands, incense burners, and table for the bread of the presence. The Holy of Holies is where the ark of the covenant had been kept in Solomon's Temple. Because the ark seems to have disappeared either during or prior to the Babylonian exile—it may have been taken by the Babylonians or hidden by the Temple priests—no mention of the ark is made here. After the ark was removed, the Holy of Holies contained only a stone in the Second Temple period (*m. Yoma* 5:2), where tradition maintains that Abraham attempted to sacrifice Isaac (Gen 22). Ezekiel does not enter the Holy of Holies since only the high priest may enter and only on Yom Kippur (Lev 15; *m. Yoma* 5:1). As in Solomon's Temple, Ezekiel's Temple is decorated with cherubim and palm trees to symbolize the Garden of Eden and the role of the Temple as the holy center of creation.

With the instruction concerning the Temple at its courts complete, the vision then depicts the return of YHWH's glory in

Ezek 43:1-12 (cf. Ezek 1-3; 8-11). The divine presence returns through the east gate from which it had earlier departed (see Ezek 10:19). YHWH informs Ezekiel that the Temple will be the place of the divine throne, and that Israel will sanctify the divine name. Ezekiel's task is to inform the people of YHWH's requirements, including the plan and laws for the Temple.

Ezekiel 43:13–47:12 presents instructions concerning the Temple complex and its activities. It begins with a description of the altar, which is a four-stepped structure that resembles a Mesopotamian ziggurat (contra Exod 20:21-23). The seven-day consecration of the altar takes place at the festival of Sukkot (1 Kgs 8:65-66; Ezra 3:1-7), and closely resembles the seven-day ordination of priests (Exod 29; Lev 8). Both altar and priests are sprinkled with blood as part of the process of their sanctification for holy service (cf. Lev 16:18-19; Exod 29:16), although the use of goat as a sin offering for the dedication of the Temple is otherwise unknown.

Ezekiel's guide brings him back to the eastern gate, which will remain closed to all except for YHWH. Once again, Ezekiel sees the glory of YHWH, who informs him that those who engage in idolatry and abomination are not to be admitted to the Temple. Foreigners who are uncircumcised of heart are not to enter, but the Levites may serve in secondary functions. This instruction apparently presupposes the distinction between the Levitical priests who served outside of Jerusalem and the Zadokite priests who served in the Jerusalem Temple (see 1 Kgs 2:26-27 concerning Solomon's expulsion of the Elide priest Abiathar, whereas Zadok was permitted to remain in Jerusalem as high priest). Because the Levites were considered to have compromised their holiness (cf. the portrayal of Eli and his sons in 1 Sam 2), they may perform certain functions in the Temple although they are not permitted to serve at the altar. By contrast the Zadokite line will serve at the altar and abide by the regulations for holy life in the Temple.

A series of instructions then defines the holy precincts of the Temple, the prince, and the people, proper weights and measures, Temple offerings to be made by the people, and observance of the Temple festivals. Once the Temple is established, water wells up from below the threshold of the Temple to water the entire land. This points to the role of the Temple as the center of creation, insofar as the Temple becomes the source of rain, fertility, and life for the created world. The water flows down into the Jordan Valley and the Dead Sea to restore life in the formerly desolate region.

The final subunit in Ezek 47:13–48:35 portrays the reestablishment of the land and the people of Israel. The boundaries of the land are an idealized portrayal of the greatest extent of the kingdoms of David or Jeroboam ben Joash (2 Sam 8:5-12; 2 Kgs 14:25; cf. Num 34). The tribes of Israel are assigned equal portions of land that are aligned along its entire length from north to south. The priestly and Levitical allotment is placed in the center of the tribes together with that of Judah and surrounded by the portion allotted to the prince. The concluding statement that the name of the city shall be, "YHWH is there," signifies the return of YHWH's presence to Jerusalem, and thereby closes the circle that began at the outset of the book with YHWH's departure from Jerusalem.

In sum, the book of Ezekiel represents an attempt to interpret the fall of Jerusalem and the Temple—and their anticipated restoration—through the eyes of the Zadokite priesthood. Ezekiel is a Zadokite priest who was raised and educated to serve in the Jerusalem Temple, but his exile to Babylonia together with King Jehoiachin of Judah in 597 B.C.E. removed him from the holy precincts of the Temple and brought him instead to a foreign land. Beginning with his thirtieth birthday, which would have initiated his twenty-year service as an active priest, Ezekiel sought to interpret the significance of the divine will in relation to YHWH's efforts to resanctify the Temple at the center of all creation. The result is a scenario in which Ezekiel maintains that divine presence and sanctity are evident and active throughout all creation, and that YHWH will restore both Israel and the Temple at the center of a renewed creation.

SELECTED BIBLIOGRAPHY

Blenkinsopp, Joseph. *Ezekiel.* Interpretation. Louisville: Westminster John Knox, 1990.

Block, Daniel. *The Book of Ezekiel.* 2 vols. New International Commentary on the Old Testament. Grand Rapids: Eerdmans, 1997–1998.

Darr, Katheryn Pfisterer. "Ezekiel." Pages 1073-1607 in *The New Interpreter's Bible*. Edited by L. Keck, et al. Nashville: Abingdon, 2001.

Davis, Ellen. *Swallowing the Scroll: Textuality and the Dynamics of Discourse in Ezekiel's Prophecy.* Bible and Literature Series 21. Sheffield: Almond, 1989.

Galambush, Julie. *Jerusalem in the Book of Ezekiel: The City as YHWH's Wife.* SBLDS 130. Atlanta: Scholars Press, 1992.

Greenberg, Moshe. *Ezekiel 1–20.* AB 22. Garden City: Doubleday, 1983.

———. *Ezekiel 21–37.* AB 22A. New York: Doubleday, 1997.

Hals, Ronald M. *Ezekiel.* FOTL 19. Grand Rapids: Eerdmans, 1989.

Kutsko, John F. *Between Heaven and Earth: Divine Presence and Absence in the Book of Ezekiel.* Biblical and Judaic Studies 7. Winona Lake: Eisenbrauns, 2000.

Mein, Andrew. *Ezekiel and the Ethics of Exile.* Oxford Theological Monographs. Oxford: Oxford University Press, 2001.

Odell, Margaret S., and John T. Strong, editors. *The Book of Ezekiel: Theological and Anthropological Perspectives.* SBLSymS. Atlanta: Society of Biblical Literature, 2000.

Renz, Thomas. *The Rhetorical Function of the Book of Ezekiel.* VTSup 76. Leiden: Brill, 1999.

Sweeney, Marvin A. "Ezekiel: Zadokite Priest and Visionary Prophet of the Exile." *Occasional Papers of the Institute for Antiquity and Christianity* 41. Claremont: Institute for Antiquity and Christianity, 2001.

Zimmerli, Walther. *Ezekiel: A Commentary on the Book of the Prophet Ezekiel.* 2 vols. Hermeneia. Philadelphia: Fortress, 1979–1983.

CHAPTER 6

THE BOOK OF THE TWELVE PROPHETS

The Book of the Twelve Prophets is a very unusual literary composition that functions simultaneously as a collection of twelve individual prophetic works and as a single prophetic book. According to the masoretic version of the book, the twelve individual prophets include Hosea, Joel, Amos, Obadiah, Jonah, Micah, Nahum, Habakkuk, Zephaniah, Haggai, Zechariah, and Malachi. The Septuagint version of the book presents a different order: Hosea, Amos, Micah, Joel, Obadiah, Jonah, Nahum, Habakkuk, Zephaniah, Haggai, Zechariah, and Malachi. Other sequences were also known in antiquity.[1] The Judean Wilderness scrolls, for example, generally present the same order as the masoretic tradition, although one manuscript (4QXII[a]) places Jonah after Malachi.[2] Each individual work within the Book of the Twelve begins with its own superscription or narrative introduction that identifies the prophet in question and frequently provides information concerning the historical background of the work, its literary characteristics, and its overall concerns. No common material binds the twelve together; they simply stand according to the order presupposed by the version of the Bible in

165

which they appear, but they invariably function together as a single work.

The Book of the Twelve tends to be counted as one of the twenty-four books of the Tanak in Jewish tradition and as twelve of the thirty-nine (or more) books of the Old Testament in Christianity. The book is generally called *trey 'āśār* in Jewish tradition, which is Aramaic for "the twelve prophets." Early Christian tradition refers to it as *hoi dōdeka prophētai* or *ton dōdekaprophēton*, both of which mean, "the twelve prophets," in Greek. The Latin term, *prophetae minores*, "the minor prophets," first appears in early Latin patristic sources, such as Augustine's "City of G-d," where it refers only to the relatively small size of the individual prophetic works that appear within. The Twelve Prophets generally appear as the fourth book of the "Latter Prophets" in the Tanak (*b. Baba Batra* 14b), but the Talmud also stipulates that only three lines separate the individual books of the Twelve Prophets whereas four lines normally separate biblical books (*b. Baba Batra* 13b). Christian canons generally place the Twelve Prophets after Isaiah, Jeremiah, Ezekiel, and Daniel in the "Prophets" of the Old Testament. Although Greek versions of the Christian Old Testament tend to reflect the Septuagint order noted above, the arrangement varies among the manuscripts. With the increasing use of the Vulgate, first produced in the fourth century C.E. by Saint Jerome in an effort to provide a Latin text based upon the Hebrew, the Roman Catholic Church and its Protestant offshoots tended to adopt the order of books found in the Masoretic Text.

Although some interpreters have argued that the sequence of books in the Book of the Twelve is based upon their relative size or thematic concerns, most interpreters contend that the sequence is based on chronological factors.[3] Such a claim is based on the LXX sequence, which begins with the three eighth-century prophets, Hosea, Amos, and Micah, and the consistent groupings of seventh-century prophets, Nahum, Habakkuk, and Zephaniah, and sixth-century prophets, Haggai and Zechariah, in both the MT and LXX sequences. The books of Joel, Obadiah, Jonah, and Malachi, however, are very problematic because they do not provide clear internal evidence concerning the historical setting in which their respective prophets are to be placed. It is therefore striking that three of these prophets appear to be associated with events of the ninth century B.C.E. The reference to the valley of Jehoshaphat in Joel 4:12 (= NRSV 3:12) suggests the Judean king Jehoshaphat's (873–849 B.C.E.) defeat of Ammon, Moab, and Edom as indicated in 2 Chr 20. Obadiah is the name of an Israelite official and associate of the prophet Elijah who hid the prophets of YHWH in the reign of King Ahab of Israel (869–850 B.C.E.). Malachi is also associated with the ninth century prophet Elijah in Mal 3:1, 23-24. If the sequence of Twelve Prophets was based on chronology, we would expect to see these figures at the beginning of the book. Second Kings 14:25 identifies Jonah ben Ammitai as a prophet during the reign of the Israelite king Jeroboam ben Joash (786–746 B.C.E.), which would place him among the eighth century prophets. The LXX tradition nevertheless places him apart from the other eighth century figures, and MT mixes him with ninth and eighth century prophets. We might also note that Zephaniah, who spoke during the early reign of Josiah (640–609 B.C.E.), should appear as the first of the seventh century prophets, whereas Nahum celebrates the downfall of Nineveh in 612 B.C.E. and Habakkuk focuses on the rise of the Chaldean or Neo-Babylonian Empire which took control of Judah in 605 B.C.E. Hosea, who is placed in the reigns of the Israelite king Jeroboam (786–746 B.C.E.) and the Judean kings Uzziah (783–742 B.C.E.), Jotham (742–735 B.C.E.), Ahaz (735–715 B.C.E.), and Hezekiah (715–687 B.C.E.), would have to follow Amos, whose work is placed only in the reigns of Jeroboam and Uzziah.

Clearly, neither the LXX nor the MT version of the Book of the Twelve is arranged according to a chronological scheme. Both sequences do, however, appear to represent concerns with the punishment of both Israel and Judah during the monarchic period and with the restoration of Jerusalem and the Temple in the post-exilic period. It is noteworthy, therefore, that both versions begin with Hosea, which metaphorically portrays YHWH as a husband who divorces his bride Israel to portray the disruption of their relationship as Israel is destroyed by the Assyrians in the eighth century B.C.E. Both versions also conclude with Malachi, who categorically states that YHWH hates divorce and calls upon the people to hold firm to the covenant as YHWH's messenger approaches. The theme of the Day of YHWH as a day of punishment for both Israel/Judah and the nations when YHWH's sovereignty is manifested at Zion permeates the books of the Twelve

Prophets in both versions. Nevertheless, the progression from judgment to restoration is configured differently in each.

The LXX version of the Book of the Twelve presents an initial concern with the punishment of the northern kingdom of Israel, which then provides a model for understanding the experience of Jerusalem/Judah and the nations. Hosea, Amos, and Micah each take up the judgment of the northern kingdom as its primary concern although each also indicates concern with Jerusalem and Judah. Hosea condemns Israel, but calls for it to return to YHWH and notes that Israel and Judah will be reunited under the rule of a Davidic king. Amos likewise focuses on condemnation of the northern Israelite sanctuary at Beth El, and looks forward to the rise of a new Davidic king. Micah explicitly compares Israel to Judah, and anticipates restoration after both suffer punishment. The fourth book in the LXX sequence, Joel, marks a transition within the sequence of books insofar as it focuses specifically on Jerusalem and the threat of attacking nations. It portrays YHWH's defeat of the nations and restoration of Jerusalem on the Day of YHWH. Obadiah, Jonah, and Nahum then follow with specific concerns for YHWH's judgment of the nations. Obadiah relates YHWH's judgment of Edom on the Day of YHWH. Jonah focuses on YHWH's mercy for Nineveh when it repents, and Nahum focuses on YHWH's judgment of Nineveh for its abuse of Israel and defiance of YHWH. Habakkuk, Zephaniah, Haggai, and Zechariah, then focus specifically on Jerusalem. Habakkuk raises the question of theodicy in asking why YHWH brings the Neo-Babylonian Empire against Judah, and answers the question by stating that YHWH will destroy the oppressor. Zephaniah calls for a purge of Jerusalem and Judah on the Day of YHWH and thereby alludes to the fall of Jerusalem to Babylon. Haggai demands that the people rebuild the Temple in order to realize YHWH's worldwide sovereignty and blessing. Zechariah points to the eschatological combat that will engulf the world following the reconstruction of the Temple as YHWH's sovereignty is ultimately recognized by Israel, Judah, and the nations at Zion. The book of Malachi concludes the sequences with an exhortation to hold to the covenant in anticipation of YHWH's manifestation on the Day of YHWH.

The masoretic version of the Book of the Twelve presents a very different sequence in which the books concerned with the fate of the northern kingdom of Israel are interspersed among those concerned primarily with Jerusalem and Judah. This results in a sequence that emphasizes the fate of Jerusalem from the outset, particularly since the books concerned with northern Israel also signal an ultimate concern with Israel's relationship and reunification with Jerusalem/Judah. Like the LXX version, the MT begins with Hosea and ends with Malachi, so that it too employs the metaphorical portrayal of marriage to depict the tension in the relationship between YHWH and Israel and the concern to call upon the people to maintain the relationship despite suffering of conquest and exile that the people have endured. Although Hosea addresses the fate of northern Israel, its frequent references to Judah (Hos 1:7; 5:5, 10, 14; 6:4, 11; 8:14; 10:11; and 12:3) and its concern for reunification of Israel and Judah under a Davidic monarch (Hos 3:5) facilitate a reading of the book in relation to a larger concern with Jerusalem. The placement of Joel in the second position ensures that the questions of Jerusalem and the threat posed by the nations will set the agenda for the rest of the sequence. Insofar as Joel depicts YHWH's intention to defend Jerusalem on the Day of YHWH from the threats posed by the nations, it demonstrates how the reunification signaled in Hosea will take place and establishes the concern from which the remaining books will be read. In filling such an agenda, the ahistorical portrayal of the nations allows the scenario presented in Joel to serve as a typological model for the historically based models that appear throughout the rest of the sequence, i.e., YHWH will bring the nations to punish Jerusalem for wrongdoing, but YHWH will deliver the city once the punishment is complete as YHWH's sovereignty is revealed to the entire world. Amos then calls for judgment against the northern kingdom of Israel and its reunification with Judah under the rule of a restored Davidic monarchy. Obadiah calls for the punishment of Edom and its submission to Israel at Zion on the Day of YHWH. Jonah tempers Obadiah's message with a contention that YHWH will show mercy to Nineveh when it repents, but later books also indicate YHWH's judgment against Nineveh when it oversteps its bounds in acting against Israel. Micah takes up such a concern by presupposing that Assyria and later Babylon will be YHWH's agents of punishment against Israel and Judah prior to their restoration around Jerusalem under the rule of a righteous Davidic monarch. The rest of the sequence is identical to that of the LXX version. Nahum celebrates the downfall of the oppressive Nineveh as an example of YHWH's justice. Habakkuk reassures readers of YHWH's justice by pointing to YHWH's plans to punish the Chaldeans or Neo-Babylonians for their oppression even though YHWH authorized them to enter Judah in the first place. Zephaniah again calls for a purge of Jerusalem on the Day of YHWH, which would represent the Babylonian destruction of the city. Haggai calls for the restoration of the Temple and the house of David under Zerubbabel. Zechariah outlines the significance of the restoration of the Temple as Israel, Judah, and the nations will ultimately recognize YHWH at the Jerusalem Temple. Finally, Malachi calls for its audience to maintain the covenant while waiting for YHWH's manifestation on the Day of YHWH.

The differences in sequence and hermeneutical perspective in the two versions of the Book of the Twelve raise questions concerning the diachronic formation of each. The LXX form of the Twelve, with its interest in viewing the experience of northern Israel as a model for that of Jerusalem and Judah, appears to reflect the concerns of Judah in the late monarchic, exilic, and early postexilic periods when the nations were attempting to come to grips with the theological significance of the threat posed by Babylon. Such a concern begins in the Josianic reform, when Israel's destruction is understood as YHWH's judgment, which in turn motivates the purification of the Temple as a part of a national effort at restoration and rededication to YHWH in the aftermath of the fall of Assyria. With Josiah's death and the realization, particularly by Jeremiah, that Jerusalem and Judah would also suffer at the hands of the Babylonians, the ground work was laid for the hermeneutical perspective now apparent in the LXX form of the Book of the Twelve. Similar perspectives are evident in the LXX form of Jeremiah, which emphasizes YHWH's judgment against Israel as a model for Jerusalem and Judah beginning in LXX Jer 2–6 and extending through chapter 25. The placement of books concerning the nations in the LXX version of the Twelve (Joel, Obadiah, Jonah, Nahum) appears also in the LXX arrangement of Jeremiah, in which the oracles concerning the nations appear immediately after Jer 1–25. The fate of Jerusalem then appears in LXX Jer 32–52, following the oracles concerning the nations. Similar concerns appear in the posited early forms of Isa 5–32, which begins with concern for the Assyrian invasion of Israel as a model for that of Jerusalem in chapters 5–12. The oracles concerning the nations follow in Isa 13–23, and the focus on Jerusalem appears in Isa 28–32. Second Isaiah likewise develops the theme of northern Israel's experience as a model for that of Jerusalem by placing the material concerned with the exile and return of Jacob in Isa 41–48 prior to the material concerned with the restoration of Jerusalem or Bat Zion in Isa 49–54. Although the question of punishment is foundational to this pattern, the prophetic works ultimately draw upon Josianic visions of restoration to posit the restoration of Israel, Judah, and Jerusalem in the postexilic period.

The masoretic version of the Book of the Twelve, with its emphasis on the fate of Jerusalem, appears to reflect the concerns of Judean elements during the Persian period from the time of the rebuilding of the Temple through the reforms of Ezra and Nehemiah, who focused on the restoration of Jerusalem as the holy center of Persian period Judah and perhaps the world at large. At this point, concern with the north fades, particularly since northern figures are viewed with suspicion due to charges that they represent a syncretistic population that accepts the influence of pagan religious practices and deities. Such concerns are evident in the Deuteronomistic History, particularly 2 Kgs 17, which contends that Israel was destroyed for its syncretistic practice, but continues to focus on Jerusalem and Judah. Such concern is particularly evident in Ezra–Nehemiah and 1–2 Chronicles, which focus especially on Jerusalem and the Temple in their respective presentations of the restoration of Jerusalem in the Persian period and their historical focus on the history of Judah with special emphasis on the role of the Jerusalem Temple. Similar concerns are evident in the masoretic version of Jeremiah, which focuses on Jerusalem from the outset in chapters 2–45 before presenting the oracles concerning the nations in chapters 46–51. It is also evident in the sixth and fifth century editions of Isaiah, which begin in Isa 1 and 2–4 and conclude in Isa 49–54 and 55–66 with specific focus on Jerusalem. Ezekiel likewise emphasizes the question of Jerusalem by portraying its destruction as a purging of the city so that the Temple might be purified to serve once again as the holy center of creation.

Although the two versions of the Book of the Twelve have different sequences of books that point to differing hermeneutical
agendas, both share an intertextual relationship with the book of
Isaiah in particular that points to a very different understanding
of the significance of world events for understanding divine purpose.[4] Like both versions of the Book of the Twelve, Isaiah contends that YHWH brought the nations to punish Israel and Judah
for wrongdoing and to reveal YHWH's sovereignty throughout the
world. But Isaiah identifies the manifestation of YHWH's sovereignty with the rise of the Persian Empire, particularly the rise of
the Persian monarch Cyrus who is identified as YHWH's Messiah
and Temple builder (Isa 44:28; 45:1). It thereby calls upon its
audience to accept this state of affairs and to submit to the
Persian Empire as the will of YHWH. The Book of the Twelve is
very different. Although it, too, presupposes that YHWH brought
the nations to punish Israel and Judah as part of the process by
which YHWH's sovereignty is revealed to the world, it calls upon
its audience to fight against the nations that oppress
Israel/Judah/Jerusalem under the rule of YHWH and the Davidic
monarch in order to realize the promised restoration of
Jerusalem. Such a scenario is particularly evident when one considers the role of the very famous swords into plowshares passage
in Isaiah and the Twelve. Isaiah 2:2-4 envisions a scenario of
world peace in which Israel will join the nations in a pilgrimage
to Zion to learn YHWH's Torah and to end war. Israel and the
nations alike will suffer YHWH's judgment on the Day of YHWH
before this idyllic scenario is realized. The Book of the Twelve
cites this passage at three points, and presents a very different
scenario of YHWH's or Israel's warfare against the nations in
order to realize this goal. Within the sequence of the Twelve, it
first appears in Joel 4:10 (= NRSV 3:10), which calls for the people
to beat their plowshares into swords and their pruning hooks into
spears to carry out YHWH's judgment against the nations on the
Day of YHWH. Micah 4:1-5 cites the passage as a whole, but states
categorically that Israel and the nations will serve their own
deities prior to the rise of the Davidic monarch who will lead
Israel and Judah in battle to subdue the nations that oppressed
them. Zechariah 8:20-23 likewise cites the nations' call to make a
pilgrimage to Zion as an introduction to its apocalyptic scenario
of YHWH's battle against the nations in Zech 9–14 that will result

in their recognition of YHWH at the Jerusalem Temple at the festival of Sukkot. Whereas Isaiah calls for submission to Persia, the Book of the Twelve calls for warfare against the oppressive nations—which would presumably include Persia—to realize the recognition of YHWH's sovereignty at Zion. Such differences point to debate within the Second Temple period Jewish community, expressed through the writing and redaction of prophetic (and other) biblical literature, concerning its relationship with the Persian Empire.

The balance of this chapter will focus on each of the prophetic books that comprise the Book of the Twelve. It will follow the order presented by the masoretic version of the Twelve, since that version commonly appears in both Jewish and Western Christian Bibles.

HOSEA

The book of Hosea begins the sequence of the Twelve in both the masoretic and Septuagint traditions with a metaphorical portrayal of Hosea's strained relationship with his wife Gomer that serves as a metaphor for the strained relationship between YHWH and Israel.

The superscription for the book (Hos 1:1) places the prophet in the reigns of the Israelite monarch Jeroboam ben Joash (786–746 B.C.E.) and the Judean monarchs Uzziah (783–742 B.C.E.), Jotham (742–735 B.C.E.), Ahaz (735–715 B.C.E.), and Hezekiah (715–687 B.C.E.). The reason for the chronological discrepancy between the reigns of the Israelite and Judean kings is not known, although it may be that Hosea was forced to leave Israel for Judah because of his severe criticism of the dynastic house of Jehu, of which Jeroboam was a member. The period given for Hosea's career was particularly bloody, as four of Israel's last six monarchs were assassinated, as Israel veered between a policy of alliance with Assyria and alliance with Aram before finally suffering invasion by the Assyrians. The Jehu Dynasty (842–815 B.C.E.) began in revolt against the house of Omri, and shifted Israel's political position from a very troubled alliance with Aram to a far more stable alliance with Assyria that ensured Israel's power and prosperity for the balance of the Jehu Dynasty's reign. In the aftermath of Jeroboam's reign, his son Zechariah (746 B.C.E.) was assassinated by Shallum (746 B.C.E.), who sought to break Israel's alliance with Assyria so that it might ally with Aram instead. Shallum in turn was assassinated by Menahem (745–738 B.C.E.), who returned the nation to its alliance with Assyria. Menahem's son Pekahiah (738–737 B.C.E.) was assassinated by Pekah (738–732 B.C.E.), who broke relations with Assyria once again to ally with Aram. Pekah was killed during the course of the Syro-Ephraimitic War, when Assyria invaded Aram and Israel following their attack on Judah in 734–732 B.C.E. Although Assyria subdued Israel, the country revolted in 724 B.C.E. under the leadership of King Hoshea. The result was the complete destruction of Israel by 722/1 B.C.E. and the deportation of many surviving Israelites.

Based upon Israel's experience of bloodshed and invasion during this period, the book of Hosea is designed to address the problem of such evil by positing that the nation was suffering punishment because it had abandoned YHWH. By employing his own marriage to Gomer bat Diblaim and the birth of their children as a metaphor for YHWH's relationship with Israel, Hosea draws upon the traditional portrayal of Israel as the bride of YHWH to charge that Gomer/Israel had engaged in harlotry by pursuing other lovers, prompting Hosea/YHWH to punish the wayward bride with divorce.[5] Such a portrayal presupposes Israelite conceptions of pagan Canaanite religious fertility rites and Israel's political relations with Assyria and Egypt. Indeed, the book does not consider judgment to be the final word, but calls upon its audience to repent and return to YHWH. For Hosea, such a return called for both religious and political action, including a rejection of Canaanite religion and a return to YHWH together with a rejection of Assyia and a return to alliance with Aram, the homeland of the biblical ancestors.

Although many interpreters employ a broadly thematic approach in their assessment of the structure of the book as Hos 1–3 (narratives concerning Hosea's marriage); 4–11 (oracles of judgment followed by restoration); and 12–14 (additional oracles of judgment followed by restoration),[6] close attention to the Hebrew syntax and narrative perspective of the book and the role of repentance in its presentation indicates a very different structure that is designed to convince its audience to reject alliance with Assyria and to return to YHWH and alliance with Aram.[7] An anonymous narrative provides the superscription for the book in Hos 1:1, introduces the main body of the book in Hos 1:2–14:9, and provides the concluding exhortation in Hos 14:10:

HOSEA'S CALL FOR ISRAEL'S RETURN TO YHWH

Following the superscription in Hos 1:1, which identifies the prophet in relation to his historical setting, the body of the book appears in Hos 1:2–14:9 (NRSV 1:2–14:8). The anonymous narrative introduces this section with a portrayal of YHWH's instructions to Hosea to marry a harlot and to have children with her in Hos 1:2–2:2 (NRSV 1:2-11). This narrative establishes the metaphorical portrayal of YHWH as the husband of the wayward wife Israel in order to illustrate Hosea's understanding of the tension in Israel's relationship with YHWH as a cause for the dangers that Israel faces in its relationship with Assyria. By arguing that Gomer/Israel is acting as a harlot, the prophet contends that the threats posed to Israel are punishment for abandoning YHWH and that Israel must return to YHWH (and an alliance with Aram) in order to ensure its well-being. The names given to each of the children symbolize the tension. The name of Jezreel, the first son, recalls the site where Jehu overthrew the house of Omri and established his own dynasty (see 2 Kgs 9–10). Although Israel was allied with the Arameans at this time, tension with Aram prompted Jehu and his successors to turn to the Assyrians for support, which provided the basis for Israel's power and prosperity during the Jehu Dynasty's reign (see 2 Kgs 13–14). The name of the daughter, Lo Ruhamah, means, "No mercy," to signify YHWH's lack of mercy for the purportedly recalcitrant bride. Likewise, the name of the second son, Lo Ammi, "Not my people," signifies YHWH's willingness to break the relationship. Readers often overlook the fact that neither Gomer nor Israel speaks in this narrative, and are therefore not able to defend themselves against these charges.

The book turns to Hosea's own prophetic speeches in Hos 2:3–14:9 (NRSV 2:1–14:8). Each subunit of this section begins with an imperative in which the prophet addresses his Israelite audience. The first appears in Hos 2:3–3:5 (NRSV 2:1–3:5) with the prophet's appeal to his children for their mother's return. Given the metaphorical character of the speech,[8] the appeal is directed to the people of Israel so that the nation as a whole might return to YHWH. By employing the names Ammi, "my people," and Ruhamah, "mercy," for the children, Hosea signals his interest in restoration. Although the speech begins by depicting Hosea's portrayal of Gomer, the language shifts to YHWH's portrayal of Israel. He begins with descriptions of punishment for marital infidelity, but the references to parched land, thorns, grain, wine, festivals, Baals, and so on, make it clear that he is ultimately concerned with Israel's life in the land, its agricultural produce, its festivals, and its gods. Ultimately, the prophet/YHWH envisions a restoration of the relationship when Israel returns to the wilderness to renew the marriage/covenant as in the days of the exodus from Egypt and the wilderness period when Israel was formed as a nation. The passage concludes with YHWH's instructions to Hosea to marry the adulterous woman. Interpreters debate whether or not this is Gomer, but the motif of restoration seems to presuppose that it is. The Judean setting for the final composition of the book is evident in Hos 3:5, which holds that return to YHWH entails northern Israel's return to the house of David.

The second major speech by the prophet appears in Hos 4:1–19, which lays out YHWH's basic charges against Israel. At this point, the metaphor of marriage is dropped as the prophet presents YHWH's charges that Israel has abandoned its covenant. Hosea's statements employ a verb, *yada'*, "to know," that has sexual connotations to indicate that the people lack knowledge of YHWH, but the passage also emphasizes a combination of natural images and the forensic language of the courtroom to charge that Israel has violated YHWH's commandments. Such an approach presupposes the blessings and curses of legal codes that promise rain, crops, and security in the land if the people observe YHWH's commands, and drought, famine, and exile from the land if they do not (see Deut 28–30; Lev 26). Indeed, verse 3 cites specific provisions of the Ten Commandments (see Deut 5; Exod 20) in charging that Israel's priests and prophets have not done their job in instructing the people in YHWH's expectations. The result is religious apostasy that calls for punishment if it continues.

The third speech cycle appears in Hos 5:1–14:1 (NRSV 5:1–13:16), which takes up specific discussion of the general charges made in Hos 4. Throughout this passage, Hosea and YHWH alternate as speakers. The reader must pay close attention to the use of pronouns and other indicators to determine the identity of each. Hosea begins in Hos 5:1-7 with an address to the priests, the nation, and the king to charge Israel with harlotry or abandonment of YHWH. He cites the locations of major events in Israel's history, Mizpah, where Saul was made king (1 Sam 10:17-27, N.B., kingship is portrayed negatively), Tabor, where Deborah defeated Jabin and Sisera (Judg 4–5, N.B., not all of the tribes came to battle), and Shittim, where Israel committed apostasy with the Moabites at Baal Peor (Num 25:1-5), to illustrate Israel's abandonment of YHWH. A lengthy speech by YHWH in Hos 5:8–7:16 emphasizes YHWH's reluctance to accept the people because of their alliances with Egypt and Assyia (Hos 5:13-14; 7:11-12). Overall, the passage portrays a scenario of threat as a warning trumpet is blown throughout the land to signal the approach of an enemy. Although some interpreters think this refers to the Syro-Ephraimitic invasion of Judah in 734 B.C.E. (when Israel and Aram/Syria invaded Judah to force it into an anti-Assyrian alliance; see 2 Kgs 16; Isa 7), the threat clearly encompasses both Israel and Judah. Hosea 8:1-14 focuses especially on the establishment of illegitimate kings and the golden calves in the capital city of Samaria as symbols of Israel's rebellion and return to Egypt. Northern Israel was formed by Jeroboam ben Nebat's revolt against the house of David and his establishment of calf images at Beth El and Dan (see

1 Kgs 12); Hosea contends that the house of Jehu stands in the same tradition.

The third speech cycle continues in Hos 9:1–14:1 (NRSV 9:1–13:16), which presents an overview of YHWH's relationship with Israel throughout history. Again, the words of the prophet alternate with those of YHWH. YHWH's voice frequently cites episodes of Israel's apostasy to provide background and justification for the current threat. YHWH envisions no end to the relationship, but the deity anticipates Israel's repentance. The other motif that holds this section together is the fertility and natural growth of creation, which asserts that YHWH and not Baal is the creator deity. Hosea 9:1-9 emphasizes the celebration of the festival of Sukkot, "Booths," or "Tabernacles," which marks the conclusion of the fruit and olive harvest—and indeed the entire harvest season—shortly after the New Year celebration in the fall. It anticipates the onset of the winter rains, which will provide the water that will ensure fertility and bountiful crop for the coming year. Despite the celebration, the prophet argues that Sukkot will be a time of punishment because of Israel's relationship with Assyria and Egypt. The reference to Gibeah recalls the capital of Saul (1 Sam 10:26), the first king of Israel, as a basis for the roots of YHWH's dissatisfaction. YHWH chimes in with a recollection of Israel's apostasy with the Moabite women at Baal Peor in Hos 9:10-13 (see Num 25). After the prophet calls for Israel to suffer miscarriage and dry breasts, YHWH recalls Gilgal, where Joshua made his first alliance with the Canaanites (Josh 9–10) and Israel renewed Saul's kingship (1 Sam 11). The prophet continues his criticism in Hos 9:17–10:8 with charges that YHWH will reject Israel because they continue idolatry at Beth Aven ("house of iniquity," a term used to describe Beth El and its golden calf) and see to it that the calf is carried off to Assyria. YHWH's recollection of Gibeah once again recalls Saul's capital and the rape of the Levite's concubine (Judg 19–21). The prophet's reference to Shalman's destruction of Beth Arbel likely refers to the Assyrian monarch, Shalmaneser III (858–824 B.C.E.), to whom King Jehu of Israel submitted in order to relieve Israel from pressure by the Arameans.[9]

YHWH waxes nostalgic in Hos 11:1-9 with a metaphorical recollection of Israel as a child in the wilderness, first learning to walk. After bitterly condemning them to return to Egypt under

Assyrian rule, YHWH vacillates by declaring that Israel cannot be given up like Admah and Zeboiim, two cities that were destroyed with Sodom and Gomorrah (Gen 14:2; 19:24-28). A series of statements by Hosea and YHWH culminates with the charge that Israel has made a treaty with Assyria to carry oil to Egypt (Hos 12:2; NRSV 12:1), apparently a nod to Assyria's commercial ambitions in the ancient world. The prophet once again turns to Israel's early history in Hos 12:3-9 (NRSV 12:2-8) with recollections of Jacob's wrestling with the angel at Jabbok (Gen 32:22-32) and his encounter with YHWH at Beth El (Gen 28) in order to charge that Israel engages in dishonest trade and claims to have become rich without YHWH. This serves as an introduction to YHWH's assertion in Hos 12:10-12 (NRSV 12:9-11), "I am YHWH, your G-d," which echoes the Ten Commandments. YHWH refers to the prophets sent to Israel. The passage has suffered poor translation because of its enigmatic language, that is, verse 11 (NRSV 10) should read, "through the prophets I speak in metaphors/oracles," and verse 12 (NRSV 11) should read, "if Gilead is iniquity, they (the prophets) were nothing." Gilead recalls Jacob's treaty with Laban, i.e., Israel's alliance with Aram, in Gen 31:44-46, which serves as a reminder that Israel's natural allies are the Arameans, since their ancestors came from Aram. Jacob found his beloved wife (Rachel—and Leah; Gen 29–31) in Aram, whereas the prophet (Moses) had to lead Israel out of Egyptian bondage. From Hosea's perspective, the choice between alliance with Aram and Egypt/Assyria should be obvious when one considers the past. YHWH recalls the Exodus in Hos 13:4-14, but Hosea concludes in Hos 13:15–14:1 (NRSV 13:15-16) that the east wind, which once split the Red/Reed Sea (Exod 14–15) must now come to punish Israel for rebellion against YHWH if the people do not return.

Hosea 14:2-9 (NRSV 14:1-8) concludes the lengthy segment of the prophet's speech to Israel in Hos 2:3–14:9 with an appeal for Israel's return. This constitutes the rhetorical goal of the book, and demonstrates that the prophet's images of judgment are intended to persuade the audience to return rather than to announce irrevocable judgment. He notes the political aspect of his efforts by stressing that Assyria cannot save Israel, and provides a religious dimension by claiming that reliance on Assyria is equivalent to idolatry. YHWH speaks as creator to emphasize the healing of Israel like dew, so the nation will blossom as a lily, olive tree, vine, and so forth, a final appeal for Israel to recognize its G-d.

The concluding verse of the book in Hos 14:10 (NRSV 9) is a statement by the anonymous narrator of the book that calls upon the readers of the book to recognize YHWH's righteousness in the midst of the evil that threatens the nation.

JOEL

The book of Joel appears in the second position of the masoretic sequence of the Book of the Twelve where it emphasizes the central importance of threats to Jerusalem and its deliverance from the nations on the Day of YHWH. Its typological portrayal of Jerusalem therefore serves as a Leitmotif for the theological concerns of the Book of the Twelve in the MT, and it introduces such concerns in the LXX version as well following the portrayal of the fate and significance of northern Israel. Although theologically important, Joel is notoriously difficult to interpret historically since the superscription in Joel 1:1 simply notes the otherwise unknown prophet, Joel ben Pethuel, without reference to historical setting. Although a plethora of dates have been suggested based on enigmatic references within the book, only the extensive references to other biblical literature, for example, Exod 10:1-20, 21-29 (Joel 1–2); Isa 13:6 (Joel 1:15); Ezek 30:2-3 (Joel 1:15); Amos 1:2; 9:13 (Joel 4:16, 18, NRSV 3:16, 18); Obadiah; Mic 4:1-4/Isa 2:2-4 (Joel 4:10, NRSV 3:10); Zeph 1:14-15 (Joel 2:1-2); and 2 Chr 20:20-26 (Joel 3–4, NRSV 2:28–3:21), have provided any secure foundation for claims that the book must date to a relatively late period in the fifth or fourth century B.C.E.[10]

Because Joel lacks specific historical referents and emphasizes elements of nature, it is frequently perceived to be a proto-apocalyptic book. Its portrayal of the portents in heaven and earth on the Day of YHWH, i.e., the darkened sun and stars, the moon turned to blood, the pouring out of the divine "spirit" (literally, "wind") on all flesh prior to judgment against the nations suggests an apocalyptic scenario of cosmic disruption. But familiarity with the climate of the land of Israel indicates that this is no cosmic upheaval, but a description of the very real effects of the so-called "east wind" or sirocco (Hebrew, Sharav; Arabic, Ḥamsin), a phenomenon like the Santa Ana wind of the American southwest, which typically appears in Israel at the transitions between the dry and wet seasons.[11] The Sharav blows so much dust and dirt that it obscures the sun during the day and gives the moon a reddish cast at night. It threatens crops and people, and therefore frequently serves as a natural agent of divine action in the Hebrew Bible (e.g., at the Red Sea in Exod 14–15). Overall, Joel portrays the threat posed by hostile nations to Jerusalem as a locust plague that is defeated by the east wind. Joel serves as an enduring assurance of YHWH's pledge of protection for Jerusalem.

Although many scholars argue that the original material in Joel 1–2 was expanded by later authors in Joel 3–4, such claims are based on the purported apocalyptic character of the later chapters. Indeed, the book displays a coherent literary pattern of YHWH's response to national lamentation at a time of threat. Joel's use of liturgical forms marks him as a figure who stands within priestly circles, perhaps as a prophetic Temple singer.[12] The structure of Joel may be portrayed as follows[13]:

YHWH'S RESPONSE TO JUDAH'S APPEALS FOR RELIEF FROM THREAT

I. Superscription   1:1
II. Body of the Book: YHWH's response to
    Judah's appeal   1:2–4:21
    A. Prophet's call to communal complaint concerning
        the threat of the locust plague   1:2-20
    B. Prophet's call to communal complaint concerning
        the threat of invasion   2:1-14
    C. Prophet's announcement of YHWH's response to
        protect people from the threat   2:15–4:21

The superscription identifies the following material as "the word of YHWH which came to Joel ben Pethuel" without further elaboration. The following material is organized to present YHWH's response and reassurance of protection to Judah's complaint concerning the threat posed by the nations, here portrayed as locusts that threaten both crop and city. The initial call for communal complaint by the prophet in Joel 1:2-20 presupposes the typical form and setting of the psalms of complaint or lamentation (e.g., Ps 7), which appeal to YHWH for deliverance at a time of threat. Because of the conception of YHWH as creator and Jerusalem as the holy center of creation, the initial complaint draws heavily on the Exodus locust plague tradition (Exod 10:1-20) to portray the threat against Jerusalem. Such portrayals are typical of the Day of YHWH tradition, in which YHWH's judgment is frequently expressed in natural or cosmic terms (see, e.g., Isa 2; 13; 34; Obadiah; Zeph 1).

The prophet's discourse then shifts to the imagery of military invasion with a second call for communal complaint in Joel 2:1-14. Such a shift effectively demonstrates the correlation between the natural and human worlds that is so frequently articulated in biblical tradition (e.g., the Exodus and Wilderness traditions, which draw upon the natural world to depict YHWH's deliverance of the people from Egyptian bondage). The second call continues the Day of YHWH imagery, but the enemy clearly appears to be hostile nations. The prophet announces YHWH's deliverance in Joel 2:15–4:21. Although many argue that this section should begin in Joel 2:18, the command to blow the trumpet in Zion parallels the similar command in Joel 2:1, but this time, the assembly of people looks forward to deliverance. The call to spare the people is about to be realized, and the question, "Where is their G-d?" is about to be answered. YHWH's response culminates in warfare in the Valley of Jehoshaphat against the nations that threaten Jerusalem. The tradition reverses Micah's and Isaiah's calls to turn swords into plowshares and recalls Jehoshaphat's victory over the Ammonites and Moabites who threatened Jerusalem in the Valley of Beracah/Blessing (2 Chr 20:20-26). The passage also draws heavily on Obadiah's portrayal of YHWH's judgment against Edom on the Day of YHWH. Altogether, Joel upholds the tradition of YHWH's role as creator and protector, who defends Zion from evil.

AMOS

The book of Amos follows Joel in the masoretic order of the Twelve, but it focuses its interest on the northern kingdom of Israel. Like Joel, it employs the metaphor of locusts to portray threats against the land, and its vision of restoration includes mountains dripping sweet wine as well. It follows Hosea in the LXX version of the Twelve, and like Hosea calls for a return to

YHWH and a restoration of Davidic rule. The book is set against the background of the rise of the Israelite state under the rule of Jeroboam ben Joash (786–746 B.C.E.) and his Judean vassal, Uzziah ben Amaziah (783–742 B.C.E.). As noted above, this was a period of wealth and power for the northern kingdom that was brought about by the Jehu Dynasty's policy of alliance with the Assyrian Empire. According to 2 Kgs 14:25, Jeroboam's kingdom extended from Lebo Hamath in Aram to the sea of the Arabah (Gulf of Aqabah) in the south. This would make the kingdom about as large as that of Solomon.

Although northern Israel was powerful during this period, the prophet Amos points to problems in the kingdom that in his estimation will bring about disaster for the state. Amos does not mention the rising power of the Assyrian Empire, although his oracles are set in the period immediately prior to the time of Assyria's westward expansion beginning in 745 B.C.E. Rather, the reasons for his condemnation of Israel appear to lie in his Judean identity. Amos was a sheepherder and tender of sycamore trees who lived in the Judean town of Tekoa, located south of Jerusalem in the Judean wilderness overlooking the Dead Sea. Following the Judean king Amaziah's failed attempt to revolt against the more powerful northern Israel (2 Kgs 14:8-14), Judah remained a vassal of Israel, and apparently was compelled to pay a heavy tribute. Such a tribute fell upon the Judean population at large, and Amos appears to have traveled to Beth El, the royal sanctuary of the northern kingdom of Israel, in order to pay a portion of Judah's tribute. The major festivals, Pesach (Passover), Shavuot (Weeks), and Sukkot (Booths), marked the times of harvest in the agricultural season, and people were required to bring a portion of their flocks and harvest to the Temple at that time as a form of taxation that would support Temple and state.[14] We moderns must recall that ancient Judah had a subsistence-level agricultural economy, and the imposition of such a tax had grave implications for the people, particularly when natural catastrophes, such as drought, locusts, seasonal fires, and so forth, took their toll from the annual harvest. Amos points repeatedly to the poverty of his people who have suffered these disasters and yet still have to pay tribute to the north. For the north's part, we must recall that Israel would have been forced to pay tribute to Assyria as well.

The book is organized rhetorically to present an argument for the overthrow of the sanctuary at Beth El and an exhortation to seek YHWH. Following the superscription in Amos 1:1 and the associated motto in 1:2, which emphasizes YHWH's association with Zion or Jerusalem, the book begins broadly with a focus on judgment against the nations that surround Israel, and then it narrows its focus to Israel at large and finally to Beth El, before concluding with a call for the restoration of Davidic rule over all Israel. Although the prophet's oracles emphasize judgment against the northern kingdom, they include calls to seek YHWH (Amos 5:4, 6) to indicate the prophet's ultimate intentions. The structure of Amos may be outlined as follows:[15]

AMOS'S EXHORTATION TO SEEK YHWH

I. Introduction		1:1-2
A. Superscription		1:1
B. Motto: YHWH roars from Zion		1:2
II. Exhortation proper		1:3–9:15
A. Oracles against the nations (culminating in northern Israel)		1:3–2:16
1. Damascus/Aram		1:3-5
2. Gaza/Philistia		1:6-8
3. Tyre/Phoenicia		1:9-10
4. Edom		1:11-12
5. Ammon		1:13-15
6. Moab		2:1-3
7. Judah		2:4-5
8. Israel		2:6-16
B. Indictment of northern Israel		3:1–4:13
C. Call for repentance of northern Israel		5:1–6:14
D. Amos's vision reports: call for destruction of Beth El and rise of the house of David		7:1–9:15

The introduction for the book of Amos appears in Amos 1:1-2 as a combination of the superscription for the book and the following motto. As noted above, the superscription sets the book in the reigns of Jeroboam ben Joash of Israel (786–742 B.C.E.) and Uzziah ben Amaziah of Judah (783–742 B.C.E.), a period of great power for northern Israel. It identifies Amos as a sheepherder from the Judean town of Tekoa, and notes that his work is placed two years prior to a major earthquake. The motto indicates the prophet's Judean identity by stating that YHWH roars from Zion/Jerusalem, so that the top of Carmel (a very fertile northern Israelite chain of hills along the Mediterranean coast) withers. Insofar as Judah was subjugated to Israel during this period, Amos's Judean identity becomes a foundational issue throughout the book.

The initial set of oracles against the nations begins the prophet's discourse with a very broad perspective. Although many claim that it represents YHWH's or Amos's universal moral perspective, the nations listed here are all Israel's neighbors and the events noted all stem from their interrelationships with Israel during the ninth century B.C.E. During that period, Aram successfully attacked its ally, Israel, and the various nations listed actively supported the move or failed to come to Israel's aid as expected. The rhetorical strategy of the prophet in his indictment of each nation is clear, namely, he condemns each one for its past transgressions against Israel and YHWH, and thereby wins over his Israelite audience. Although Judah is mentioned in the sequence, we must recall that Judah was Israel's vassal at this time. It is only after Amos has won over his audience that he begins to focus on his true target, and concludes the sequence with a lengthy diatribe against Israel that highlights its abuses against the poor, in this case, the people of Judah. It is ironic that the sequence of nations reflects the later Assyrian (and the Aramean) strategy for conquering Israel, namely, take Aram first and then take Philistia to block any aid from Egypt, which enables the easy conquest of the coast and the surrounding inland nations before striking at the isolated Israelite center.

The second segment of the prophetic discourse in Amos 3:1–4:13 focuses specifically on the prophet's charges against the northern kingdom of Israel. He points to signs of coming judgment, apparently the locust plague and seasonal fires from his vision reports, and claims that YHWH is bringing judgment against the nation as in the past (e.g., Sodom and Gomorrah). The third segment of the prophetic discourse in Amos 5:1–6:14 continues to emphasize his charges against Israel, but he couples them with calls for the people to seek YHWH and to reject Beth El and the other northern temples. Overall, Amos envisions the Day of YHWH, perhaps a day that signals YHWH's defense of the nation (see Joel) as a day of YHWH's judgment against Israel (Amos 5:18-20).

The final segment of Amos's discourse appears in his vision reports of Amos 7:1–9:15. Here, the prophet relates the experiences that apparently prompted him to speak his message at the Beth El sanctuary. It is striking that in each case Amos cites an image or an event that would represent a common experience of the ancient Israelite/Judean farmer, but he sees in each an expression of the will of YHWH. Indeed, throughout the book, we see his observations of common images, such as a cart laden with sheaves (Amos 2:13) or lions roaring in the wild when they catch prey (Amos 3:4). His observation that horses cannot run on rocks (Amos 6:12) shows the reader how Amos observes the world around him, much like the wisdom tradition (see Prov 30) to determine the will of YHWH.[16] He notes the plague of locusts (Amos 7:1-3), a common and recurring threat to ancient (and modern) farmers, that eat the crop and leave little behind after the king's portion of the harvest has been taken. He notes the fires that dry up the deep (Amos 7:4-6), a common occurrence at the end of Israel's dry summer season. In both cases, he sees them as communications from YHWH, and successfully appeals to YHWH to show mercy. The third vision, YHWH holding a plumb line (7:7-9) again employs a common image of a weighted line used to measure the straightness of a wall—an essential tool in a society in which house walls were built by hand from stone foundations and mud brick—an error would quickly result in the collapse of the typical Israelite two-story house. Here it serves as a metaphor for measuring Israel's moral straightness. A brief editorial narrative in Amos 7:10-17 informs the reader of the circumstances of Amos's speech at the Beth El Temple, and how he is expelled from Israel for his charges against Temple and monarch. The fourth vision employs a pun on Amos's presentation of a basket of summer fruit *(qayiṣ)*, which YHWH states represents the end *(qeyṣ)* of Israel. Such a presentation explains why Amos, a dresser of fig trees, appears at the Beth El altar in the first place, that is, to present the fruit harvest at the sanctuary. The final image of YHWH calling for the destruction of the Beth El capitals draws upon the imagery of a Temple altar in operation, with the carcasses of sacrificial animals, the knives, the blood, the fire, and the smoke, that all evoke images of destruction. For Amos, such images call for the destruction of the sanctuary itself. He concludes his vision sequence with a call for the fallen booth of David. Although many see this as a postexilic addition, it expresses the prophet's Judean viewpoint and hopes for a restoration of Davidic/Judean rule over the north as it was in the days of Solomon.[17]

OBADIAH

The book of Obadiah follows Amos as the fourth book of the masoretic sequence and Joel as the fifth book of the Septuagint sequence. In the MT, it builds upon the concern with the Day of YHWH in Joel and Amos, but focuses on Edom as the object of punishment rather than on the nations at large (Joel 1:15) or Israel (Amos 5:18-20; but cf. 9:11-12). In the LXX, the theme of judgment against Edom specifies Edom as the threat against Jerusalem announced generally in Joel (N.B., Joel refers repeatedly to Obadiah).

The superscription simply identifies the book as "the vision of Obadiah." Although some traditional authorities identify Obadiah with the ninth century Israelite official who assisted Elijah and hid the prophets from persecution by Ahab and Jezebel (1 Kgs 18), there is no conclusive evidence that the present work is to be identified with the ninth century figure. Some elements of Obad 8-18 could be read in relation to the Judean king Amaziah's (800–783 B.C.E.) attack against the Edomites (2 Kgs 14:7, 10), but the dependence of Obad 1-7 on Jer 49:7-22 and the explicit references to the exiles of Israel and Jerusalem in Obad 19-21 indicate a late-exilic or early postexilic dating for the book.[18] In this case, it is read in relation to other texts that indicate Edom's assistance in the capture and destruction of Jerusalem by the Babylonians (see Ps 137:7; Isa 34:5-17; 63:1-6; Jer 49:7-22; Lam 4:21-22; and so on). Following the superscription in Obad 1a, the balance of the book in Obad 1b-21 presents an oracular condemnation of Edom for its treachery against Jerusalem. The oracle begins with a prophetic messenger formula in Obad 1ba$^{1-5}$, which introduces the prophet's call to punish Edom in Obad 1ba^{6-12}-7 and the prophet's announcement of punishment against Edom in Obad 8-21. The structure of Obadiah appears as follows:[19]

PROPHETIC ANNOUNCEMENT OF JUDGMENT
AGAINST EDOM

I. Superscription   1a
II. Oracle concerning the condemnation of Edom   1b-21
  A. Prophetic messenger formula   1ba^{1-5}
  B. Oracle proper   1ba^{6-12}-21
    1. call to punish Edom   1ba^{6-12}-7
    2. announcement of punishment against Edom   8-21

JONAH

The book of Jonah is the fifth book in the masoretic sequence of the Twelve and the sixth book of the Septuagint sequence. In both the MT and the LXX, it follows Obadiah and tempers the portrayal of YHWH's judgment against Edom with a portrayal of YHWH's mercy for a repentant Nineveh. In the MT, it precedes Micah, which calls for restoration of the people around a new Davidic king, who will defeat the nations that oppress Israel and Judah. In the LXX, it precedes Nahum, which celebrates the downfall of Nineveh, one of the greatest oppressors in the Bible alongside Babylon. Jonah demonstrates that YHWH shows mercy to Nineveh when it repents, but brings punishment when it sins.

The portrayal of the prophet draws on 2 Kgs 14:25, which presents Jonah ben Amittai as an eighth century prophet who foresees the greatness of Jeroboam ben Joash's restored kingdom of Israel (786–746 B.C.E.). There is nevertheless no evidence that the book of Jonah presents a historical account of the prophet's life.[20] The narrative makes extensive use of irony, parody, and exaggeration, for example, a prophet of YHWH attempts to flee from YHWH; the pagan characters of the narrative do not hesitate to acknowledge YHWH; a great fish swallows Jonah for three days; YHWH saves Nineveh, which ultimately destroys the northern kingdom of Israel; and so on. The book is not designed to present a historical account of the prophet. It is designed to examine the question of YHWH's justice and mercy.

Many interpreters maintain that the book poses a conflict between the universalism of YHWH and the particularism of the Jewish community, but such a construction of the issue depends largely on a misreading of the book informed by anti-Jewish stereotypes. Jonah is not a selfish and petulant figure who questions why YHWH's mercy should be shown to Gentiles. He is a prophet who has foreseen the greatness of Jeroboam II, and presumably he also has foreseen that Nineveh, the capital of the Assyrian Empire, will see to the destruction of his own nation in 722–721 B.C.E. only a few years after the reign of the great monarch. Even if one argues what Jonah may or may not know, the reader of the Bible knows what Nineveh will ultimately do, and it is to the readers of biblical tradition that the book is addressed. Why should YHWH show mercy to a nation that will ultimately serve such a destructive purpose? Such a question fundamentally entails the question of YHWH's righteousness and fidelity to the covenant with Israel. Ultimately, the book argues that YHWH responds to repentance with mercy, which has important implications for the exilic or postexilic Judean audience of the book. Repentance brings YHWH's mercy and the possibility of restoration.

Indeed, the questions posed by the book of Jonah make a great deal of sense in relation to the Babylonian exile and its aftermath. Contrary to the assertions of Isaiah and Jeremiah, YHWH did not destroy Babylon (Isa 13–14; 21; Jer 50–51) until 486 B.C.E., after the Second Temple had already been built. The Persian Empire took control of Babylon peacefully, and continued to rule Judah from the former Babylonian capital. Although some have argued that the Psalm of Jonah in chapter 2 is an independent composition, it functions as an integral part of the book that emphasizes Jonah's piety in the context of a Temple setting. The book differs from most prophetic literature in that it is fundamentally a narrative and not a presentation of prophetic oracles. It appears in two distinct and yet parallel parts to emphasize the contrast between Jonah's attempt to flee his initial commission to condemn Nineveh in Jonah 1–2 and his frustration over YHWH's mercy when Nineveh repented in Jonah 3–4. The structure of Jonah appears as follows:[21]

NARRATIVE CONCERNING YHWH'S MERCY TOWARD
A REPENTANT NINEVEH

I. Jonah's attempt to flee from YHWH   1:1–2:1
  A. Jonah's attempt to flee YHWH's initial commission
                                                      1:1-3
  B. Jonah's encounter with the sailors during the storm
                                                  1:4-16
  C. Jonah's prayer to YHWH from the belly of the fish
                                                  2:1-11
II. Encounter between YHWH and Jonah concerning
    YHWH's mercy toward a repentant Nineveh   3:1–4:11
  A. YHWH's renewed commission to Jonah and its
    outcome   3:1-10
  B. YHWH's assertion of the right to mercy in
    encounter with Jonah   4:1-11

The narrative includes two parallel episodes that are designed to highlight the contrast (and comparisons) between YHWH's two commissions to Jonah. In each half, YHWH commissions Jonah to condemn Nineveh, but something entirely unexpected happens, i.e., Jonah, the prophet of YHWH, attempts to flee from the sovereign of the universe in chapters 1–2, and YHWH reverses judgment and grants mercy to Nineveh in chapters 3–4.

The first half of the book, Jonah 1–2, is designed to prepare the reader for the primary examination of issues in Jonah 3–4. Jonah 1–2 includes three basic episodes, each of which begins with action by YHWH that serves as the basis for action by the other major protagonists of the narrative. Jonah 1:1-3 presents YHWH's initial commission to Jonah and his unexpected attempt to flee. The reader knows that Jonah is a prophet and that YHWH is sovereign of the universe, so that such an attempt is patently absurd. The absurdity of the situation is highlighted by the portrayal of Jonah's experiences on board ship in Jonah 1:4-16. YHWH brings a storm that threatens to sink the ship. While Jonah, the prophet of YHWH, sleeps soundly in the hold while attempting to escape his G-d, the pagan sailors call upon Jonah to pray to YHWH and offer sacrifice themselves in a futile attempt to stop the storm. They finally and reluctantly accede to Jonah's advice that they throw him into the sea. In Jonah 2:1-11, Jonah finally acknowledges YHWH and prays for mercy until YHWH prompts the fish to vomit him out onto dry land.

The second half of the book, Jonah 3–4, then focuses on the primary questions of YHWH's righteousness and fidelity in relation to the questions of judgment and mercy. YHWH commissions Jonah once again to announce judgment against Nineveh in chapter 3. The prophet obeys, and the unexpected happens when Nineveh actually listens to the prophet and repents. The hyperbole of the narrative is such that even the animals of the city repent. Jonah 4 presents Jonah's indignation at YHWH's mercy toward Nineveh and the key examination of the issues posed in the book. Jonah cites the merciful aspects of the formulaic characterization of YHWH from Exod 34:6-7, and demands that YHWH take his life in his exasperation at having his message of judgment reversed. But such a reversal highlights the purposes of the prophetic judgment speech, namely, it is designed to convince people to change, not serve as irreversible judgment as some contend. To illustrate the principle of pity or mercy, YHWH provides a castor bean plant to give Jonah shade and comfort, and then sends a worm to destroy it. Despite his sorrow at the loss of the plant, Jonah still contends that he would rather die than give up his anger at YHWH. At this point, YHWH concludes the book by asking Jonah (and the audience of the book) if YHWH should not pity Nineveh with its one hundred twenty thousand people and many animals, just as Jonah had pitied the plant. The answer to YHWH's rhetorical question of course is yes. Such an answer is of particular importance to the postexilic Jewish community, which viewed the Babylonian exile as an expression of divine judgment, and the restoration as an expression of divine mercy that resulted from community repentance. Such a portrayal is designed to call for the people to repent and rebuild as exilic and postexilic Judah sought restoration.

MICAH

The book of Micah is the sixth book in the masoretic sequence of the Twelve and the third book in the Septuagint version. It follows Jonah in the MT, and emphasizes the restoration of Jerusalem and Judah at the center of the nations following the experience of the Babylonian exile. It follows Amos in the LXX sequence of the Twelve, and thereby concludes the pattern of viewing the experience of northern Israel as a model for that of Jerusalem and Judah.

The superscription attributes the book to Micah the Morashtite, who lived in the days of the Judean kings Jotham (742–735 B.C.E.), Ahaz (735–715 B.C.E.), and Hezekiah (715–687 B.C.E.). It states that his words concern Samaria and Jerusalem, which indicates the correlation between the experiences of the northern and southern kingdoms. Micah's home town is identified with Moresheth-Gath, a town on the southwestern border of Judah and Philistia, near the Philistine city of Gath. Moresheth-Gath is identified with Tell Judeidah, located in the Judeah Shephelah (a region of descending hills) about 21 miles southwest of Jerusalem and 9 miles east of Gath.[22] This location is significant because it is precisely where the Assyrian king Sennacherib concentrated his attack against Judah at the time of Hezekiah's revolt in 701 B.C.E.[23] It enables us to understand that Micah was a war refugee, who had to flee his home for Jerusalem as the Assyrians advanced. Such a portrayal informs his images of suffering on the part of the people and his anger at the monarchies of Israel and Judah for bringing such disaster on the heads of the Judean population. Unlike his better-known colleague Isaiah, Micah calls for the destruction of Jerusalem (Mic 3:12).

Micah appears to have a very different perspective than the urbane Isaiah, and the book does not hesitate to let the differences be known. Both include nearly identical versions of the famous oracle in Isa 2:2-4 and Mic 4:1-5 that calls for nations to come to Zion to learn YHWH's Torah and turn their swords into plowshares to bring about world peace, but each book has a very different perspective as to how such an idyllic scenario is to be brought about.[24] Isaiah maintains that YHWH will judge all the world (Isa 2:6-21), and invites Jacob/Israel to join the pilgrimage of the nations to Zion to submit to YHWH (Isa 2:5). Ultimately, the book of Isaiah calls for Israel/Judah to submit to punishment by Assyria and Babylon, and finally to the rule of Persian monarch Cyrus, who is identified as YHWH's messiah (Isa 44:28; 45:1). Micah, however, notes that Israel/Judah and the nations all follow their respective gods (Mic 4:5). The prophet's scenario of punishment by the nations in the form of the Babylonian exile (Mic 4:10) and the rise of a new Davidic king who will punish the oppressive nations then follows as the means to achieve the ideal scenario of

Mic 4:1-5. Whereas Isaiah calls for submission to the rule of the nations, most notably Persia, as the will of YHWH, Micah calls for the overthrow of the oppressive nations and restoration of a righteous Davidic monarch. The reference to the Babylonian exile in Mic 4:10 and the intertextual references to Isa 2:2-4; 14:24-27; and 2:6-21 in Mic 4:1-5 and 5:4, 9-14 indicate that the book was edited during the early Second Temple period when the question of Judah's relationship with the Persian Empire was in question. Although the Persians had allowed the return to Jerusalem and the rebuilding of the Temple, many would have followed Haggai in viewing warfare against the Persian monarch Darius (522–517 B.C.E.) as a sign that YHWH was going to overthrow the Persian Empire. Otherwise, Micah's oracles fit easily into the late eighth century B.C.E.

Many interpreters follow a diachronic composition-historical model for the structure of the book, which posits that Micah's purportedly authentic oracles appear in Mic 1-3, and collections of later materials appear in Mic 4-5 and 6-7. Such a view does not take into account the synchronic literary features of the book, such as the syntactic connectors that join chapters 2-5 into a single unit, and that leave chapters 1, 6, and 7 as discrete units within the larger framework of the book. It also postulates that chapters 6 and 7 must be later in large measure because of their liturgical features, although such a view overlooks the fact that Judean religion was Temple-based in the monarchic period, and liturgical poetry could be expected from an early time. When these features are taken into consideration, the literary structure of the book is designed to raise the question of Jerusalem's (or Israel's) future in the aftermath of the Babylonian exile. It begins in typical fashion with the superscription in Mic 1:1, and the balance of the book in Mic 1:2–7:20 is formulated as a prophetic announcement concerning YHWH's future exaltation of Jerusalem at the center of the nations. Micah 1:2-16 begins with a portrayal of YHWH's punishment of Samaria as a paradigm for that of Jerusalem. Micah 2:1–5:14 provides a detailed overview of the process of punishment and restoration for Jerusalem. Micah 6:1-16 appeals to the people of Israel/Judah to return to YHWH as a prelude for this process, and Mic 7:1-20 expresses the prophet's trust that YHWH will act to bring the restoration about once the punishment is complete. The structure of Micah may be portrayed as follows:[25]

MICAH'S ANNOUNCEMENT CONCERNING YHWH'S FUTURE EXALTATION OF JERUSALEM AT THE CENTER OF THE NATIONS

Following the superscription in Mic 1:1, the body of the book is designed to take its audience through a literary progression of subunits that are organized to convince the reader that YHWH will act to exalt Jerusalem at the center of the nations after having brought punishment upon it for the erroneous decisions of the kings of Israel and Judah. Micah 1:2-16 begins the sequence with a trial scenario in which the prophet accuses Samaria and Jerusalem, respectively the capitals of Israel and Judah of transgression that brought conquerors against both nations. The passage does not specify the transgression, but one may surmise that the transgression was Israel's and Judah's individual decisions to go to war against Assyria in the latter half of the eighth century B.C.E. The result was disaster for both as the Assyrians invaded Israel and subjugated Judah in the Syro-Ephraimitic War of 734–732 B.C.E., destroyed Israel when it revolted in 724–722/1 B.C.E., and devastated Judah when it revolted in 701 B.C.E.

The second major component of the book appears in Mic 2:1–5:14, which is held together by syntactical connectors at 3:1, "and I said," 4:1, "and it shall come to pass," and 5:1 (NRSV 5:2), "but you, O Bethlehem Ephrata." In addition, it presents the exile of the northern kingdom as the model and impetus for that of the south in the later Babylonian period. The initial subunit of this section is a woe speech in Mic 2:1-13 that accuses the leadership of Israel with lack of concern for the people. The prophet accuses the leaders of rising against the people as an enemy (v. 8), and the portrayals of suffering among the people appear to represent the experience of people fleeing for their lives from their homes as the leaders act as if they were drunk. The chapter ends with a portrayal of the king leading the people like sheep out of their fold and into exile. The prophet then turns to the future of Jerusalem in Mic 3:1–5:14. He begins in Mic 3:1-8 with accusations of injustice and disregard for the welfare of the people in general, and then turns specifically to Jerusalem in Mic 3:9–5:14. The claim in Mic 3:9-12 that Jerusalem and Zion will be destroyed introduces his concern with Jerusalem and indicates that, unlike his Jerusalemite colleague, Isaiah, the rural Micah had no stake in the claims of Davidic or Zion theology that YHWH would protect Jerusalem forever. Micah 4–5 begins with the above-mentioned portrayal of world peace as the nations stream to Zion to give up war. It shifts to the process by which that ideal is achieved when it focuses on the nations that oppressed Israel until YHWH would redeem them in Babylon (4:10) together with the rise of the Davidic monarch who would defeat the nations and restore the remnant of Jacob in the midst of the nations.

Micah 6:1-16 appeals to the people for righteous action or observance of YHWH's justice, and demands that they not act like the notorious king Ahab ben Omri of Israel (cf. 1 Kgs 17–22). Although many claim that liturgical features and the reference to Moses, Aaron, Miriam, and Balaam mark this as a late text, such features and figures appear within the earliest layers of the Pentateuch from the monarchic period.

Micah 7:1-20 concludes the book with a liturgical expression of confidence that YHWH will act to realize the plans laid out in the book. Although some see the liturgical forms and references to Abraham and Jacob as signs of late composition, liturgy would have been a part of Judean Temple-based worship throughout the bulk of the monarchic period, and the ancestral figures are well known in early pentateuchal tradition.

NAHUM

The book of Nahum is the seventh book in both the masoretic and Septuagint sequences of the book of the Twelve. Nahum follows Micah in the MT version of the Twelve, and thereby points to the ultimate downfall of Assyria following the restoration of the righteous Davidic monarch who will defeat the nations that oppress Israel/Judah. Nahum follows Joel, Obadiah, and Jonah in the LXX sequence of the Twelve, and thereby continues the focus on the nations with a depiction of Nineveh's downfall for its oppression of Israel.

The superscription of the book identifies it as "the oracle concerning Nineveh" and "the vision of Nahum the Elqoshite," but it provides no further information concerning the historical setting of the book or the prophet. Nineveh fell to a combined force of Babylonians and Medes in 612 B.C.E., two years after the fall of Assur in 614 B.C.E. and three years prior to the final defeat of the Assyrian army at Haran in 609 B.C.E. The book refers to the fall of Thebes (No-Amon; Nah 3:8-10) to the Assyrians in 663 B.C.E. Although some scholars have attempted to date the book to this period, it appears to represent a later justification for Nineveh's destruction. Nahum 3:8-10 portrays Nineveh as a city surrounded by the waters of the Nile. The Nile did run through the Egyptian city of Thebes, but the portrayal more closely resembles Nineveh, which was protected by moats formed by the Khusur canal that ran through the city.[26] Control of the water in the moats was apparently a decisive factor in the Babylonian/Median conquest of the city.

The portrayal of Nineveh's conquest is a key factor in the rhetorical strategy of the book, which is designed to convince its audience that YHWH is indeed the powerful and just sovereign of all creation who punishes Nineveh for its abusive treatment of other nations. Following the superscription in Nah 1:1, the body of the book appears as a prophetic *maśśa'*, "oracle," in which the prophet attempts to convince his audience to abandon their doubts about YHWH's justice and power to recognize YHWH as the cause of Nineveh's destruction. The prophet employs a form of the disputation speech to challenge the contention of a Judean audience that Assyria's domination of the world showed that YHWH lacks power or righteousness. The prophet attempts to refute the notion that YHWH is powerless by pointing to the fall of Nineveh as an act of YHWH.[27]

The argument proceeds with an initial masculine plural address to Judah and Assyria in Nah 1:2-10 that challenges their low estimation of YHWH's power with a partial acrostic poem in

196

verses 2-8 and a rhetorical question, "How do you reckon/consider YHWH?" that is, "What do you think about YHWH?" Nahum 1:11–2:1 follows with a second feminine singular address to Judah asserting that the fall of Nineveh and the end of its oppression is an act of YHWH. A key statement is verse 11, which reads correctly, "from you has gone forth wrong thinking about YHWH, worthless council." Nahum 2:2–3:19 then concludes the book with a second masculine singular address to Nineveh and the Assyrian king that again asserts YHWH as the true cause of Nineveh's destruction. The structure of Nahum appears as follows:

NAHUM'S ARGUMENT THAT YHWH IS THE TRUE POWER OF THE WORLD

I. Superscription	1:1
II. *Maśśa'* Proper: Refutation of Contention that YHWH is Powerless	1:2–3:19
A. Address to Judah and Assyria challenging their low estimation of YHWH	1:2-10
B. Address to Judah asserting that the end of Assyrian oppression is an act of YHWH	1:11–2:1
C. Address to Nineveh and the Assyrian king asserting that the fall of Nineveh is an act of YHWH	2:2–3:19

HABAKKUK

The book of Habakkuk is the eighth book of both the masoretic and Septuagint sequences of the Book of the Twelve. It follows the portrayal of Nineveh's fall in Nahum and precedes the portrayal of Jerusalem's upcoming punishment in Zephaniah in order to raise questions concerning YHWH's role in raising the Neo-Babylonian Empire as a threat against Jerusalem and Judah. The two superscriptions for the book in Hab 1:1 and 3:1 simply identify each portion of the book with Habakkuk the prophet. Nevertheless, the portrayal in Hab 1:6 of the rise of the Chaldeans, i.e., the Neo-Babylonian Dynasty founded in 625 B.C.E. by Nabopolassar, provides an indication of the historical context. When Nabopolassar's son Nebuchadnezzar defeated Egypt in 605 B.C.E. and took control of Judah, many in Judah saw the Babylonians as foreign oppressors rather than former allies from the days of King Josiah.[28] Habakkuk raises the question as to why YHWH would bring an oppressor against Judah. Although many interpreters have argued that Habakkuk's portrayal of the wicked must initially refer to Judeans who rejected YHWH's Torah (Hab 1:2-4), the usage of the term throughout the rest of the book indicates that it refers to the Babylonians as "the wicked who swallow the righteous" (Hab 1:13; cf. 1:12-17). The portrayal of the Babylonian king as the wicked oppressor who will be destroyed by YHWH (Hab 2:5-20) is opposed to the depiction in Hab 2:4 of "the righteous who shall live by their faith" (in YHWH).

The two-part structure of the book is indicated by the superscriptions in Hab 1:1 and 3:1.[29] Habakkuk 1:1–2:20 is a prophetic *maśśa'*, "oracle," that presents a dialogue between Habakkuk and YHWH concerning YHWH's righteousness. Habakkuk laments to YHWH over the oppression of the righteous by the wicked in 1:2-4; YHWH claims to have brought the Chaldeans in 1:5-11; Habakkuk demands to know how YHWH can tolerate such wickedness in 1:12-17; and Hab 2:1-20 portrays YHWH's assurances that the wicked oppressor will ultimately fall. The Prayer of Habakkuk in 3:1-19 draws on the imagery of theophany to assert that YHWH will respond to Habakkuk's complaint by destroying the oppressor. The structure of Habakkuk appears as follows:

HABAKKUK'S ORACLE AND PRAYER CONCERNING YHWH'S RIGHTEOUSNESS

I. Habakkuk's Oracle: Dialogue concerning YHWH's
   righteousness   1:1–2:20
   A. Superscription   1:1
   B. *Massa'* proper   1:2–2:20
     1. Habakkuk's initial complaint to YHWH
       concerning oppression of righteous by wicked   1:2-4
     2. YHWH's response: I brought the Chaldeans   1:5-11
     3. Habakkuk's second complaint: why tolerate
       evil?   1:12-17
     4. Report of YHWH's response: oppressor will fall   2:1-20
II. Prayer of Habakkuk: Petition for YHWH to act   2:1-19
   A. Superscription   3:1
   B. Prayer proper: YHWH will act   3:2-19a
   C. Instructions for the Choirmaster   3:19b

ZEPHANIAH

Zephaniah is the ninth book in both the masoretic and Septuagint sequences of the Book of the Twelve. Although the superscription for the book in Zeph 1:1 places it in the reign of King Josiah of Judah (640–609 B.C.E.), its position following Habakkuk, which relates Habakkuk's concerns over the rise of the Neo-Babylonian Empire, and Haggai, which calls for the restoration of the Temple, indicates that its scenario of judgment and restoration for Jerusalem is read in relation to the Babylonian destruction of the city and the exile of much of its surviving population.

Many interpreters argue that Zephaniah has been heavily redacted in the postexilic period to emphasize a concern with eschatological judgment and salvation of the entire world.[30] Arguments for this contention begin with the supposed typical three-part structure of the book, namely, punishment against Jerusalem/Israel (Zeph 1:2–2:3); punishment against the nations (Zeph 2:4–3:8); and eschatological salvation for Jerusalem/Israel and the nations (Zeph 3:9-20). The argument also relies on contentions for purported references to the priestly source or layer of the Pentateuch in Zeph 1:2-18, particularly the notices of punishment of the animals, fish, birds, and so on.; the supposedly universal perspective of the nations in Zeph 2:4-15; and the concerns with the restoration of the exiles in Zeph 3:8-20. Close analysis of the text indicates that the literary structure of the text does not break down so easily into the purported tripartite structure, particularly since concerns with judgment and restoration are intermixed throughout the book. The nations listed hardly represent a universal perspective, but the focus of this text is instead on nations that would have concerned Judah during Josiah's reign, i.e., Philistia (where many Israelites and Judeans had been placed by the Assyrians to support their olive oil industry), Moab and Ammon (which had encroached upon Israelite territory), Ethiopia (which once ruled Egypt), and Assyria (the major oppressor from which Josiah would attempt to free his country). The reference to returning exiles indicating that they come from Ethiopia suggests a monarchic period setting, since many northern Israelites and Judeans fled to Ethiopian-ruled Egypt to escape the Assyrian assaults of the eighth century B.C.E. The overall concern with the Day of YHWH and Temple-based or cultic matters hardly indicates the exilic or postexilic periods, particularly since Judah's religious establishment was centered at the Jerusalem Temple from the reign of Solomon on. The polemics against Baal worship evident in the text easily derive from Josiah's reign, insofar as his program of reform and restoration would call upon the population to abandon foreign worship. The language does not suggest a failure of Josiah's reforms, but a rhetorical strategy designed to convince the audience to avoid any association with foreign worship and to support the king's reforms.

Close examination of the literary features of the book indicates that, following the superscription in Zeph 1:1, the body of the book exhibits a two part structure that reflects the rhetorical effort to convince the people to support Josiah's reform. Zephaniah 1:2-18 announces the coming Day of YHWH (cf. Isa 2; 13; 34) as a day of punishment and sacrifice for those who would adhere to foreign gods. Zephaniah 2:1–3:20 presents an exhortation to seek YHWH, i.e., to support Josiah's reform. It is based upon the exhortation in Zeph 2:1-3 and the prophet's explanatory address in Zeph 2:4–3:20. Zephaniah 2:4 points to the destruction of the Philistine cities in Zeph 2:4 as the basic evidence of YHWH's actions, and Zeph 2:5-15 and 3:1-20 respectively point to YHWH's actions against selected nations and the projected restoration of Jerusalem as further reason to support the reform. The structure of Zephaniah appears as follows:

ZEPHANIAH'S EXHORTATION TO SEEK YHWH

I.	Superscription	1:1
II.	Body of Book: Exhortation to seek YHWH	1:2–3:20
	A. Announcement of the Day of YHWH against Baal worshipers	1:2-18
	B. Exhortation to seek YHWH	2:1–3:20
	1. Exhortation proper	2:1-3
	2. Substantiation: YHWH's actions	2:4–3:20
	a. basic for exhortation: destruction of Philistine cities	2:4
	b. punishment of nations	2:5-15
	c. restoration of Jerusalem	3:1-20

HAGGAI

Haggai is the tenth book in both the masoretic and Septuagint versions of the Twelve. It is set in the second year of the reign of King Darius of Persia (520 B.C.E.), and appears as the prophet's call for the people of Jerusalem to support efforts to rebuild the Jerusalem Temple (cf. Ezra 3; 6). He is mentioned together with Zechariah in Ezra 5:1; 6:14 as a prophet who called for the building of the Temple at the time that Zerubbabel ben Shealtiel, the grandson of King Jehoiachin of Judah, and Joshua ben Jehozadak, the high priest, returned to Jerusalem to commence the reconstruction efforts. During this period, the Persian Empire was wracked by internal conflict as several major figures fought to gain control of the empire following the death of Cambyses, the son of Cyrus, in 522 B.C.E. Darius, the son-in-law of Cyrus, ultimately won control of the empire.

The book of Haggai appears in narrative form, and it presents a series of oracles dated to the year 520 B.C.E., in which the prophet lays out his calls for the rebuilding of the Temple and the designation of Zerubbabel as YHWH's designated regent.[31] Haggai 1:1-15a begins with a narrative concerning the people's compliance with the prophet's first oracle that calls upon the people to rebuild the Temple so that YHWH will provide rain and good harvest. Haggai 1:15b–2:9 presents the prophet's second oracle concerning the future glory of the new Temple to which the nations will bring gifts to acknowledge YHWH's sovereignty. Haggai 2:10-23 presents two oracles that respectively call upon the people to complete the Temple to ensure community purity and announce Zerubbabel as YHWH's signet ring, a metaphor for regent, who will ensure the overthrow of the nations that subjugate Judah. The structure of Haggai appears as follows:

NARRATIVE CONCERNING HAGGAI'S ORACLES
TO REBUILD THE TEMPLE AND RECOGNIZE ZERUBBABEL
AS YHWH'S REGENT

ZECHARIAH

Zechariah appears as the eleventh book in both the masoretic and Septuagint versions of the Book of the Twelve. Following Haggai, it presents an account of the visions and the oracles of the prophet Zechariah concerning the significance of the Temple's restoration. The book appears in narrative form, and it is set in the second and fourth years of the reign of the Persian monarch Darius, i.e., in 520 and 518 B.C.E. (see Zech 1:1, 7; 7:1). Darius, the son-in-law of Cyrus, came to the throne following the unexpected death of his brother-in-law Cambyses. The empire was plunged into civil war as several figures attempted to seize control of the throne. It was during the years 520–517 B.C.E. that Darius was able to quell opposition forces and begin his campaign against the Greek colonies in Asia Minor and the Greek mainland. Darius had authorized Zerubbabel ben Shealtiel, the grandson of King Jehoiachin of Judah, and the priest Joshua ben Jehozadak to return to Jerusalem in 522 B.C.E. to begin construction of the Second Temple. The narrative setting of the book would therefore also coincide roughly with the years of the building of the Temple in 520–515 B.C.E.

Ezra 5:1 and 6:14 mention Zechariah and Haggai as the two prophets who supported the rebuilding of the Temple. It is noteworthy therefore that Zechariah is identified only as "the son of Iddo" in Ezra, but as "the son of Berechiah the son of Iddo" in Zech 1:1, 7. The descent from Iddo indicates that Zechariah is a priest, insofar as Neh 12:4 identifies Iddo as one of the priests and Levites who returned to Jerusalem with Zerubbabel and Joshua ben Jehozadak in 522 B.C.E., and Neh 12:16 identifies Zechariah as head of the priestly house of Iddo. The discrepancy in names, however, has prompted most scholars to posit that some error has been made in the recording of his name, but a closer look at the intertextual relationships of the name indicates that the discrepancy is deliberate.[32] Although the name Zechariah ben/bar Iddo appears to represent a valid name for a priestly figure in Jerusalem during the reconstruction of the Temple, Zechariah ben Berechiah ben Iddo appears related to the figure Zechariah ben Yeberechiah, one of the witnesses to the birth of Isaiah's son Maher Shalal Hash Baz, in Isa 8:1-4. Yeberechiah is a minor grammatical variant of the name Berechiah.

The book of Zechariah cites extensively from Isaiah and other prophetic books (e.g., Zech 8:20-23; cf. Isa 2:2-4), although it frequently disagrees with Isaiah's scenario of peace gained through submission to the nations (Persians; see the designation of Cyrus as YHWH's messiah and Temple builder in Isa 44:28; 45:1) to call instead for a scenario of warfare against the nations that will prompt their submission to YHWH at the newly rebuilt Temple (Zech 12–14). It would appear that Zechariah ben/bar Iddo's name has been reformulated in Zech 1:1, 7 to identify him with Zechariah ben Yeberechiah in Isa 8:1-4. This would cast Zechariah as an authentic witness to the Isaian tradition, and thereby justify his view that the construction of the Temple would lead to the submission of the nations to YHWH. Such a position is in keeping with Joel, Obadiah, and Micah (see also Nahum), who likewise cite Isaian tradition to call for warfare against the nations that oppress Jerusalem, Israel, and Judah.

Most modern interpreters argue that Zechariah is a composite book like Isaiah insofar as Zech 1–8 appears to represents the visions of the prophet Zechariah, whereas Zech 9–14 represents a later apocalyptic scenario. Many also argue that Zech 9–11 and 12–14 are separate compositions that should be designated as Second and Third Zechariah. In contrast to the narratives of Zech 1–8, each of these blocks is designated as a prophetic *maśśa'* oracle in Zech 9:1; 12:1; Zech 9 appears to represent Alexander the Great's invasion of the Near East (see the reference to the Greeks in Zech 9:13); references such as the three shepherds of Zech 11 are enigmatic; and the scenario of cosmic warfare in Zech 12–14 appears to represent an eschatological scenario. Interpreters are beginning to recognize that Zech 9–14 may well date to the Persian period. The reference to the Greeks in Zech 9:13 calls for combat between Judeans and Greeks whereas Talmudic statements indicate that Alexander was received in Jerusalem as a friend (*b. Yoma* 69a; *b. Tamid* 32a, 31b-32b; cf. Josephus, *Antiquities of the Jews* 11:329);[33] the itinerary for the king in Zech 9 does not match Alexander's route; the three shepherds appear to represent the three kings of Persia, Cyrus, Cambyses, and Darius; and the scenario of combat against the nations need not represent an eschatological scenario but an expression of Judean hopes for independence from Persian rule not unlike those expressed in Haggai.

Furthermore, a synchronic literary reading of the book of Zechariah notes the literary coherence of the book, particularly when the structural role of the date formulae in Zech 1:1, 7; and 7:1 are taken into consideration. Whereas the conventional two- or three-part structure of Zech 1–8; 9–14 or 1–8; 9–11; 12–14 is based on diachronic or historical consideration of the origins of each respective block, the date formulae indicate a two-part structure for the book in which the narrator guides the reader into a presentation of the prophet's eight visions and two major oracles.[34] Zechariah 1:1-6 presents the introduction to the book with YHWH's initial word to the prophet, and Zech 1:7–14:21 presents YHWH's later words to the prophet concerning the visions in Zech 1:7–6:15 and the oracles in Zech 7:1–14:21. The present synchronic literary structure of Zechariah appears as follows:

ACCOUNT OF ZECHARIAH'S VISIONS AND ORACLES CONCERNING THE SIGNIFICANCE OF THE RESTORATION OF JERUSALEM

I. Introduction to the Book: YHWH's initial word
to Zechariah 1:1-6

II. Narrative presentation of YHWH's later words
to Zechariah: visions and oracles 1:7–14:21

    A. Visions 1:7–6:15

        1. Divine horses: YHWH's anger against
nations and plan to restore Jerusalem and
Temple 1:7-17

        2. For horns: restoration of Temple altar;
scattering of Israel and punishment of nations ... 2:1-4

        3. City with walls of fire: restoration of Jerusalem ... 2:5-17

        4. Ordination of Joshua ben Jehozadak 3:1-10

        5. Menorah and two olive shoots: Zerubbabel
and foundation stone 4:1-14

        6. Flying scroll: justice for land from Temple ... 5:1-4

        7. Woman in ephah basket: iniquity sent to
Shinar/Babylon 5:5-11

        8. Four chariots proclaim crowning of Joshua
ben Jehozadak 6:1-15

The introduction to the book in Zech 1:1-6 signals the concern with earlier prophetic tradition by constructing Zechariah's identity in relation to the figure of Zechariah ben Yeberechiah in Isa 8:1-4 as noted above and by its references to the "former prophets" (v. 4). By referring to the calls for repentance made to the ancestors by the former prophets, the introduction emphasizes YHWH's ability to act in the world as announced by the prophets. Such an argument prepares the reading audience to anticipate the realization of the claims made in the following material concerning Zechariah's visions and oracles.

The narrative account of Zechariah's visions in Zech 1:7–6:15 lays out a sequence of the prophet's visions, each of which is based upon his observations of activities connected with the building of the new Temple and its preparation to serve as the holy center of creation. The first vision in Zech 1:7-17 draws upon the typical use of horse-mounted messengers by the Persian Empire to portray the four horsemen who announce YHWH's plans to rebuild the Temple. The second vision in Zech 2:1-4 (NRSV 1:18-21) draws upon the imagery of workmen constructing the four-horned altar for the Temple (cf. Exod 27:2) to symbolize the scattering or exile of Israel in all directions and the punishment of all nations that carried out the exile. The third vision in Zech 2:5-17 (NRSV 2:1-13) draws upon the imagery of workmen laying out the plans for the reconstruction of the Temple and the city to depict Jerusalem as an unwalled, holy city, ringed by fire, much like the Persian holy city of Pasargadae, as a representation of YHWH's presence in the center of the nations. The fourth vision in Zech 3:1-10 portrays the ordination of Joshua ben Jehozadak as high priest for service in the new Temple (cf. Exod 28–29; Lev 8–9). The fifth vision in Zech 4:1-14 describes the Temple menorah, "candelabrum," flanked by two olive branches to symbolize YHWH's presence and the role of the two anointed figures, the royal Zerubbabel and the priestly Joshua, at the foundation of the new Temple. The sixth vision in Zech 5:1-4 employs the image of the flying scroll to symbolize the reading of Torah from the ulam or "porch" of the Temple as the basis for the holy life of the people. The seventh vision in Zech 5:5-11 portrays the removal of a woman in an ephah basket to Shinar, the site of Babylon, to symbolize the purity of the priests and the offerings made at their ordination. The eighth and final vision in Zech 6:1-15 presents the images of four chariots and the priest, Joshua ben Jehozadak, seated on the throne to symbolize the reestablishment of the Temple. Many argue that the passage originally had Zerubbabel as the royal figure seated on the throne, particularly since his absence from the Temple consecration portrayed in Ezra 6 suggests to many that the Persians removed him when they concluded that he might attempt to restore Judean independence (cf. Hag 2:20-23).

The narrative account of the transmission of YHWH's word to Zechariah in Zech 7:1–14:21 poses a question concerning mourning for the lost Temple in Zech 7:1-7 and answers the question with a lengthy depiction of rejoicing and righteous action at the restoration of the Temple in Zech 7:8–14:21. Within this second section, three subunits, each introduced by the prophetic word transmission formula, lay out YHWH's concerns. Zechariah 7:8-14 begins with an initial oracle concerning YHWH's call for righteous action that reiterates concerns from the introduction of the book to emphasize the reasons for the exile. A second subunit in Zech 8:1-17 recalls the earlier words of the prophets to emphasize that restoration will follow the period of punishment. The third subunit in Zech 8:18–14:21 call for joy at the restoration of the Temple by portraying how the nations will come to seek YHWH (see Zech 8:18-23). The two major prophetic *maśśa'ot*, "oracles," in Zech 9–11 and 12–14 respectively present YHWH's judgment against the shepherds, i.e., the three Persian kings, Cyrus, Cambyses, and Darius, that failed to bring about YHWH's purposes as articulated in Isa 40–54 (see esp. Isa 44:24–45:1), and YHWH's judgment against the nations. The scenario depends upon the rise of a new shepherd or

Davidic monarch (Zech 11:16; cf. Jer 23:1-8), who would lead the combat that would eventually result in the nations' acknowledgment of YHWH at the Temple during the festival of Sukkot. Such a proposal runs counter to Isaiah, which envisions submission to the Persians as recognition of YHWH's worldwide sovereignty.

MALACHI

Finally, Malachi constitutes the twelfth book in both the masoretic and Septuagint versions of the Twelve. It is especially well suited for this role because it calls for the return of the people to YHWH and it rejects the notion of divorce, which had been employed metaphorically to represent the rupture of the relationship between YHWH and Israel at the beginning of the Book of the Twelve in Hosea. Although some argue that Malachi was composed for this position, there is little explicit evidence of direct dependence or interrelationship with the other books that comprise the Twelve.

Nothing is known of the prophet Malachi, and many suspect that he does not even exist since the name in Hebrew means simply, "my messenger, angel," and the term does not appear elsewhere in the Bible as a proper name. The book's concern with the neglect of the Temple and the marriage of Jewish men to pagan women suggests that it is to be set some time prior to the arrival of Ezra in Jerusalem. Ezra's dates are disputed, but they range from the latter half of the fifth century B.C.E. through the early fourth century. That suggests that Malachi should be dated to the fifth century, and perhaps played a role in building the case for Ezra's placement in Jerusalem. Indeed, Ezra's reforms address the issues raised in Malachi.

The literary form of Malachi supports such a contention.[35] The structure of Malachi may be represented as follows:

PARENETIC ADDRESS TO PRIESTS AND PEOPLE CALLING
FOR PROPER REVERENCE FOR YHWH

I. Superscription	1:1
II. Body of the Book: Parenetic Address Proper	1:2–3:24
A. First disputation: YHWH loves the people	1:2–5
B. Second disputation: People and Priests have Mishandled Cultic Matters	1:6–2:16

Following the superscription in Mal 1:1, which identifies the book simply as "An oracle. The word of YHWH to Israel by Malachi," the body of the book in Mal 1:2–3:24 (NRSV 1:2–4:5) appears as a parenetic address to priests and people designed to convince them to provide proper reverence and support for YHWH and the Temple. This section includes six disputation speeches that challenge popular perceptions to argue for such adherence to YHWH. Malachi 1:2-5 contends that YHWH loves the people. Malachi 1:6–2:16 argues that both people and priests have mishandled cultic matters. Malachi 2:17–3:5 answers concerns about YHWH's justice to contend that the Day of YHWH's justice is about to arrive. Malachi 3:6-12 calls for the proper treatment of YHWH's tithes. Malachi 3:13-21 (NRSV 3:13–4:3) again asserts that YHWH's justice will be realized on the Day of YHWH. The concluding statements in Mal 3:22-24 (NRSV 4:5-6) sum up the argument by calling for observance of YHWH's Torah and announcing the return of the prophet Elijah prior to the expected Day of YHWH (cf. 2 Kgs 2, which contends that Elijah did not die, but ascended to heaven in a fiery chariot).

In sum, the masoretic version of the book of the Twelve arranges the individual books of the Twelve in a sequence that emphasizes reflection on the fate of Jerusalem from the latter half of the monarchic period when the Assyrian Empire began to threaten the region, through the period of the Babylonian destruction of the city, and finally through the time of the Persian period restoration. To a certain degree, the book of the Twelve engages in debate with the book of Isaiah, which offers a similar reflection. But whereas Isaiah envisions a scenario in which Israel will join the nations at Jerusalem in submitting to YHWH and will accept Persian rule as an expression of the divine will, the book of the Twelve Prophets collectively argue that YHWH will raise a Davidic messiah who will play a role in enabling YHWH to defeat the nations that oppress Jerusalem, thereby prompting them to recognize YHWH's sovereignty. Such differing positions point to the fundamental role of dialogue among the various prophetic books, namely, the prophets do not speak with a monolithic voice. Instead, they express a variety of viewpoints in their attempts to discern divine purpose in the world of human experience.

SELECTED BIBLIOGRAPHY

THE BOOK OF THE TWELVE

Ben Zvi, Ehud. "Twelve Prophetic Books or 'The Twelve': A Few Preliminary Considerations." Pages 125-56 in *Forming Prophetic Literature: Essays on Isaiah and the Twelve in Honor of J. D. W. Watts*. Edited by J. W. Watts and P. R. House. JSOTSup 235. Sheffield: Sheffield Academic Press, 1996.

Jones, Barry Alan. *The Formation of the Book of the Twelve: Study in Text and Canon*. SBLDS 149. Atlanta: Scholars Press, 1995.

Nogalski, James D. *Literary Precursors to the Book of the Twelve*. BZAW 117. Berlin and New York: Walter de Gruyter, 1993.

———. *Redactional Processes in the Book of the Twelve*. BZAW 118. Berlin and New York: Walter de Gruyter, 1993.

Nogalski, James D., and Marvin A. Sweeney, editors. *Reading and Hearing the Book of the Twelve*. SBLSymS 15. Atlanta: Society of Biblical Literature, 2000.

Reddit, Paul L., and Aaron Schart, editors. *Thematic Threads in the Book of the Twelve*. BZAW 325. Berlin and New York: Walter de Gruyter, 2003.

Sweeney, Marvin A. *The Twelve Prophets*. 2 vols. Berit Olam. Collegeville: Liturgical, 2000.

THE BOOK OF HOSEA

Andersen, Francis I., and David Noel Freedman. *Hosea*. AB 24. Garden City: Doubleday, 1980.

Ben Zvi, Ehud. *Hosea*. FOTL XXIA, part 1. Grand Rapids and Cambridge: Eerdmans, forthcoming, 2005.

Davies, G. I. *Hosea.* NCB. Grand Rapids: Eerdmans, 1992.

Landy, Francis. *Hosea.* Readings. Sheffield: Sheffield Academic Press, 1995.

MacIntosh, A. A. *Hosea.* ICC. Edinburgh: T & T Clark, 1997.

Mays, James Luther. *Hosea.* OTL. Philadelphia: Westminster, 1969.

Wolff, Hans Walter. *Hosea: A Commentary on the Book of the Prophet Hosea.* Hermeneia. Translated by G. Stansell. Philadelphia: Fortress, 1974.

Yee, Gale A. "Hosea." Pages 195-297 in vol. 7 of *The New Interpreter's Bible.* Edited by L. E. Keck, et al. Nashville: Abingdon, 1996.

THE BOOK OF JOEL

Barton, John. *Hosea.* FOTL XXIA, part 1. Grand Rapids and Cambridge: Eerdmans, forthcoming, 2005.

———. *Joel and Obadiah: A Commentary.* OTL. Louisville: Westminster John Knox, 2001.

Coggins, Richard J. *Joel and Amos.* NCB. Sheffield: Sheffield Academic Press, 2000.

Crenshaw, James L. *Joel.* AB 24C. New York: Doubleday, 1995.

Ogden, Graham S., and Richard R. Deutsch. *Joel and Malachi: A Promise of Hope, A Call to Obedience.* International Theological Commentary. Grand Rapids: Eerdmans; London: Hansell, 1987.

Wolff, Hans Walter. *Joel and Amos.* Hermeneia. Translated by W. Janzen, et al. Philadelphia: Fortress, 1977.

THE BOOK OF AMOS

Andersen, Francis I., and David Noel Freedman. *Amos.* AB 24A. New York: Doubleday, 1989.

Coggins, Richard J. *Joel and Amos.* NCB. Sheffield: Sheffield Academic Press, 2000.

Jeremias, Jorg. *The Book of Amos: A Commentary.* OTL. Translated by D. W. Stott. Louisville: Westminster John Knox, 1998.

Mays, James Luther. *Amos: A Commentary.* OTL. Philadelphia: Wesminster, 1969.

Paul, Shalom. *Amos.* Hermeneia. Minneapolis: Fortress, 1991.

Wolff, Hans Walter. *Joel and Amos.* Hermeneia. Translated by W. Janzen, et al. Philadelphia: Fortress, 1977.

THE BOOK OF OBADIAH

Barton, John. *Joel and Obadiah: A Commentary.* OTL. Louisville: Westminster John Knox, 2001.
Ben Zvi, Ehud. *A Historical-Critical Study of the Book of Obadiah.* BZAW 242. Berlin and New York: Walter de Gruyter, 1996.
Raabe, Paul R. *Obadiah.* AB 24D. New York: Doubleday, 1996.
Wolff, Hans Walter. *Obadiah and Jonah.* ContCom. Translated by M. Kohl. Minneapolis: Augsburg, 1986.

THE BOOK OF JONAH

Limburg, James. *Jonah: A Commentary.* OTL. Louisville: Westminster John Knox, 1993.
Magonet, Jonathan. *Form and Meaning: Studies in Literary Technique in the Book of Jonah.* BBET 2. Bern: Herbert Lang. Frankfurt am Main: Peter Lang, 1976.
Sasson, Jack M. *Jonah.* AB 24B. New York: Doubleday, 1990.
Simon, Uriel. *Jonah.* JPS Bible Commentary. Philadelphia: Jewish Publication Society, 1999.
Trible, Phyllis. "Jonah." Pages 461-529 in vol. 7 of *The New Interpreter's Bible.* Edited by L. Keck, et al. Nashville: Abingdon, 1996.
Wolff, Hans Walter. *Obadiah and Jonah.* ContCom. Translated by M. Kohl. Minneapolis: Augsburg, 1986.

THE BOOK OF MICAH

Andersen, Francis I., and David Noel Freedman. *Micah.* AB 24E. New York: Doubleday, 2000.
Ben Zvi, Ehud. *Micah.* FOTL 21B. Grand Rapids and Cambridge: Eerdmans, 2001.
Hillers, Delbert. *Micah.* Hermeneia. Philadelphia: Fortress, 1984.
Jacobs, Mignon R. *The Conceptual Coherence of the Book of Micah.* JSOTSup 322. Sheffield: Sheffield Academic Press, 2001.
Mays, James Luther. *Micah: A Commentary.* OTL. Philadelphia: Westminster, 1976.

McKane, William. *Micah: Introduction and Commentary.* Edinburgh: T & T Clark, 1998.

Wolff, Hans Walter. *Micah.* ContCom. Translated by G. Stansell. Minneapolis: Augsburg, 1990.

THE BOOK OF NAHUM

Coggins, Richard J., and S. Paul Re'emi. *Israel among the Nations: Nahum, Obadiah, Esther.* International Theological Commentary. Grand Rapids: Eerdmans, 1985.

Floyd, Michael H. *Minor Prophets, part 2.* FOTL 22. Grand Rapids and Cambridge: Eerdmans, 2000.

Roberts, J. J. M. *Nahum, Habakkuk, Zephaniah: A Commentary.* OTL. Louisville: Westminster John Knox, 1991.

Spronk, Klaas. *Nahum.* HCOT. Kampen: Kok Pharos, 1997.

THE BOOK OF HABAKKUK

Andersen, Francis I. *Habakkuk.* AB 25. New York: Doubleday, 2001.

Floyd, Michael H. *Minor Prophets, part 2.* FOTL 22. Grand Rapids and Cambridge: Eerdmans, 2000.

Haak, Robert D. *Habakkuk.* VTSup 44. Leiden: Brill, 1992.

Hiebert, Theodore. "Habakkuk." Pages 621-55 in vol. 7 of *The New Interpreter's Bible.* Edited by L. Keck et al. Nashville: Abingdon, 1996.

Roberts, J. J. M. *Nahum, Habakkuk, Zephaniah: A Commentary.* OTL. Louisville: Westminster John Knox, 1991.

THE BOOK OF ZEPHANIAH

Ball, Ivan J., Jr. *Zephaniah: A Rhetorical Study.* Berkeley: BIBAL, 1988.

Ben Zvi, Ehud. *A Historical-Critical Study of the Book of Zephaniah.* BZAW 198. Berlin and New York: Walter de Gruyter, 1991.

Bennett, Robert A. "Zephaniah." Pages 657-704 in vol. 7 of *The New Interpreter's Bible.* Edited by L. Keck, et al. Nashville: Abingdon, 1996.

Berlin, Adele. *Zephaniah.* AB 25A. New York: Doubleday, 1994.

Floyd, Michael H. *Minor Prophets, part 2.* FOTL 22. Grand Rapids and Cambridge: Eerdmans, 2000.

Roberts, J. J. M. *Nahum, Habakkuk, Zephaniah: A Commentary.* OTL. Louisville: Westminster John Knox, 1991.

Sweeney, Marvin A. *Zephaniah.* Hermeneia. Minneapolis: Fortress, 2003.

Vlaardingerbroek, J. *Zephaniah.* HCOT. Leuven: Peeters, 1999.

THE BOOK OF HAGGAI

Floyd, Michael H. *Minor Prophets, part 2.* FOTL XXII. Grand Rapids and Cambridge: Eerdmans, 2000.

March, W. Eugene. "Haggai." Pages 705-32 in vol. 7 of *The New Interpreter's Bible.* Edited by L. Keck, et al. Nashville: Abingdon, 1996.

Meyers, Carol L., and Eric M. Meyers. *Haggai, Zechariah 1–8.* AB 25B. New York: Doubleday, 1987.

Petersen, David L. *Haggai and Zechariah 1–8: A Commentary.* OTL. Philadelphia: Westminster, 1984.

Reddit, Paul L. *Haggai, Zechariah, Malachi.* NCB. London: Marshall Pickering. Grand Rapids: Eerdmans, 1995.

Wolff, Hans Walter. *Haggai.* ContCom. Translated by M. Kohl. Minneapolis: Augsburg, 1988.

THE BOOK OF ZECHARIAH

Conrad, Edgar. *Zechariah.* Readings. Sheffield: Sheffield Academic Press, 1999.

Floyd, Michael H. *Minor Prophets, part 2.* FOTL 22. Grand Rapids and Cambridge: Eerdmans, 2000.

Hanson, Paul. *The Dawn of Apocalyptic.* Philadelphia: Fortress, 1975.

Meyers, Carol L., and Eric Meyers. *Haggai, Zechariah 1–8.* AB 25B. New York: Doubleday, 1987.

———. *Zechariah 9–14.* AB 25C. New York: Doubleday, 1993.

Petersen, David L. *Haggai and Zechariah 1–8: A Commentary.* OTL. Philadelphia: Westminster, 1984.

———. *Zechariah 9–14 and Malachi: A Commentary.* OTL. Louisville: Westminster John Knox, 1995.

Reddit, Paul L. *Haggai, Zechariah, Malachi.* NCB. London: Marshall Pickering. Grand Rapids: Eerdmans, 1995.

THE BOOK OF MALACHI

Floyd, Michael H. *Minor Prophets, part 2.* FOTL 22. Grand Rapids and Cambridge: Eerdmans, 2000.

Hill, Andrew E. *Malachi.* AB 25D. New York: Doubleday, 1998.

Petersen, David L. *Zechariah 9–14 and Malachi: A Commentary.* OTL. Louisville: Westminster John Knox, 1995.

Reddit, Paul L. "Haggai, Zechariah, Malachi." NCB. London: Marshall Pickering. Grand Rapids: Eerdmans, 1995.

Schuller, Eileen. "Malachi." Pages 841-77 in vol. 7 of *The New Interpreter's* Bible. Edited by L. Keck, et al. Nashville: Abingdon, 1996.

CHAPTER 7

EPILOGUE

As the preceding chapters have demonstrated, the prophets play significant roles within the canonical scriptures of both Judaism and Christianity. Indeed, both traditions understand the prophets as representatives of G-d who articulate divine expectations for Israel/Judah in particular and for humanity in general in relation to the past, present, and future of the world of creation.

Both traditions make it clear that the prophets hold an integral place in their respective worldviews. Although Jewish tradition maintains that prophecy came to a close with Malachi, it ensures their continuing relevance by including the prophets as an essential link in the chain of tradition that begins with the revelation of Torah to Moses at Sinai and continues through the major Rabbis of the Mishnah who laid the foundation for future Jewish thought. Mishnah *Pirke Avot* (Chapters of the Fathers) 1:1 states, "Moses received the Torah from Sinai and committed to Joshua, and Joshua to the elders, and the elders to the Prophets, and the Prophets committed it to the men of the Great Synagogue. They said three things: 'Be deliberate in judgment, raise up many

215

disciples, and make a fence around the Torah.'" The Prophets continue to be read as part of the regular liturgy of the synagogue. Each reading of the Torah as part of the Shabbat, Daily, and Festival synagogue service is "completed" by a reading from the Prophets called the *Haftarah* (completion), particularly since Judaism contends that the Prophets express the divine teachings that appear initially in the five books of the Torah.

Christianity also understands the Prophets to be an essential part of Christian revelation and identity. As noted in the discussion of the structure of the Christian canon above, the Prophets point to the New Testament and its revelation of Jesus Christ. But the Prophets are also understood to point beyond the New Testament to the second coming of Christ that will mark the eschatological end of the world as we know it and the inauguration of the kingdom of G-d when Christ presides over a world in which the ideals of the prophets are realized, namely, when all the nations shall stream to Zion to recognize G-d, beat their swords into plowshares, and learn war no more (Isa 2:2-4; Mic 4:1-5). The Prophets appear regularly in the various forms of the Christian lectionary. Even today, prophetic identity is essential to the self-understanding of Christians, particularly since Prophets are perceived to act in accordance with the divine spirit to witness to G-d and to bring about justice and peace in the world.

Many surveys of prophecy point to the apocalyptic or eschatological realization of the prophetic ideal beyond the normal scope of human history. Although apocalyptic or proto-apocalyptic texts, such as Isa 24–27; 34–35; Ezek 38–39; Joel; Zech 9–14, and others, clearly point to a concern with the future realization of divine purpose, they are well integrated into the prophetic books that constitute both the Jewish and Christian versions of the Bible. In this respect, recent study has demonstrated that the apocalyptic texts are as much concerned with influencing people in this world as they are with articulating a future that might extend beyond this world. Even Daniel, the only fully apocalyptic book of the Hebrew Bible, appears as part of the Prophets in Christian canons. Indeed, Daniel is written from a priestly perspective to support the Hasmonean revolt against Seleucid Syria that began in 167 B.C.E.

Our treatment of the Prophets emphasizes the impact that the Prophets were expected to have upon their own societies and the events of their day. Without dispensing with the concerns for the future articulated in the Prophets, it is also essential for us to consider the impact of the Prophets for our own times. To ignore such a dimension potentially marginalizes the Prophets in our thinking about the present when in fact they have important insights for the contemporary world.

As our survey of the Prophets demonstrates, they were essentially concerned with the problem of evil, whether of divine or human origin, in their own day. Most fundamentally, they are concerned with the Babylonian exile in 587 B.C.E. and the restoration of Jerusalem and the Jewish people that took place in the early Second Temple period from 539 B.C.E. on. Although earlier manifestations of evil also were of concern, the Aramean invasions of Israel in the ninth century B.C.E. and the Assyrian destruction of northern Israel in 722/1 B.C.E. among others, the Babylonian exile and the subsequent restoration have come to play a dominant role in the structure and outlook of the Hebrew Bible in both Judaism and Christianity. Of course, both traditions also read the Bible in relation to the destruction of the Second Temple and the exile of Jews by the Romans in 70 C.E. (and following the Bar Kochba revolt of 132–135 C.E.). For Judaism, this second destruction and exile inaugurated the Rabbinic period of reflection upon the Torah tradition and the definition of Jewish life in the diaspora. For Christians, it marked the spread of Christianity throughout the world.

The Prophets address the challenges posed by the problem of exile and the possibility of restoration. Although the destruction of Jerusalem and the Temple, the deaths of many thousands of people, and the exile of even more raise questions about the righteousness, power, and commitment of YHWH to the covenant with Israel, the Prophets chose to assert divine righteousness and argue instead that human beings bear responsibility for the events of their time. Isaiah, the Jerusalemite, contends that the monarchy and the people did not put their trust in YHWH in accordance with the Davidic tradition of divine protection for Jerusalem, the house of David, and the nation Israel. The process of punishment and restoration pointed to the revelation of YHWH as divine sovereign of all creation, and the book itself calls for Israel to take its place among the nations as YHWH's representative in the holy center of creation at Zion. Jeremiah, the Levitical

217

priest, contends that the disaster suffered by Israel and Judah was due to a failure to observe YHWH's Torah, and he embarks on a program of teaching Torah in an effort to bring Israel back to its foundations with a restoration that will see YHWH's Torah inscribed upon the people's hearts. Ezekiel, the Zadokite priest, claims that the holy center of creation, the Jerusalem Temple, has become defiled by the people's wrongdoing and must be purified to place creation back on its proper foundations. The Twelve Prophets, whether individually or collectively, likewise point to the actions of the people as the basis for punishment and postulate a restoration in which the oppressors will be defeated and Jerusalem or Israel restored at the center of creation. The Prophets may disagree with each other, at times explicitly, but they all remain true to their calling even in the most challenging of circumstances. In all cases, the Prophets point to fundamental human responsibilities to work with YHWH to ensure the future of the world.

We live in a time very much like that of the Babylonian exile in 587 B.C.E. or even the aftermath of the destruction of the Second Temple in 70 C.E. The past century has seen a deliberate attempt to murder the entire Jewish people, and it has seen attempted genocides against other nations and peoples as well. It has seen two world wars and a so-called Cold War that have nearly wrought the destruction of our own world. It has seen the introduction of nuclear weapons and threats to our natural environment that have the potential to bring our lives to an end. This hardly exhausts the problems that we face—racism, misogyny, economic exploitation, and fundamental hypocrisy and betrayal all come to mind—but it provides examples of the sorts of challenges that we must confront as we now find ourselves in a new century or even a new millennium.

Many choose to argue that G-d is dead, impotent, unconcerned, or even malicious. Even the Prophets raise these possibilities, for example, Habakkuk asks how YHWH can look upon evil; Isaiah fails to challenge YHWH like Abraham and Moses when faced with the possibility of divine evil; Jeremiah accuses YHWH of overpowering him like a rapist; Ezekiel portrays the destruction of Jerusalem as a sacrifice that consumes all without distinction. Others choose to focus on the prophetic accusation of human wrongdoing in an effort to contend that the punishments we suffer are well deserved. Again, the prophets are replete with examples that hardly need to be repeated here. Both of these choices represent elements of truth; both G-d and human beings do bear a measure of responsibility for the disasters of the past. But ultimately, both choices represent a fundamental misunderstanding of the Prophets, who consistently demand righteous action from the people that they address. The question is not one of the past, i.e., what evil did G-d commit, or what evil did we commit, but one of the future, i.e., what responsibility will we take for the future? Perhaps one of the prophets says it best:

"Let justice roll down like waters, and righteousness like a mighty stream" (Amos 5:24).

It is up to us to see that Amos's words are realized in our own time.

SELECTED BIBLIOGRAPHY

Braiterman, Zachary. *(G-d) After Auschwitz: Tradition and Change in Post-Holocaust Jewish Thought.* Princeton: Princeton University Press, 1998.

Fackenheim, Emil L. *The Jewish Bible after the Holocaust: A Rereading.* Bloomington and Indianapolis: Indiana University Press, 1990.

Linafelt, Tod, ed. *Strange Fire: Reading the Bible after the Holocaust.* BibSem 71. Sheffield: Sheffield Academic Press, 2000.

Williamson, Clark M. *A Guest in the House of Israel: Post-Holocaust Church Theology.* Louisville: Westminster John Knox, 1993.

NOTES

Chapter 1: The Prophets in Jewish and Christian Scripture

1. For discussion of the theological issues posed by the Shoah (Holocaust), see now Zachary Braiterman, *(G-d) After Auschwitz: Tradition and Change in Post-Holocaust Jewish Thought* (Princeton: Princeton University Press, 1998); Clark M. Williamson, *A Guest in the House of Israel: Post-Holocaust Church Theology* (Louisville: Westminster John Knox, 1993); Tod Linafelt, editor, *Strange Fire: Reading the Bible after the Holocaust* (BibSem 71; Sheffield: Sheffield Academic Press, 2000).

2. For an overview concerning the study of prophetic literature during the nineteenth and twentieth centuries, see esp. Joseph Blenkinsopp, *A History of Prophecy in Israel* (2nd ed.; Louisville: Westminster John Knox, 1996), 16-26.

3. See Marvin A. Sweeney, "Tanak versus Old Testament: Concerning the Foundation for a Jewish Theology of the Bible," in *Problems in Biblical Theology: Essays in Honor of Rolf Knierim* (ed. H. T. C. Sun et al.; Grand Rapids: Eerdmans, 1997), 353-72.

4. For discussion of the formation of the Christian Bible, particularly with regard to the role of the Old Testament, see now Roger T. Beckwith, *The Old Testament Canon of the New Testament Church and Its Background in Early Judaism* (Grand Rapids: Eerdmans, 1986).

5. For discussion of the Tanak, see Beckwith, *The Old Testament Canon;* Sid Leiman, *The Canonization of Hebrew Scripture: The Talmudic and Midrashic Evidence* (Hamden: Connecticut Academy of Arts and Sciences/Archon, 1972).

6. Although the Hebrew term *tôrâ* (Torah) is frequently translated "Law," this is a mistranslation based on Paul's attempts to characterize Torah as an unbending relic of past revelation that is incapable of facilitating salvation. The term is derived from the *hiphil* (causative) form of the Hebrew verb root, *yrh*, "to guide, instruct," and is best rendered, "Instruction, Teaching." Torah includes not only legal material, but a

221

comprehensive history of the world from creation through the emergence of the people Israel. It thereby instructs ancient Israel and modern Judaism in divine purpose, the significance and character of the created world, and the place, identity, and responsibilities of Israel/Judaism and all humanity within that world.

Chapter 2: Reading Prophetic Books

1. For discussion of the social roles of prophecy in ancient Israel and Judah, see esp. David L. Petersen, *The Roles of Israel's Prophets* (JSOTSup 17; Sheffield: Sheffield Academic Press, 1981); Robert Wilson, *Prophecy and Society in Ancient Israel* (Philadelphia: Fortress, 1980).

2. For discussion of the basic forms of prophetic literature and speech, see now Marvin A. Sweeney, *Isaiah 1–39, with an Introduction to Prophetic Literature* (FOTL 16; Grand Rapids and Cambridge: Eerdmans, 1996), 1-30, 512-47.

3. For a survey of prophecy in the ancient Near Eastern world, see Blenkinsopp, *A History of Prophecy*, 40-48; Herbert B. Huffman, "Prophecy; Ancient Near Eastern Prophecy," *ABD* 5:477-82.

4. For discussion of the professional nature and training of prophets and oracle diviners in ancient Mesopotamia, see Frederick H. Cryer, *Divination in Ancient Israel and Its Near Eastern Environment* (JSOTSup 142; Sheffield: Sheffield Academic Press, 1994).

5. For an English translation, see James B. Pritchard, editor, *Ancient Near Eastern Texts Relating to the Old Testament* (3rd ed. with supplement; Princeton: Princeton University Press, 1969), 441-44.

6. Ibid., 443.

7. Ibid., 444-46.

8. Ibid., 445.

9. Ibid., 449.

10. Ibid.

11. For discussion of the Mespotamian *baru* priest, see esp. Cryer, *Divination*.

12. Herbert B. Huffman, "Prophecy in the Mari Letters," in *Biblical Archaeologist Reader 3* (ed. D. N. Freedman; Garden City, N.Y.: Doubleday, 1970), 199-224, 205-6.

13. Huffman, "Prophecy in the Mari Letters," 211-12.

14. Ibid., 209.

15. *ANET*, 25-29.

16. For a discussion of parody in the Balaam narrative, see David Marcus, *From Balaam to Jonah: Anti-Prophetic Satire in the Hebrew Bible* (Brown Judaic Studies 301; Atlanta: Scholars Press, 1995).

17. For transcription, translation, and discussion of the Deir 'Alla inscription, see Meindert Dijkstra, "Is Balaam also among the Prophets?" *JBL* 114 (1995): 43-64.

18. Dijkstra, "Is Balaam," 47.

19. For discussion of the superscriptions for prophetic books, see Gene M. Tucker, "Prophetic Superscriptions and the Growth of the Canon," in

Canon and Authority (ed. G. W. Coats and B. O. Long; Philadelphia: Fortress, 1977), 56-70.

20. For discussion of the Levitical singers, see David L. Petersen, *Late Israelite Prophecy: Studies in Deutero-Prophetic Literature and in Chronicles* (SBLMS 23; Missoula: Scholars Press, 1977), 55-96.

21. See Burke O. Long, "Reports of Visions among the Prophets," *JBL* 95 (1976): 353-65; Sweeney, *Isaiah 1-39*, 542.

22. See Samuel M. Meier, *Speaking of Speaking: Marking Direct Discourse in the Hebrew Bible* (VTSup 46; Leiden: Brill, 1992), 314-19; Sweeney, *Isaiah 1-39*, 547.

23. See W. D. Stacey, *Prophetic Drama in the Old Testament* (London: Epworth, 1990); Sweeney, *Isaiah 1-39*, 536-37.

24. See Norman Habel, "The Form and Significance of the Prophetic Call Narratives," *ZAW* 77 (1965): 297-323; Sweeney, *Isaiah 1-39*, 542-43.

25. For full discussion of the prophetical stories and their various types, see Alexander Rofé, *The Prophetical Stories* (Jerusalem: Magnes, 1988); cf. Sweeney, *Isaiah 1-39*, 535-36.

26.Richard D. Weis, "Oracle," *ABD* 5:28-29; Sweeney, *Isaiah 1-39*, 526.

27. Ibid. "A Definition of the Genre *Maśśa'* in the Hebrew Bible" (Ph.D. dissertation; Claremont Graduate School, 1986); Michael H. Floyd, "The משא (*Maśśa'*) as a Type of Prophetic Book," *JBL* 121 (2002): 401-22; Sweeney, *Isaiah 1-39*, 534-35.

28. Meier, *Speaking of Speaking*, 273-98; Sweeney, *Isaiah 1-39*, 524.

29. Sweeney, *Isaiah 1-39*, 529.

30. Claus Westermann, *Basic Forms of Prophetic Speech* (Cambridge: Lutterworth; Louisville: Westminster John Knox, reprint edition, 1991); Sweeney, *Isaiah 1-39*, 533-34.

31. Walther Zimmerli, "The Word of Divine Self-Manifestation (Proof-Saying): A Prophetic Genre," in *I Am YHWH* (Atlanta: John Knox, 1982), 99-110.

32. Claus Westermann, *Prophetic Oracles of Salvation in the Old Testament* (Louisville: Westminster John Knox, 1991); Sweeney, *Isaiah 1-39*, 531.

33. Ibid., 514.

34. Ibid., 528-29.

35. Ibid., 532.

36. Ibid., 542.

37. Adrian Graffy, *A Prophet Confronts His People* (AnBib 104; Rome: Pontifical Biblical Institute, 1984); D. 37; F. Murray, "The Rhetoric of Disputation: Re-examination of a Prophetic Genre," *JSOT* 38 (1987): 95-121; Sweeney, *Isaiah 1-39*, 519.

38. Erhard Gerstenberger, "The Woe-Oracles of the Prophets," *JBL* 81 (1962): 249-63; Westermann, *Basic Forms*, 190-98; Sweeney, *Isaiah 1-39*, 543-44.

39. Sweeney, *Isaiah 1-39*, 522.

40. A. Vanlier Hunter, *Seek the L-rd! A Study of the Meaning and Function of the Exhortations in Amos, Hosea, Isaiah, Micah, and Zephaniah* (Baltimore: St. Mary's Seminary and University, 1982);

Sweeney, *Isaiah 1–39*, 520; cf. Gene M. Tucker, "Prophetic Speech," *Int* 32 (1978): 31-45, who cautions against making comparisons with modern addresses.

41. Sweeney, *Isaiah 1–39*, 524.

Chapter 3: The Book of Isaiah

1. For discussion of the composition of Isaiah, see Sweeney, *Isaiah 1–39*, 31-62.

2. For discussion of the Davidic covenant tradition, see esp. Moshe Weinfeld, "Covenant, Davidic," *IDBSup*, 188-92; idem, "Zion and Jerusalem as Religious and Political Capital: Ideology and Utopia," in *The Poet and the Historian: Essays in Literary and Historical Biblical Criticism* (ed. R. E. Friedman; HSS 26; Chico, Calif.: Scholars Press, 1983), 75-115.

3. See Hans Wildberger, *Isaiah 1–12: A Commentary* (ContCom; Minneapolis: Fortress, 1991), 246-78.

4. For discussion of the literary structure of Isaiah, see Sweeney, *Isaiah 1–39*, 31-62; Rolf Rendtorff, "The Book of Isaiah: A Complex Unity. Synchronic and Diachronic Reading," in *New Visions of Isaiah* (ed. R. F. Melugin and M. A. Sweeney; JSOTSup 214; Sheffield: Sheffield Academic Press, 1996), 32–49; H. G. M. Williamson, *The Book Called Isaiah: Deutero-Isaiah's Role in Composition and Redaction* (Oxford: Clarendon, 1984).

5. The classic model for the modern interpretation of a First, Second, and Third Isaiah was developed by Bernhard Duhm, *Das Buch Jesaia* (HKAT 3/1; Göttingen: Vandenhoeck & Ruprecht, 1892), esp. v-xxi. An English translation of Duhm's commentary is in progress.

6. For discussion of the interrelationship between Isa 6:1–9:6 and 36–39, see Peter R. Ackroyd, "Isaiah 36–39: Structure and Function," in *Studies in the Religious Tradition of the Old Testament* (London: SCM, 1987), 105-20, 274-78.

7. See also Marvin A. Sweeney, "The Book of Isaiah as Prophetic Torah," in *New Visions of Isaiah*, 50-67; Craig A. Evans, "On the Unity and Parallel Structure of Isaiah," *VT* 38 (1988): 129-47.

8. Cf. Peter R. Ackroyd, "Isaiah 1-12: Presentation of a Prophet," *Studies*, 79-104, 266-74.

9. See also Marvin A. Sweeney, *King Josiah of Judah: The Lost Messiah of Israel* (Oxford and New York: Oxford University Press, 2001).

10. For much of the interpretation of Isaiah presented here see my *Isaiah 1–39*, ad loc., and *Isaiah 1–4 and the Post-Exilic Understanding of the Isaianic Tradition* (BZAW 171; Berlin and New York: Walter de Gruyter, 1988).

11. See also Roy F. Melugin, "Figurative Speech and the Reading of Isaiah 1 as Scripture," in *New Visions of Isaiah*, 282-305.

12. Cf. Ronald E. Clements, "The Prophecies of Isaiah and the Fall of Jerusalem in 587 B.C.," *VT* 30 (1980): 421-36.

13. See also Wildberger, *Isaiah 1–12*, 81-96.

14. See also Bernhard W. Anderson, "'G-d with Us'—in Judgment and in Mercy: The Editorial Structure of Isaiah 5–10(11)," in *Canon, Theology, and Old Testament Interpretation* (ed. Gene M. Tucker et al.; Philadelphia: Fortress, 1988), 230-45.

15. See esp. Stuart A. Irvine, *Isaiah, Ahaz, and the Syro-Ephraimitic Crisis* (SBLDS 123; Atlanta: Scholars Press, 1990).

16. See esp. Wildberger, *Isaiah 1–12*, 246-78.

17. For discussion of the parallels between the structures of temples and royal palaces, see Baruch Halpern, *The First Historians: The Hebrew Bible and History* (San Francisco: Harper and Row, 1988), 46-54.

18. Victor Hurowitz, "Isaiah's Impure Lips and Their Purification in Light of Akkadian Sources," *HUCA* 60 (1989): 39-89.

19. See Marvin A. Sweeney, "Isaiah and Theodicy after the Shoah," in *Strange Fire*, 208-19.

20. See Irvine, *Isaiah, Ahaz, and the Syro-Ephraimitic Crisis*.

21. E.g., Dan G. Johnson, *From Chaos to Restoration: An Integrative Reading of Isaiah 24–27* (JSOTSup 61; Sheffield: Sheffield Academic Press, 1988).

22. See now Donald C. Polaski, *Authorizing an End: The Isaiah Apocalypse and Intertextuality* (BibInt 50; Leiden: Brill, 2001).

23. For discussion of the role of blindness and deafness within the whole of the book of Isaiah, see esp. Ronald E. Clements, "The Unity of the Book of Isaiah," *Int* 36 (1982): 117-29; idem, "Beyond Tradition-History: Deutero-Isaiah's Development of First Isaiah's Themes," *JSOT* 31 (1985): 95-113.

24. See esp. W. A. M. Beuken, "Jesaja 33 als Spiegeltext im Jesajabuch," *ETL* 67 (1991): 5-35; for discussion of Beuken, see Sweeney, *Isaiah 1–39*, 420-33.

25. For analysis of the literary structure of Isa 34–66, including 40–54; 55–66, see Sweeney, *Isaiah 1–39*, 31–62; idem, *Isaiah 1–4*. For discussion of Isa 40–55 in general, see esp. Roy F. Melugin, *The Formation of Isaiah 40–55* (BZAW 141; Berlin and New York: Walter de Gruyter, 1976).

26. E.g., Ackroyd, "Isaiah 36–39."

27. For discussion of Isa 36–39, see esp. Sweeney, *Isaiah 1–39*, 454-511; see also Christopher R. Seitz, *Zion's Final Destiny: The Development of the Book of Isaiah. A Reassessment of Isaiah 36–39* (Minneapolis: Fortress, 1991).

28. An English translation of Sennacherib's account appears in Pritchard, *ANET*, 287-88.

29. See the standard introductions and commentaries, e.g., John J. Collins, *Introduction to the Hebrew Bible* (Minneapolis: Fortress, 2004), 379-400, esp. 380-89.

30. See now Patricia Tull Willey, "The Servant of YHWH and Daughter Zion: Alternating Visions of YHWH's Community," in *Society of Biblical Literature 1995 Seminar Papers* (ed. Eugene H. Lovering, Jr.; Atlanta: Society of Biblical Literature, 1995), 267-303.

31. See T. N. D. Mettinger, *A Farewell to the Servant Songs: A Critical Examination of an Exegetical Axiom* (Lund: Gleerup, 1983).

32. See Patricia Tull Willey, *Remember the Former Things: The Recollection of Previous Texts in Second Isaiah* (SBLDS 161; Atlanta: Scholars Press, 1997), 229-61. For further discussion concerning intertextuality in Isa 40–66, see now Benjamin D. Sommer, *A Prophet Reads Scripture: Allusion in Isaiah 40–66* (Stanford: Stanford University Press, 1998).

33. Marvin A. Sweeney, "The Reconceptualization of the Davidic Covenant in the Book of Isaiah," in *Studies in the Book of Isaiah: Festschrift Willem A. M. Beuken* (ed. J. van Ruiten and M. Vervenne; BETL 132; Leuven: Leuven University Press and Peeters, 1997), 41-61.

34. See now Joseph Blenkinsopp, *Isaiah 56–66* (AB 19B; New York: Doubleday, 2003), 25-66.

35. See Marvin A. Sweeney, "Prophetic Exegesis in Isaiah 65–66," in *Writing and Reading the Scroll of Isaiah: Studies of an Interpretive Tradition* (ed. Craig C. Broyles and Craig A. Evans; VTSup 70/1-2; Leiden: Brill, 1997), 1:455-74.

Chapter 4: The Book of Jeremiah

1. For discussion concerning the composition of the book of Jeremiah, see esp. Jack R. Lundbom, *Jeremiah 1–20* (AB 21A; New York: Doubleday, 1999), 92-101; Douglas R. Jones, *Jeremiah* (NCB; London: Marshall Pickering; Grand Rapids: Eerdmans, 1992), 17-37.

2. Nahman Avigad, *Hebrew Bullae from the Time of Jeremiah: Remnants of a Burnt Archive* (Jerusalem: Israel Exploration Society, 1986), 28-29.

3. See, e.g., E. W. Nicholson, *Preaching to the Exiles: A Study of the Prose Traditions in the Book of Jeremiah* (New York: Schocken, 1971).

4. For discussion of the confessions of Jeremiah, see A. R. Diamond, *The Confessions of Jeremiah in Context: Scenes of a Prophetic Drama* (JSOTSup 45; JSOT Press, 1987); Kathleen M. O'Connor, *The Confessions of Jeremiah: Their Interpretation and Role in Chapters 1–25* (SBLDS 94; Atlanta: Scholars Press, 1988); Mark S. Smith, *The Laments of Jeremiah and Their Contexts* (SBLMS 42; Atlanta: Scholars Press, 1990).

5. Christopher R. Seitz, "The Prophet Moses and the Canonical Shape of Jeremiah," *ZAW* 101 (1989): 3-27; cf. idem, *Theology in Conflict: Reactions to the Exile in the Book of Jeremiah* (BZAW 176; Berlin and New York: Walter de Gruyter, 1989), esp. 222-35.

6. Emmanuel Tov, "Some Aspects of the Textual and Literary History of the Book of Jeremiah," in *Le livre d'Jérémie. Le prophète et son milieu. Les oracles et leur transmission* (BETL 54; Leuven: Leuven University Press and Peeters, 1981), 145-67; cf. J. Gerald Janzen, *Studies in the Text of Jeremiah* (HSM 6; Cambridge: Harvard University Press, 1973); Andrew G. Shead, *The Open and the Sealed Book: Jeremiah 32 in Its Hebrew and Greek Recensions* (JSOTSup 347; London: Sheffield Academic Press, 2002).

7. For discussion of the Qumran evidence, see Janzen, *Studies*; George J. Brooke, "The Book of Jeremiah and its Reception in the Dead Sea Scrolls," in *The Book of Jeremiah and Its Reception* (ed. A. H. W. Curtis and T. Römer; BETL 128; Leuven University Press and Peeters, 1997), 183-205. The Cave 2 text of Jeremiah is published in M. Baillet et al., *Les 'Petits Grottes' de Qumran* (DJD 3; Oxford: Clarendon, 1962), 62-69, and the texts from Cave 4 appear in E. Ulrich et al., *Qumran Cave 4. X: The Prophets* (DJD 15; Oxford: Clarendon, 1997), 145-207.

8. E.g., Otto Kaiser, *Introduction to the Old Testament: A Presentation of Its Results and Problems* (trans. J. Sturdy; Minneapolis: Augsburg, 1977), 239.

9. For discussion of superscriptions, see Tucker, "Prophetic Superscriptions."

10. See Sweeney, *King Josiah of Judah*, 208-33.

11. See J. Philip Hyatt, "The Beginning of Jeremiah's Prophecy," in *A Prophet to the Nations: Essays in Jeremiah Studies* (ed. L. G. Perdue and B. W. Kovacs; Winona Lake, Ind.: Eisenbrauns, 1984), 63-72 (originally published in *ZAW* 78 [1966]: 204-14).

12. Jon D. Levenson, "The Temple and the World," *JR* 64 (1984): 275-98; cf. idem, *Sinai and Zion: An Entry into the Jewish Bible* (Minneapolis: Winston, 1985).

13. For discussion of the literary structure, theological outlook, and compositional history of Jer 2–6, see my "Structure and Redaction in Jeremiah 2–6," in *Troubling Jeremiah* (ed. A. R. Pete Diamond et al; JSOTSup 260; Sheffield: Sheffield Academic Press, 1999), 200-18.

14. See my study, "The Truth in True and False Prophecy," in *Truth: Interdisciplinary Dialogues in a Pluralist Age* (ed. C. Helmer and K. De Troyer; Studies in Philosophical Theology 22; Leuven: Peeters, 2003), 9-26, which examines Jeremiah's reading of the Isaian tradition.

15. For discussion of Levitical sermons, see esp. Rex Mason, *Preaching the Tradition: Homily and Hermeneutics after the Exile* (Cambridge: Cambridge University Press, 1990), although he fails to see that the sermonic form has antecedents prior to the exile.

16. For discussion of the entrance liturgies, see Sweeney, *Isaiah 1–39*, 520.

17. See the treatment of Jeremiah's Temple Sermon in the commentaries by Carroll, Holladay, Jones, Lundbom, and McCane.

18. See the studies on Jeremiah's confessions or laments by Diamond, O'Connor, and Smith noted above. For discussion of the complaint psalms that influence Jeremiah's confessions, see Erhard S. Gerstenberger, *Psalms, Part 1, with an Introduction to Cultic Poetry* (FOTL 14; Grand Rapids: Eerdmans, 1988), 11-14.

19. See Duane F. Watson, "Hinnom Valley," *ABD* 3:202-03; Philip C. Schmitz, "Topheth," *ABD* 6:600-01.

20. For discussion of the political background of the last years of the kingdom of Judah and Jeremiah's own political viewpoints and alliances, see Jay Wilcoxen, "The Political Background of Jeremiah's Temple Sermon," in *Scripture in History and Theology: Essays in Honor of J. Coert*

Rylaarsdam (ed. A. Merrill and T. Overholt; Pittburgh: Pickwick, 1977), 151-66.

21. See Stacey, *Prophetic Drama,* 151-57; Sweeney, "The Truth"; see also James A. Sanders, "Hermeneutics in True and False Prophecy," in *Canon and Authority,* 21-41.

22. See my studies, "Jeremiah 30–31 and King Josiah's Program of National Restoration and Religious Reform," *ZAW* 108 (1996): 569-83; idem, *King Josiah,* 225-33.

23. For discussion of gender imagery here and in Jer 31:15, 22 below, see Phyllis Trible, *G-d and the Rhetoric of Sexuality* (OBT; Philadelphia: Fortress, 1978), 46-50.

24. For study of the covenant formula, see now Rolf Rendtorff, *The Covenant Formula: An Exegetical and Theological Study* (trans. M. Kohl; Edinburgh: T & T Clark, 1998).

25. See esp. Yohanan Goldman, *Prophétie et royauté au retour de l'exil* (OBO 118; Freiburg: Universitätsverlag; Göttingen: Vandenhoeck & Ruprecht, 1992), 9-64.

26. Wilcoxen, "The Political Background."

27. Seitz, "The Prophet Moses."

28. Richard N. Jones and Zbigniew T. Fiema, "Tahpanhes," *ABD* 6:308-9.

29. Bezalel Porten, "Elephantine Papyri," *ABD* 2:445-55.

30. For a study of Baruch ben Neriah in Jeremiah and the development of his image in later tradition, see now J. Edward Wright, *Baruch Ben Neriah: From Biblical Scribe to Apocalyptic Seer* (Columbia: University of South Carolina Press, 2003).

31. See Amélie Kuhrt, *The Ancient Near East, c. 3000–330 BC* (London and New York: Routledge, 1998), 2:636-44; Donald B. Redford, *Egypt, Canaan, and Israel in Ancient Times* (Princeton: Princeton University Press, 1992), 430-69.

32. History 1:105; see A. D. Godley, *Heroodotus, Books I-II* (Loeb Classical Library; London and Cambridge: Harvard University Press, 1996), 1:136-37.

33. Sweeney, "Truth."

Chapter 5: The Book of Ezekiel

1. For surveys of discussion on the book of Ezekiel, see Katheryn Pfisterer Darr, "Ezekiel Among the Critics," *CurBS* 2 (1994): 9-24.

2. Henry O. Thompson, "Chebar," *ABD* 1:893.

3. See Yoshitaka Kobayashi, "Tel-Abib," *ABD* 6:344.

4. Matthew W. Stolper, "Murashû, Archive of," *ABD* 4:927-28.

5. For discussion of the thirtieth year, see Moshe Greenberg, *Ezekiel 1–20* (AB 22; Garden City, N.Y.: Doubleday, 1983), 39-40; Katheryn Pfisterer Darr, "Ezekiel," in *The New Interpreter's Bible* (ed. L. Keck et al.; Nashville: Abingdon, 2001), 6:1110.

6. See Margaret S. Odell, "You Are What You Eat: Ezekiel and the Scroll," *JBL* 117 (1998): 229-48; Marvin A. Sweeney, "Ezekiel: Zadokite

Priest and Visionary Prophet of the Exile," *OPIAC* 41 (2001), to be republished in *Form and Intertextuality in the Study of Prophetic and Apocalyptic Literature* (Forschungen zum Alten Testament; Tübingen: Mohr Siebeck, 2005).

7. For discussion of Ezek 29:17, see Moshe Greenberg, *Ezekiel 21–37* (AB 22A; New York: Doubleday, 1997), 616-17; Walther Zimmerli, *Ezekiel 2: A Commentary on the Book of the Prophet Ezekiel, Chapters 25–48* (Hermeneia; trans. J. D. Martin; Philadelphia: Fortress, 1983), 210-11.

8. For discussion of the Zadokite (and Levitical) priests, see Merlin D. Rehm, "Levites and Priests," *ABD* 297-310.

9. For an introduction to the worldview and perspectives of the Zadokite priesthood, see Jon D. Levenson, *Sinai and Zion: An Entry into the Jewish Bible* (Minneapolis: Winston, 1985).

10. See esp. Odell, "You Are What You Eat."

11. Cf. Greenberg, *Ezekiel 1–20*, 3-27. Others, e.g., Walther Zimmerli, *Ezekiel 1: A Commentary on the Book of the Prophet Ezekiel, Chapters 1–24* (Hermeneia; trans. R. E. Clements; Philadelphia: Fortress, 1979), 68-77; Ronald M. Hals, *Ezekiel* (FOTL 19; Grand Rapids: Eerdmans, 1989), 2-7, suggest a longer process of composition and redaction.

12. See the Ugaritic Baal Cycle, which refers frequently to the storm god Baal as "the Rider of the Clouds" (e.g., Baal Cycle IIAB 3:11; *ANET*, 132; I*AB 2:7, *ANET*, 138).

13. See, e.g., *ANEP*, 534, 535, 536.

14. See Odell, "You Are What You Eat."

15. Israel Knohl, *The Sanctuary of Silence: The Priestly Torah and the Holiness School* (Minneapolis: Fortress, 1994).

16. Jon D. Levenson, "The Temple and the World," *JR* 64 (1984): 275-98.

17. See Marvin A. Sweeney, "The Destruction of Jerusalem as Purification in Ezekiel 8–11," in *Form and Intertextuality*, forthcoming.

18. For discussion of these offerings, see Jacob Milgrom, "Sacrifices and Offerings, OT," *IDBSup*, 763-71, esp. 766-69.

19. See Greenberg, *Ezekiel 1–20*, 177.

20. L. I. Rabinowitz, "Synagogue," *EncJud* 15:579-84, esp. 580.

21. Cf. Sanders, "Hermeneutics of True and False Prophecy."

22. For an English translation of the Aqhat legend, see *ANET*, 149-55.

23. See esp. Julie Galambush, *Jerusalem in the Book of Ezekiel: The City as YHWH's Wife* (SBLDS 130; Atlanta: Scholars Press, 1992).

24. For a survey of the marriage metaphor in the Hebrew Bible, see Gerlinde Baumann, *Love and Violence: Marriage as Metaphor for the Relationship between YHWH and Israel in the Prophetic Books* (trans. L. Maloney; Collegeville: Liturgical, 2003).

25. Knohl, *Sanctuary*; Gordon H. Matties, *Ezekiel 18 and the Rhetoric of Moral Discourse* (SBLDS 126; Atlanta: Scholars Press, 1990).

26. Graffy, *A Prophet Confronts His People*, 58-64.

27. See Galambush, *Jerusalem as YHWH's Wife*.

28. See Marvin A. Sweeney, "The Assertion of Divine Power in Ezekiel 33:21–39:29," in *Form and Intertextuality*, forthcoming.

29. These chapters draw heavily on earlier pentateuchal and prophetic tradition; see my "The Priesthood and the Proto-apocalyptic Reading of Prophetic and Pentateuchal Texts," in *Knowing the End from the Beginning: The Prophetic, the Apocalyptic, and Their Relationships* (ed. L. L. Grabbe and R. D. Haak; JSPSup 46; London: T & T Clark, 2003), 167-78.

30. For an overview of suggestions, see Darr, "Ezekiel," 1515.

31. See now Jon D. Levenson, *Theology of the Program of Restoration of Ezekiel 40–48* (HSM 10; Missoula: Scholars Press, 1976); Steven Shawn Tuell, *The Law of the Temple in Ezekiel 40–48* (HSM 49; Atlanta: Scholars Press, 1992).

32. Halpern, *The First Historians*, 46-54.

Chapter 6: The Book of the Twelve Prophets

1. For discussion of the different versions of the Book of the Twelve extant in the ancient world, see Ehud Ben Zvi, "Twelve Prophetic Books or 'The Twelve': A Few Preliminary Considerations," in *Forming Prophetic Literature: Essays on Isaiah and the Twelve in Honor of J. D. W. Watts* (ed. J. W. Watts and P. R. House; JSOTSup 235; Sheffield: Sheffield Academic Press, 1996), 125-56.

2. For discussion of the Book of the Twelve in the Judean Wilderness Scrolls, see Barry Alan Jones, *The Formation of the Book of the Twelve: Study in Text and Canon* (SBLDS 149; Atlanta: Scholars Press, 1995).

3. For discussion of the sequence of the books in the MT and LXX versions of the Book of the Twelve Prophets, see my "Sequence and Interpretation in the Book of the Twelve," in *Reading and Hearing the Book of the Twelve* (ed. J. D. Nogalski and M. A. Sweeney; SBLSymS 15; Atlanta: Society of Biblical Literature, 2000), 49-64; idem, *The Twelve Prophets* (Berit Olam; Collegeville: Liturgical, 2000), 1:xv-xxix.

4. Cf. Odil Hannes Steck, *The Prophetic Books and Their Theological Witness* (trans. J. D. Nogalski; St. Louis: Chalice, 2000).

5. See Bauman, *Love and Violence*, 85-104, for discussion of this theme in Hosea; cf. Francis Landy, *Hosea* (Readings; Sheffield: Sheffield Academic Press, 1995), 21-52.

6. E.g., Hans Walter Wolff, *Hosea* (Hermeneia; trans. G. Stansell; Philadelphia: Fortress, 1974); Gale Yee, *Composition and Tradition in the Book of Hosea: A Redaction-Critical Investigation* (SBLDS 102; Atlanta: Scholars Press, 1987).

7. See Sweeney, *The Twelve Prophets*, 3-7; idem, *King Josiah*, 256-72.

8. For discussion of metaphor in Hosea, see, e.g., Göran Eidevall, *Grapes in the Desert: Metaphors, Models, and Themes in Hosea 4–14* (ConBOT 43; Stockholm: Almqvist & Wiksell, 1996).

9. Sweeney, *Twelve Prophets*, 111-12; Moshe Elat, "The Campaigns of Shalmaneser III against Aram and Israel," *IEJ* 25 (1975): 25-35.

10. For discussion of the intertextual references in Joel, see Siegfried Bergler, *Joel als Schriftinterpret* (BEATAJ 16; Frankfurt: Peter Lang, 1988);

for discussion in English, see the commentaries by Wolff, Crenshaw, and Sweeney.

11. For discussion of the Hamsin/Sharav, see "Israel, Land of (Geographical Survey)," *EncJud* 9:189-90.

12. Gösta W. Ahlström, *Joel and the Temple Cult of Jerusalem* (VTSup 21; Leiden: Brill, 1971).

13. For discussion of the structure of Joel, see Sweeney, *Twelve Prophets*, 1:147-52.

14. See Moshe Weinfeld, "Tithe," *EncJud* 15:1156-62.

15. For discussion of the structure of Amos, see Sweeney, *Twelve Prophets*, 1:191-95; idem, *King Josiah*, 273-86.

16. For discussion of Amos's relation to the wisdom tradition, see esp. Hans Walter Wolff, *Amos the Prophet: The Man and His Background* (trans. F. McCurley; Philadelphia: Fortress, 1973).

17. See the treatment of this passage in the commentaries by Paul and Sweeney; cf. Max Polley, *Amos and the Davidic Empire* (New York and Oxford: Oxford University Press, 1989).

18. See esp. Ehud Ben Zvi, *A Historical-Critical Study of the Book of Obadiah* (BZAW 242; Berlin and New York: Walter De Gruyter, 1996), 99-109; Hans Walter Wolff, *Obadiah and Jonah* (ContCom; trans. M. Kohl; Minneapolis: Fortress, 1986), 37-42.

19. See Sweeney, *Twelve Prophets*, 1:279-85.

20. See now the treatment of Jonah in J. William Whedbee, *The Bible and the Comic Vision* (Cambridge: Cambridge University Press, 1998); Ehud Ben Zvi, *Signs of Jonah: Reading and Rereading Jonah in Ancient Yehud* (JSOTSup 367; London: Sheffield Academic Press, 2003).

21. Sweeney, *Twelve Prophets*, 1:303-07.

22. Lamontte M. Luker, "Moresheth," *ABD* 4:904-5.

23. See Sennacherib's account of his invasion of Judah in 701 B.C.E. in *ANET*, 287-88; cf. Isa 36–37/2 Kgs 18–19.

24. See my study, "Micah's Debate with Isaiah," *JSOT* 93 (2001): 111-24.

25. Sweeney, *Twelve Prophets*, 2:339-43; idem, *King Josiah*, 287-300.

26. See Kuhrt, *The Ancient Near East*, 540-46.

27. For discussion of the formal features and rhetorical strategy of Nahum, see Sweeney, *The Twelve Prophets*, 2:419-47.

28. For discussion of the political situation presupposed in Habakkuk, see Wilcoxen, "The Political Background"; cf. Robert D. Haak, *Habakkuk* (VTSup 44; Leiden: Brill, 1992), 107-49.

29. See Sweeney, *The Twelve Prophets*, 2:453-58; idem, *King Josiah*, 301-10.

30. For full discussion of these issues, see now my *Zephaniah* (Hermeneia; Minneapolis: Fortress, 2003).

31. For discussion of the literary form of Haggai, see the commentaries by Petersen, Meyers and Meyers, and Sweeney.

32. See my study, "Zechariah's Debate with Isaiah," in *The Changing Face of Form-Criticism for the Twenty-First Century* (ed. M. A. Sweeney and E. Ben Zvi; Grand Rapids and Cambridge: Eerdmans, 2003), 315-50.

33. "Alexander the Great," *EncJud,* 577-80.

34. Sweeney, *The Twelve Prophets,* 2:561-567; cf. Edgar W. Conrad, *Zechariah* (Readings; Sheffield: Sheffield Academic Press, 1999).

35. For discussion of the literary form of Malachi, see the commentaries by Petersen and Sweeney.

INDEX

LaVergne, TN USA
20 January 2011
213176LV00004B/30/P